LONDON'S RIVERSIDE IN PHOTOGRAPHS

The Thames from Hampton Court to the Barrier

FRANCO PFALLER

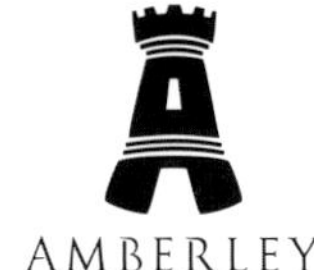

AMBERLEY

First published 2024

Amberley Publishing
The Hill, Stroud
Gloucestershire, GL5 4EP

www.amberley-books.com

Copyright © Franco Pfaller, 2024

The right of Franco Pfaller to be identified as the Author of this work has been
asserted in accordance with the Copyrights, Designs and Patents Act 1988.

ISBN 978 1 3981 1614 6 (print)
ISBN 978 1 3981 1615 3 (ebook)

British Library Cataloguing in Publication Data.
A catalogue record for this book is available from the British Library.

Typesetting by SJmagic DESIGN SERVICES, India.
Printed in the UK.

INTRODUCTION

If you live or work in London, or have visited as a tourist, then at some stage you have probably stood along the Thames and marvelled at the presence of this river. You've strolled along the South Bank, from the London Eye towards Borough Market, passing via the National Theatre, the British Film Institute, and on to the Tate Modern and Shakespeare's Globe Theatre. You may have bought an ice cream along the way, all the while counting your blessings. If you continue walking, it just gets better. You can't help but admire the HMS Belfast with the backdrop of the City of London and, further down, you behold the Tower of London and the iconic Tower Bridge in all of their glory. Or perhaps you walked in the other direction, where Big Ben and the Houses of Parliament stand, making you feel like you are a central character in current affairs.

The views from Waterloo Bridge are always stunning. Head there before sunset, look downstream, and the City of London and, further away, Canary Wharf will shine in the last sunlight. Or look in the opposite direction and take a snapshot of the London Eye, the Jubilee Bridges, Westminster Palace, and Big Ben. If you don't like that view, well, this book is not for you.

But there is far more to love along the Thames than just the world-famous buildings. I love hiking from Putney towards Richmond and beyond, where the south side of the river still feels rural and you can walk miles (in my case, kilometres) on a dirt track. There is plenty to see on the way, be it the wildlife, the rowers, Kew Gardens, or Syon House in the distance – one somehow ends up discovering something new on most walks. And once you've arrived in Richmond, sit down in one of the pubs by the river and have a well-deserved drink.

This book is a collection of photos I have taken between 2016 and 2022 from the Hampton Court Bridge to the Thames Barrier. It includes pictures of every bridge and many other beautiful sights along the way. My hope is that you like the photos and feel inspired to go and discover some of the areas that are new to you.

ABOUT THE PHOTOGRAPHER

Franco is a Swiss photographer who has been living in London since 1994. After a long career in banking (some might say too long), he changed direction and in 2014 launched www.yourpanorama.ch, a website initially focused solely on 'labelled panoramas'. Other products followed, including a trilingual photo book published in Switzerland called *Mein Wallis – Mon Valais – My Valais*. You can find him on most social media platforms under @yourpanorama.

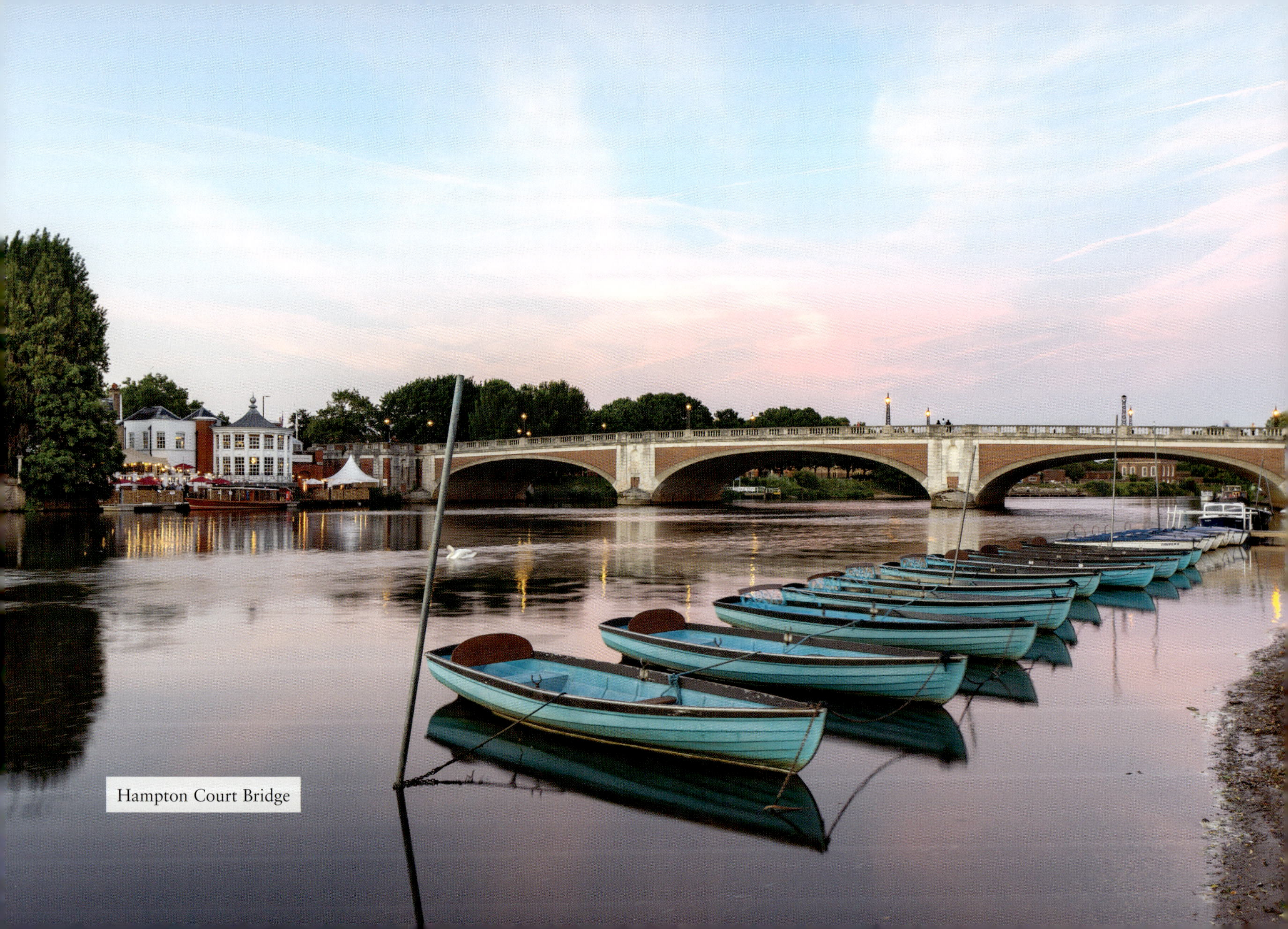
Hampton Court Bridge

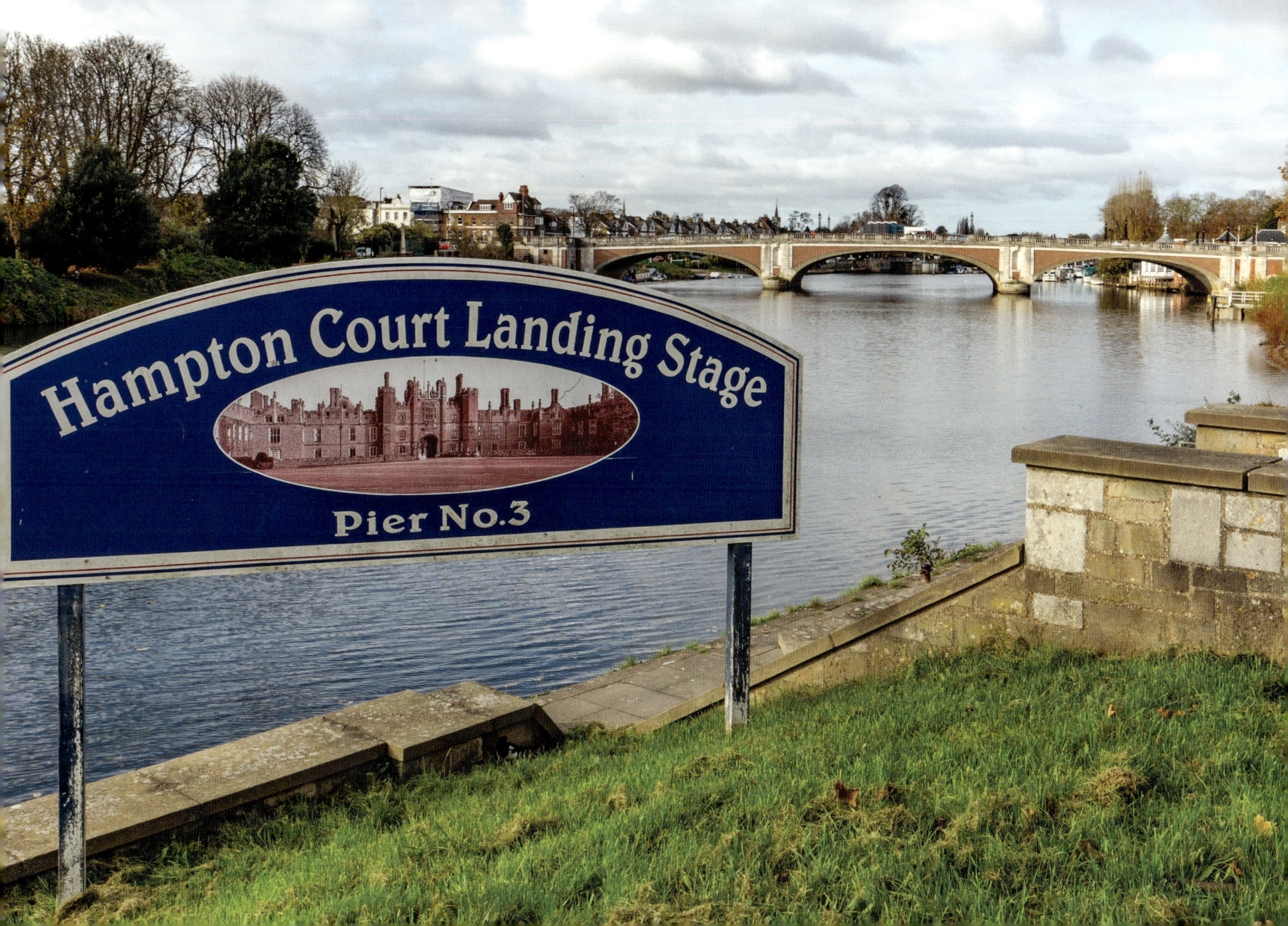
Hampton Court Landing Stage
Pier No.3

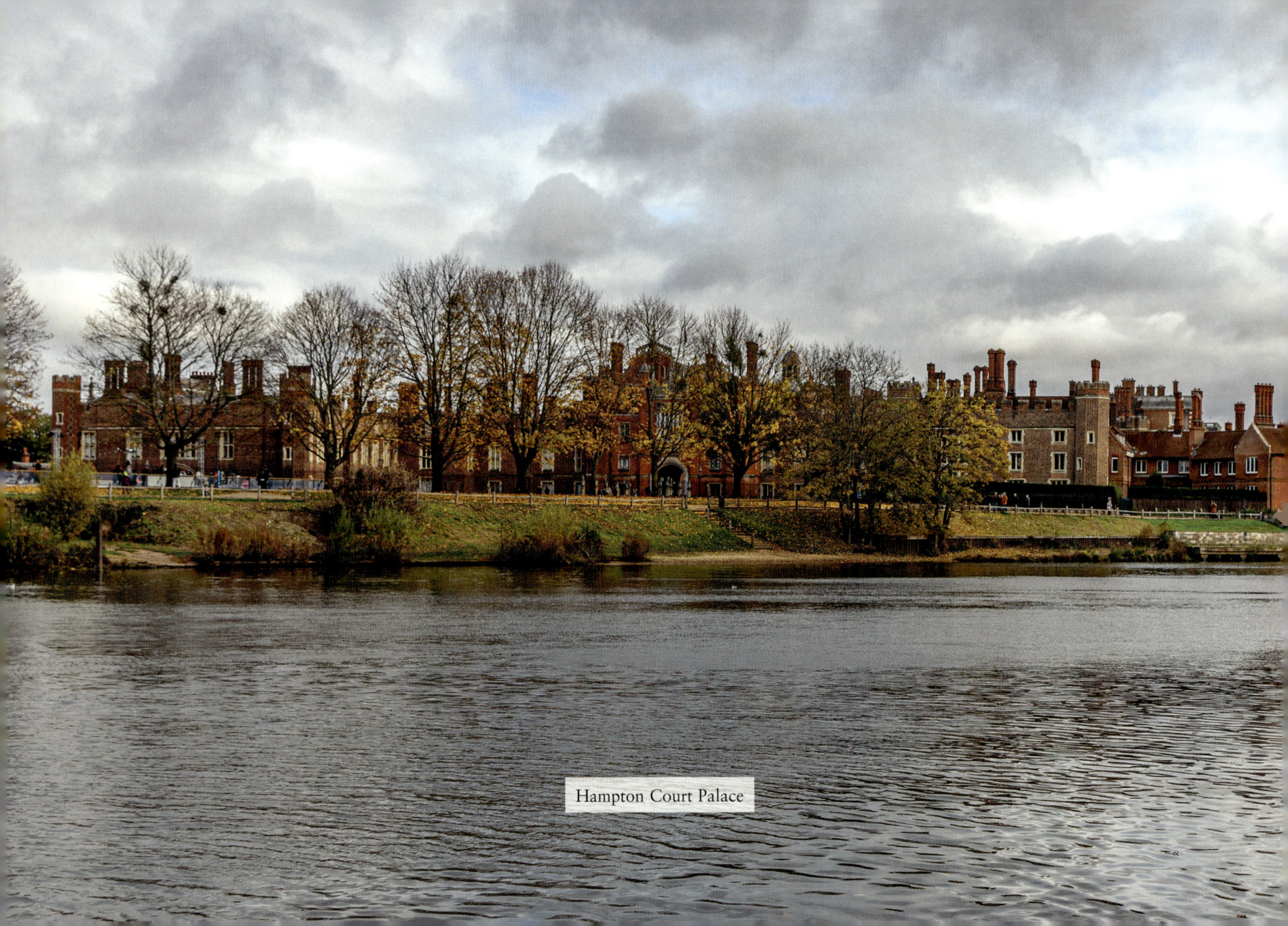

Hampton Court Palace

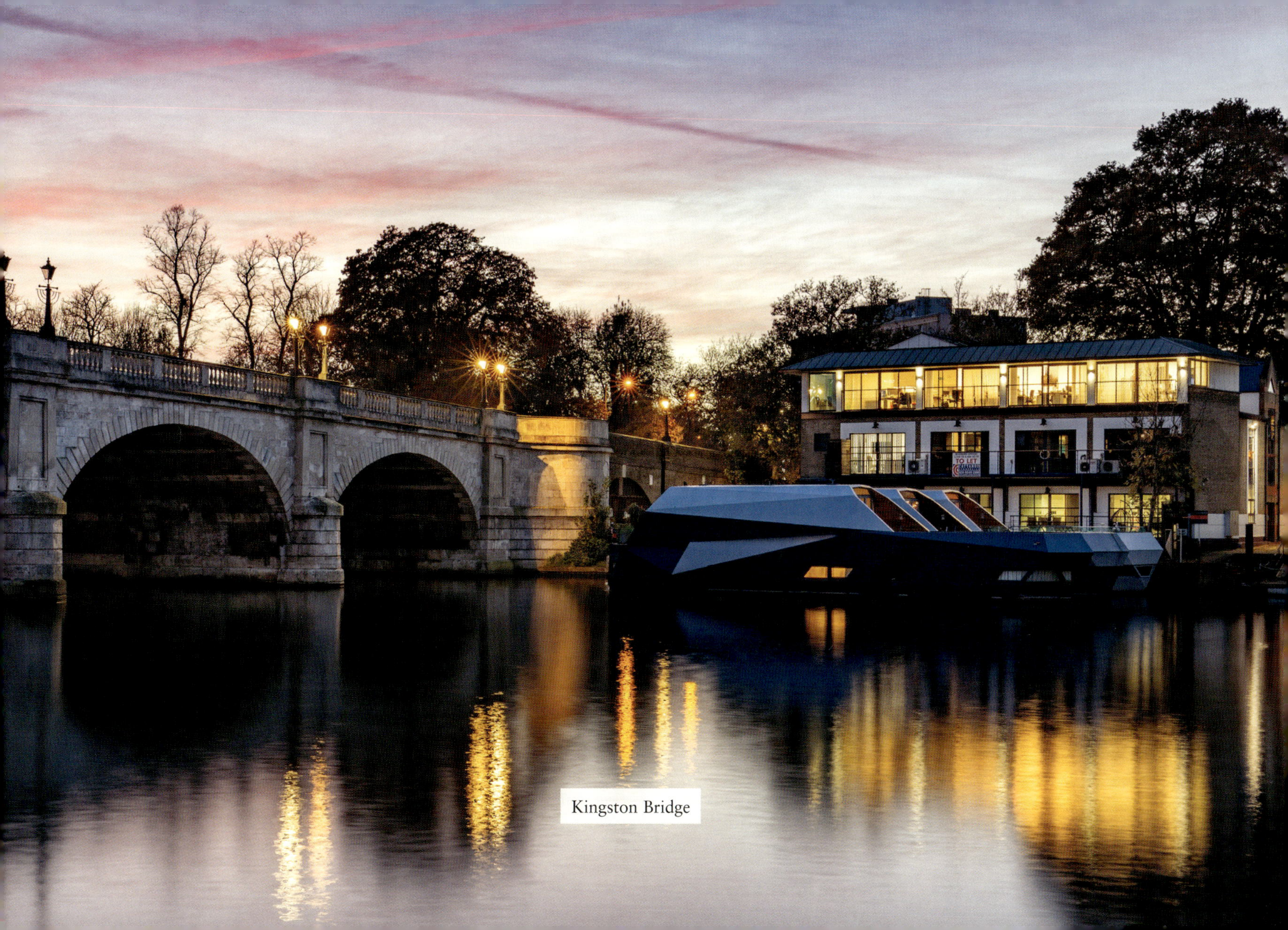

Kingston Bridge

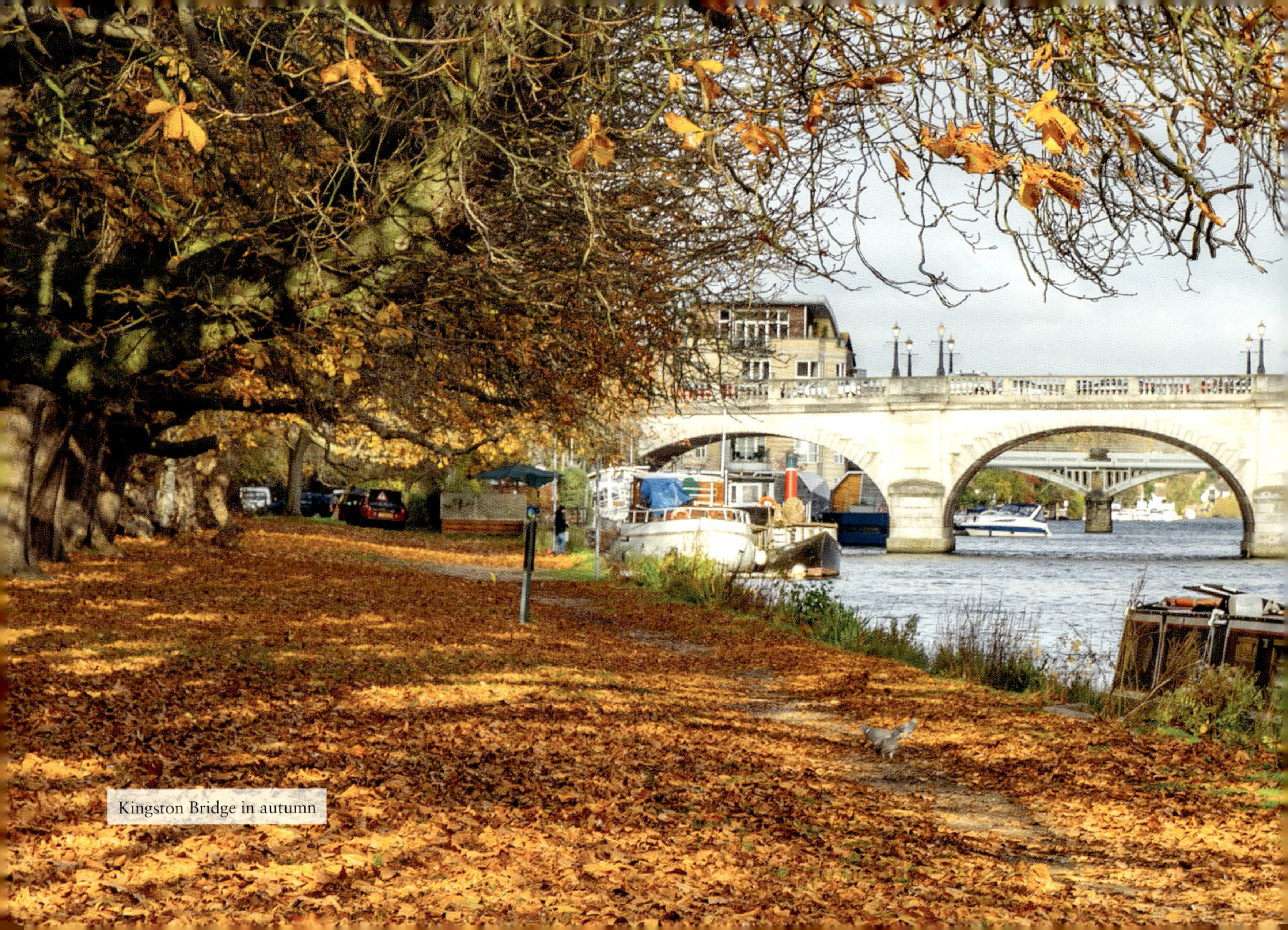
Kingston Bridge in autumn

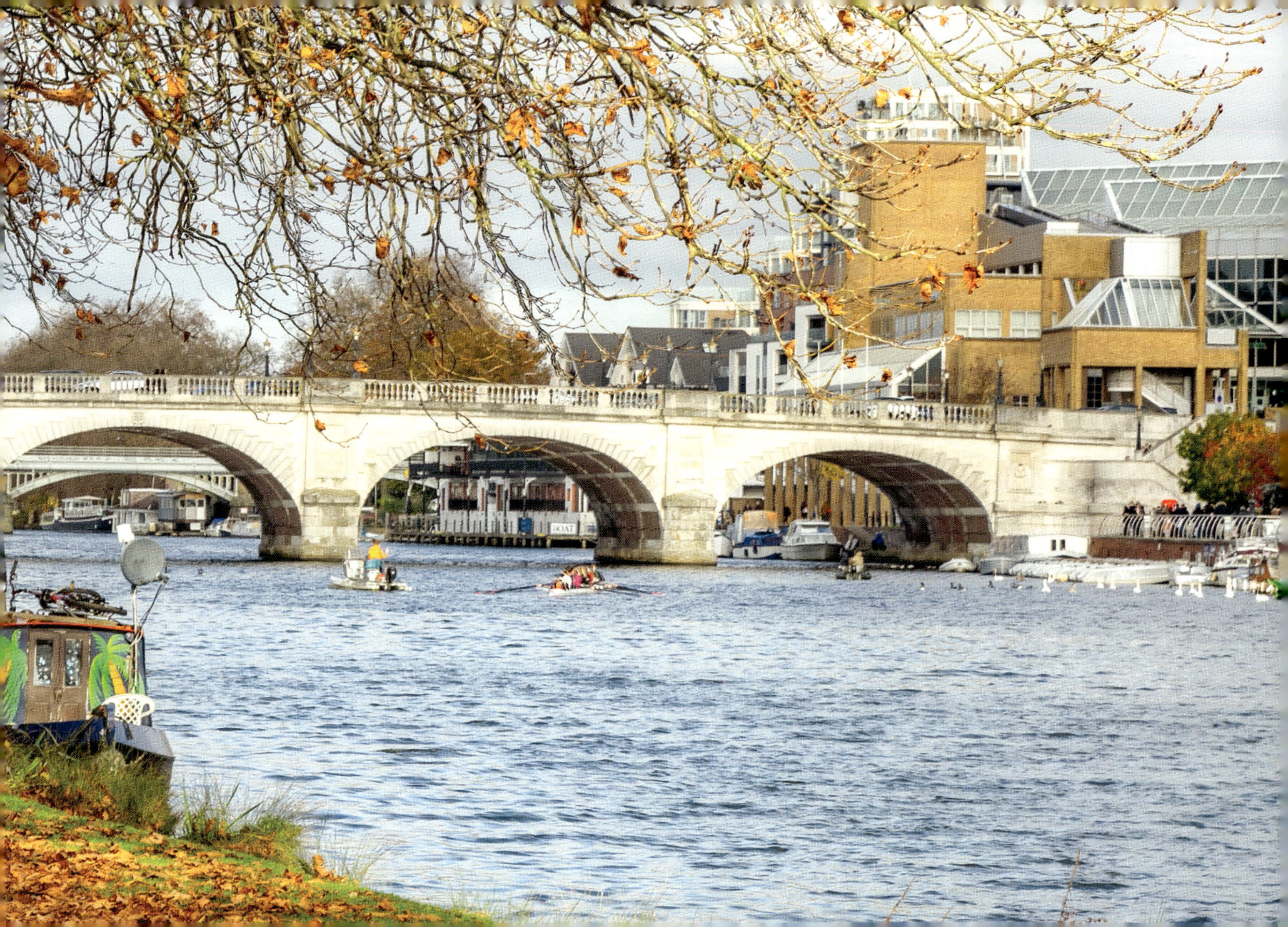

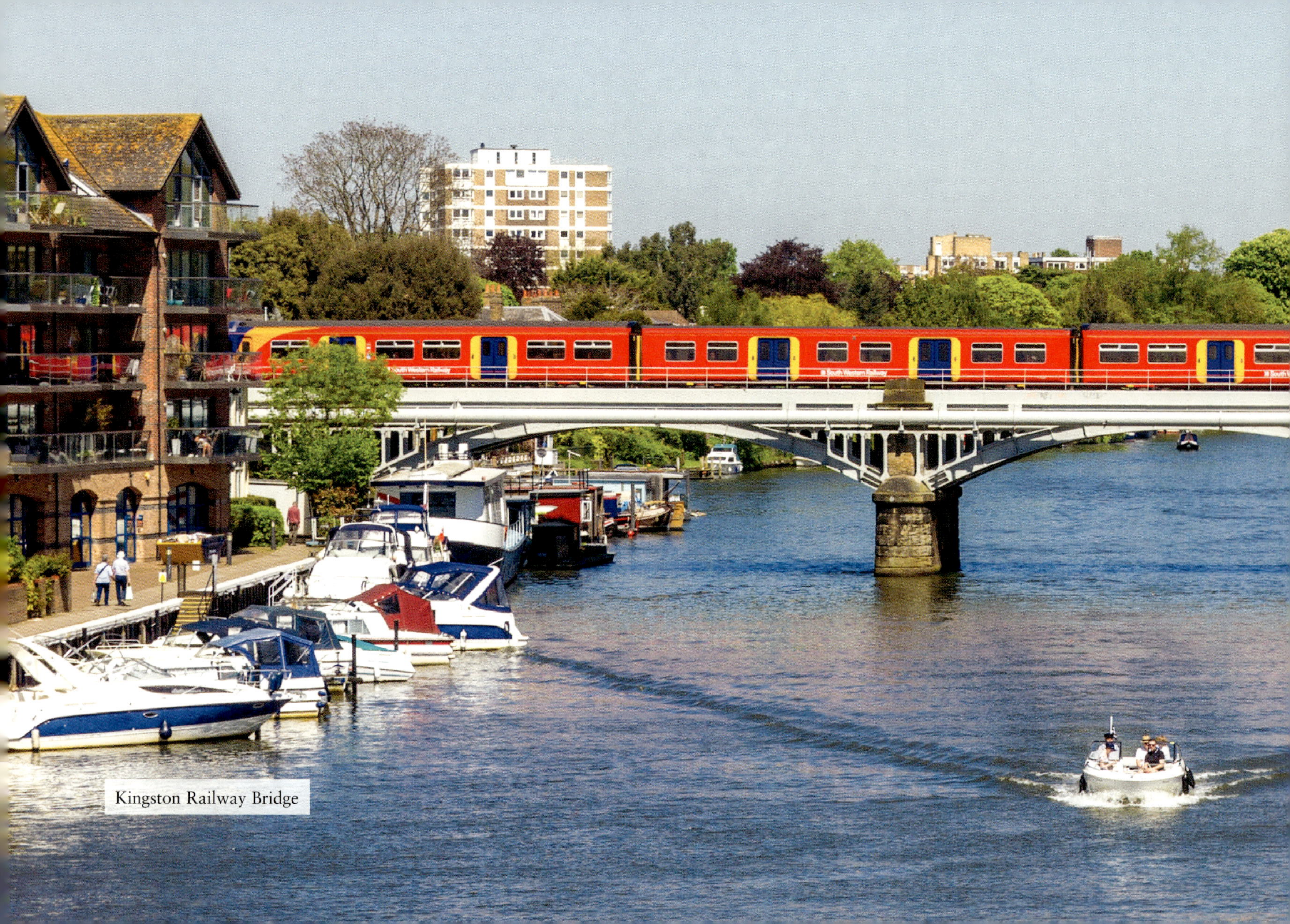

Kingston Railway Bridge

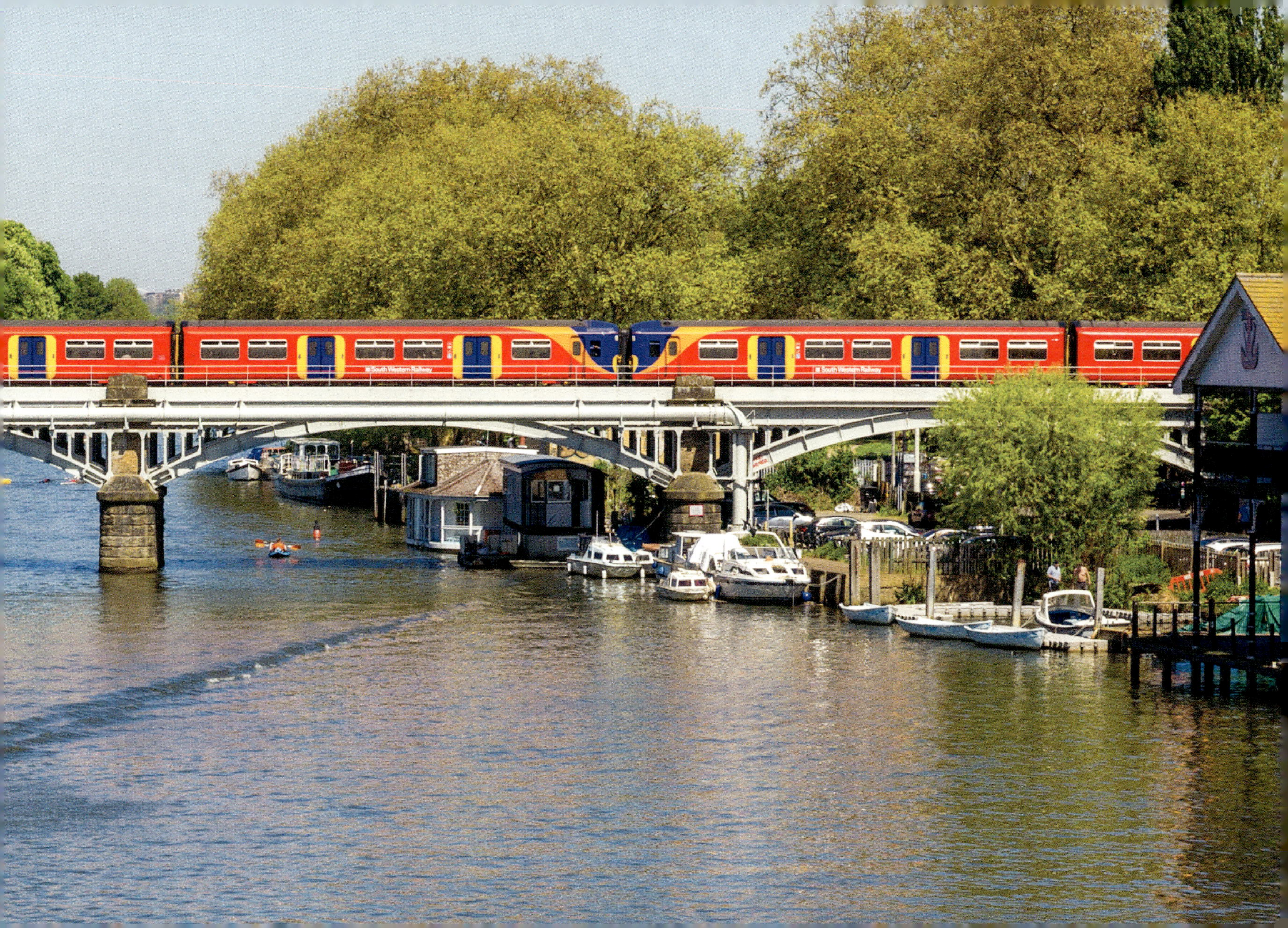

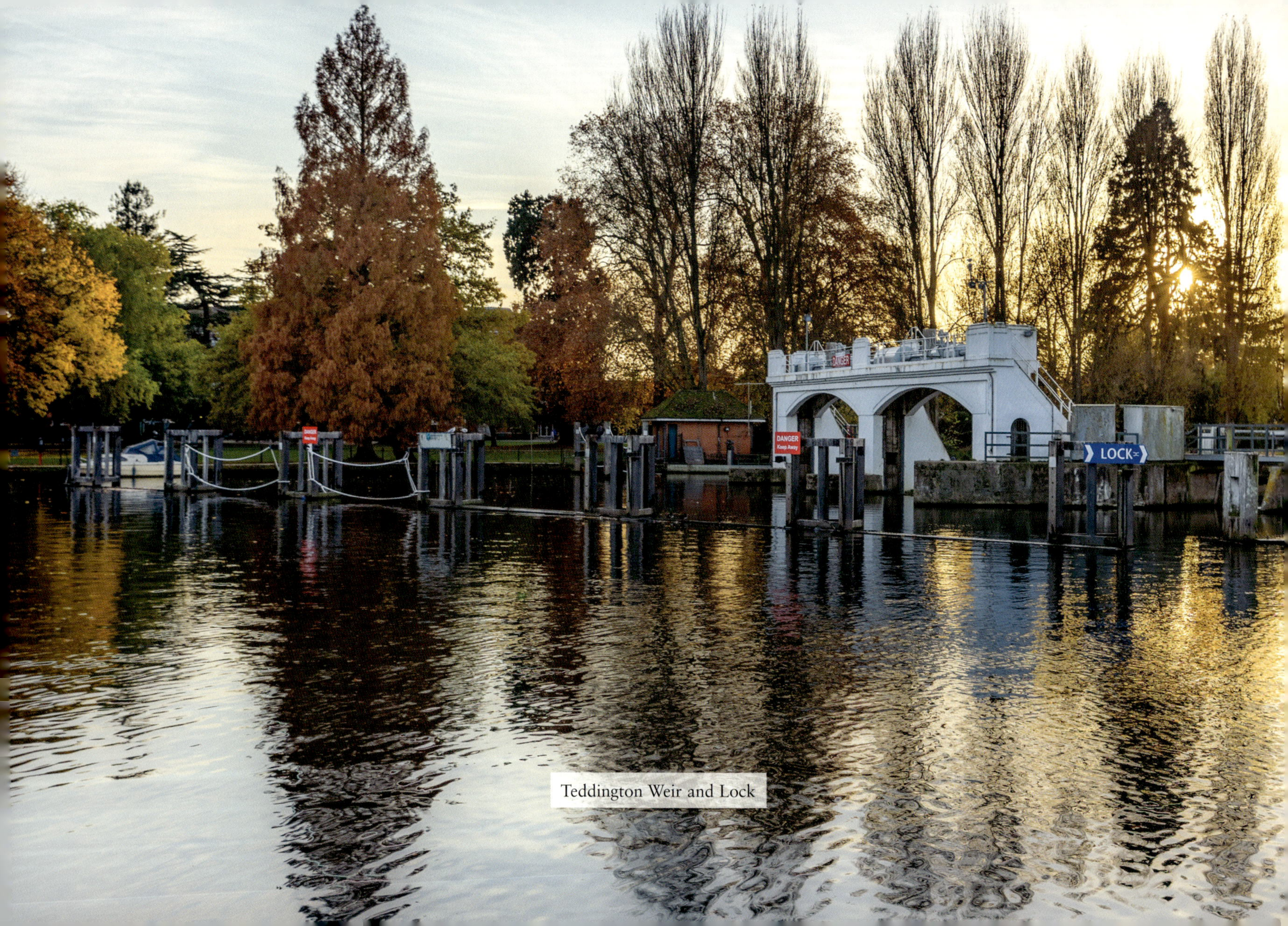

Teddington Weir and Lock

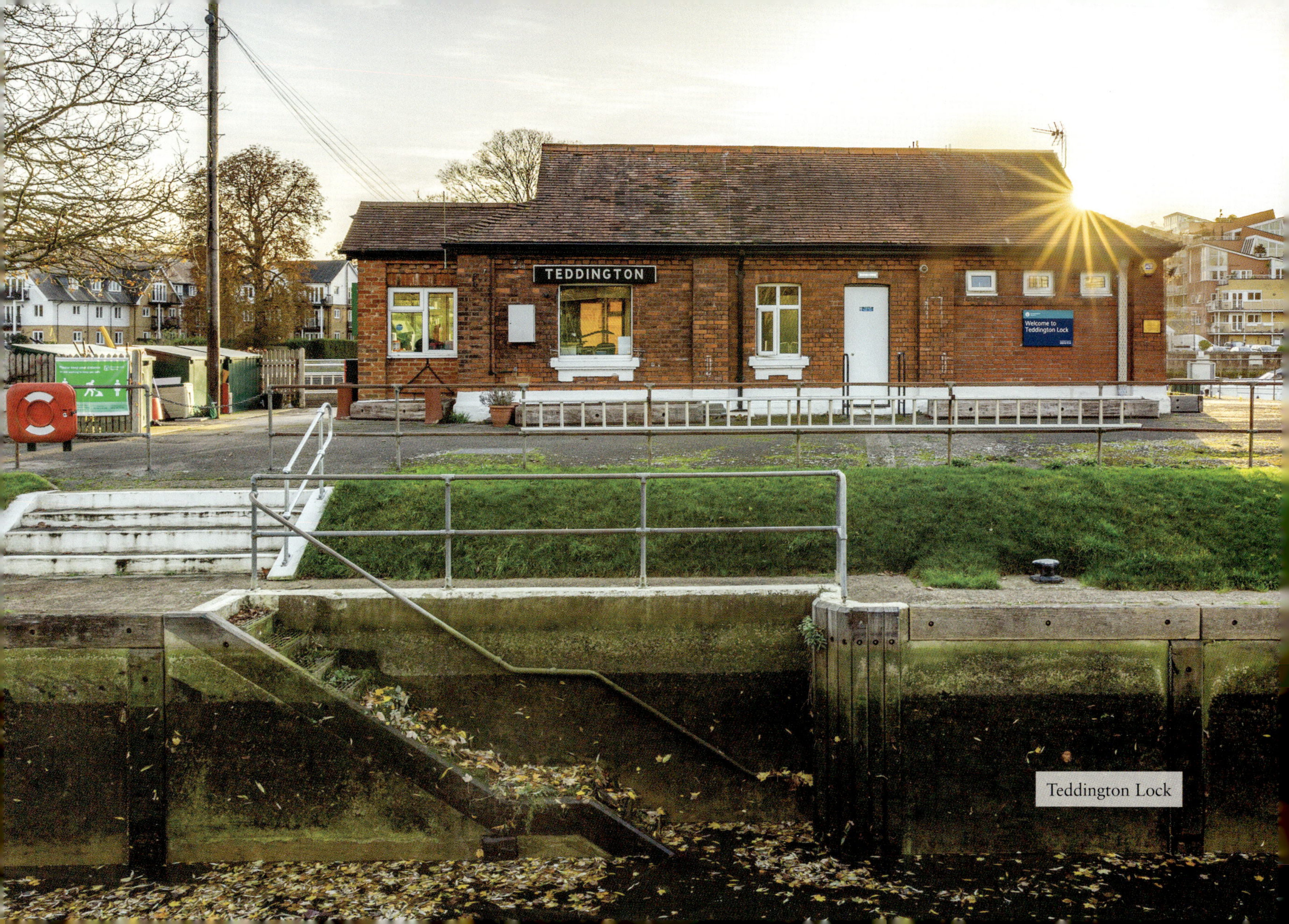
TEDDINGTON
Welcome to
Teddington Lock
Teddington Lock

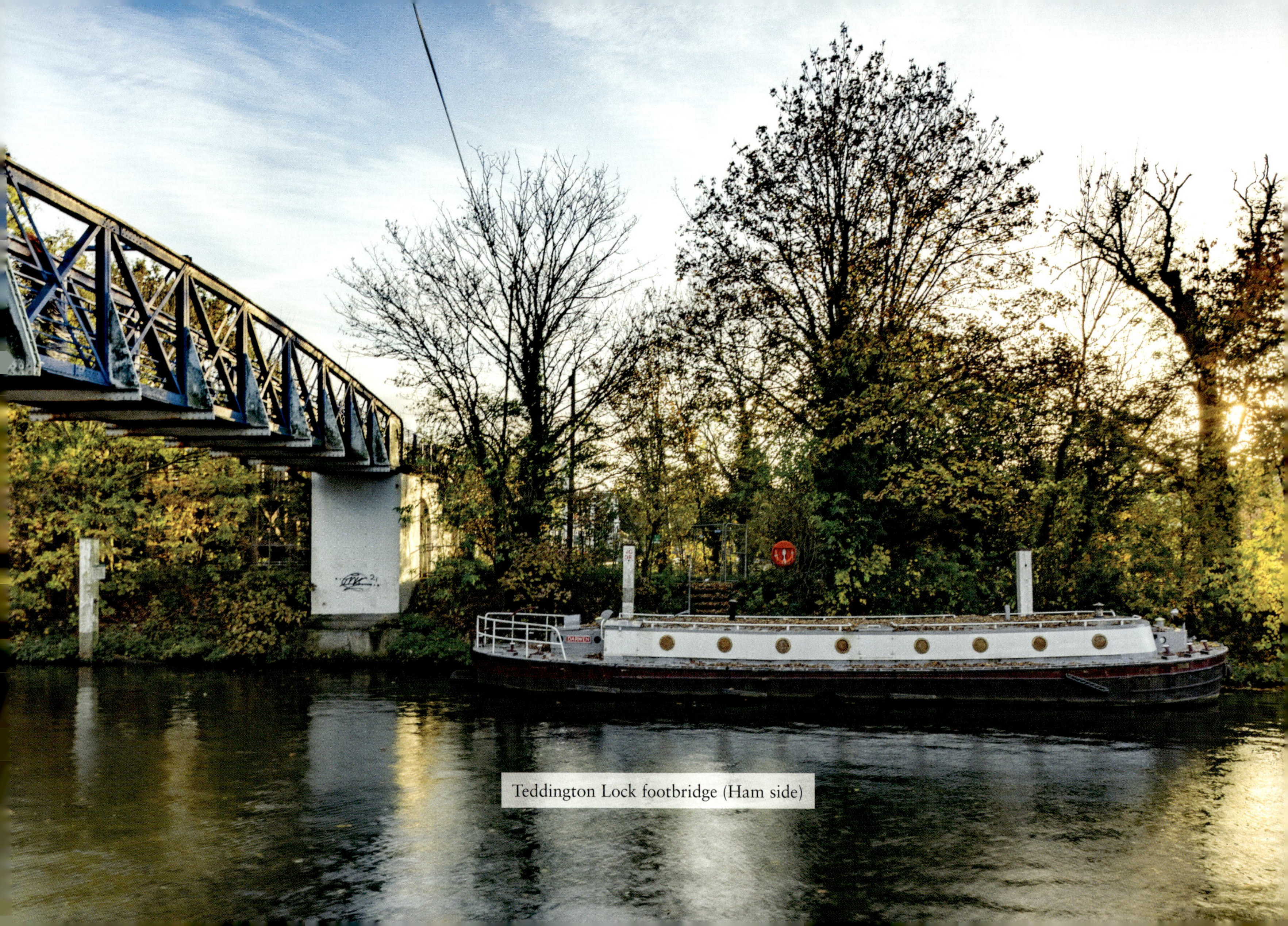

Teddington Lock footbridge (Ham side)

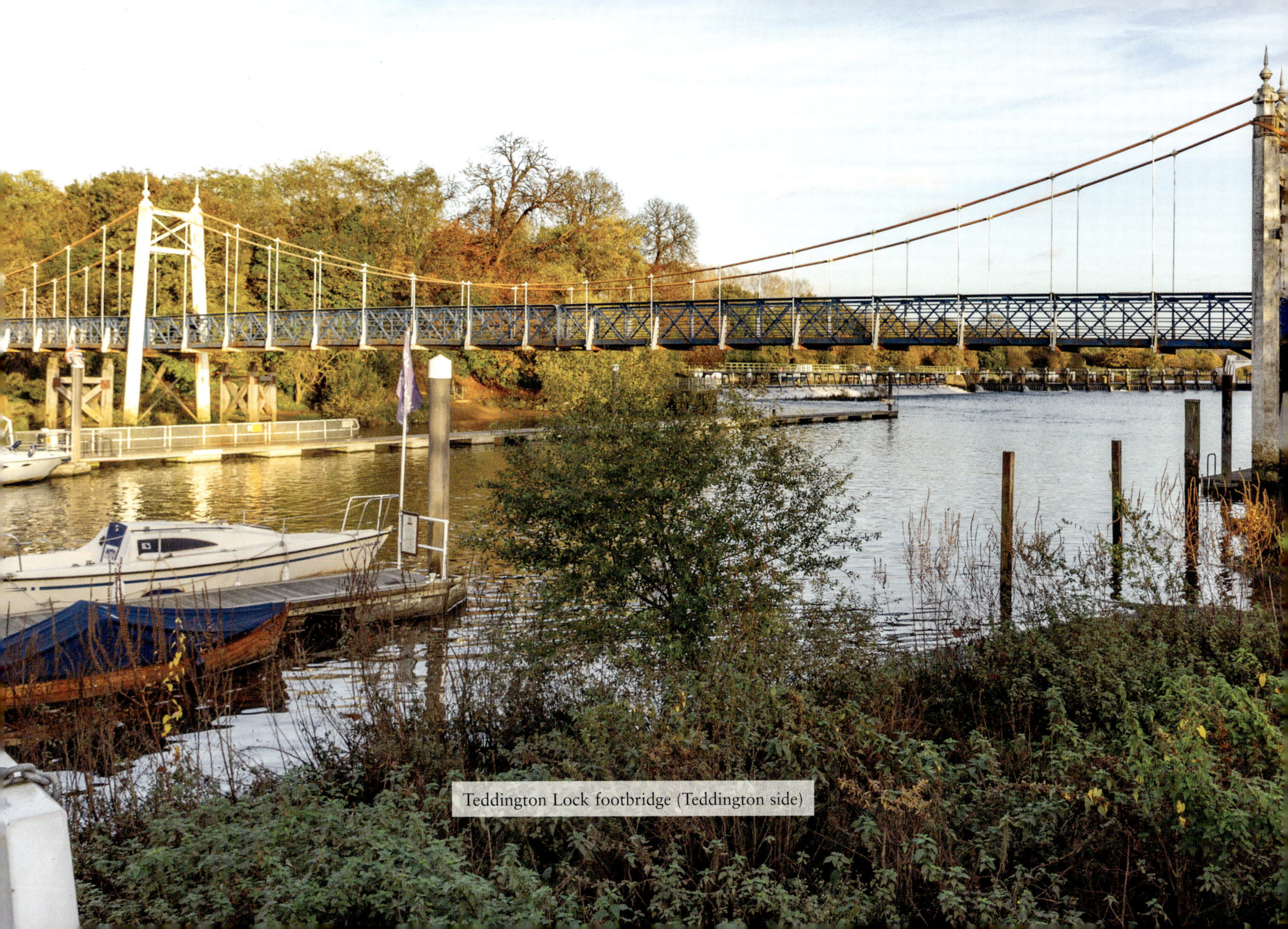

Teddington Lock footbridge (Teddington side)

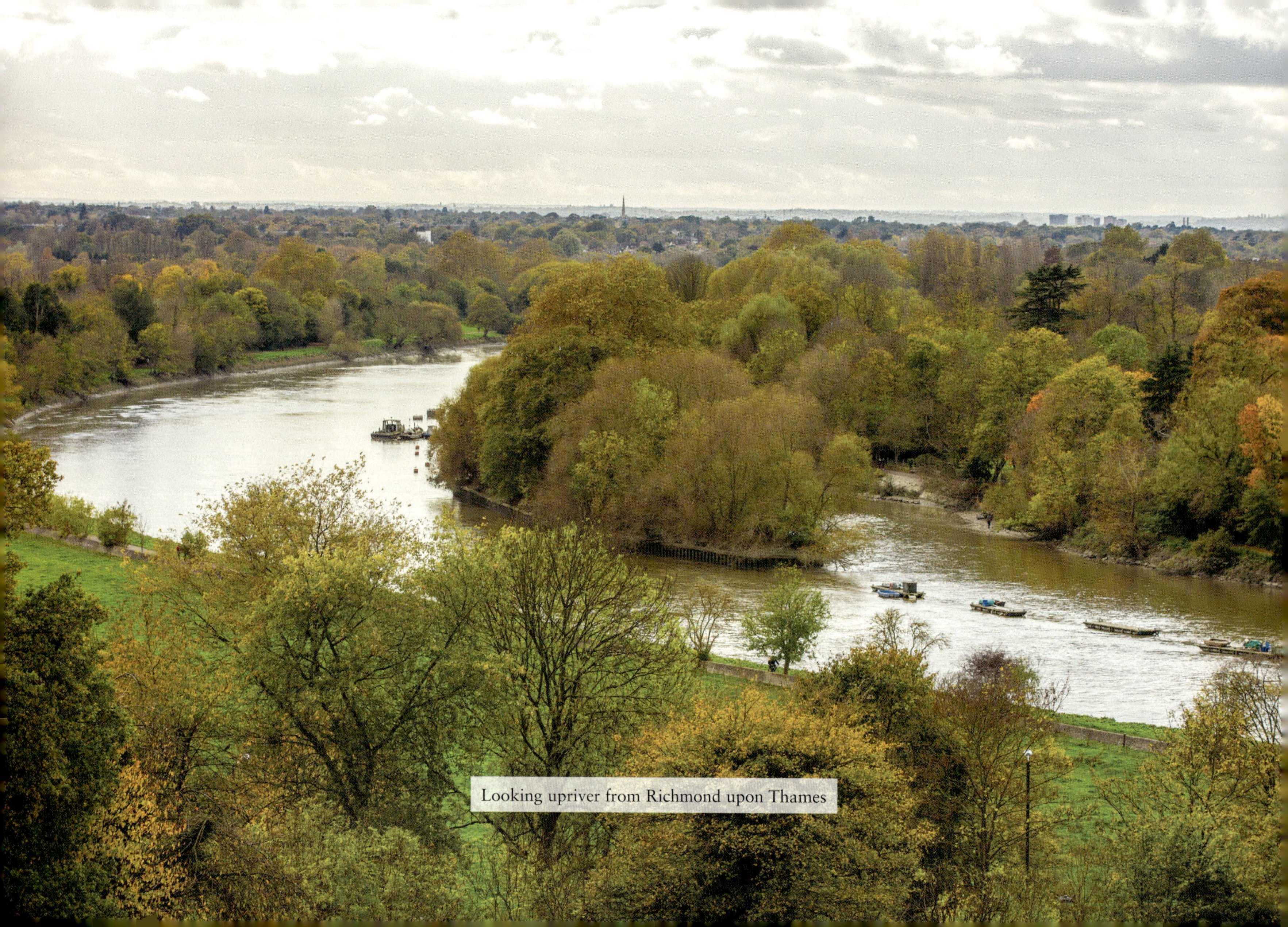

Looking upriver from Richmond upon Thames

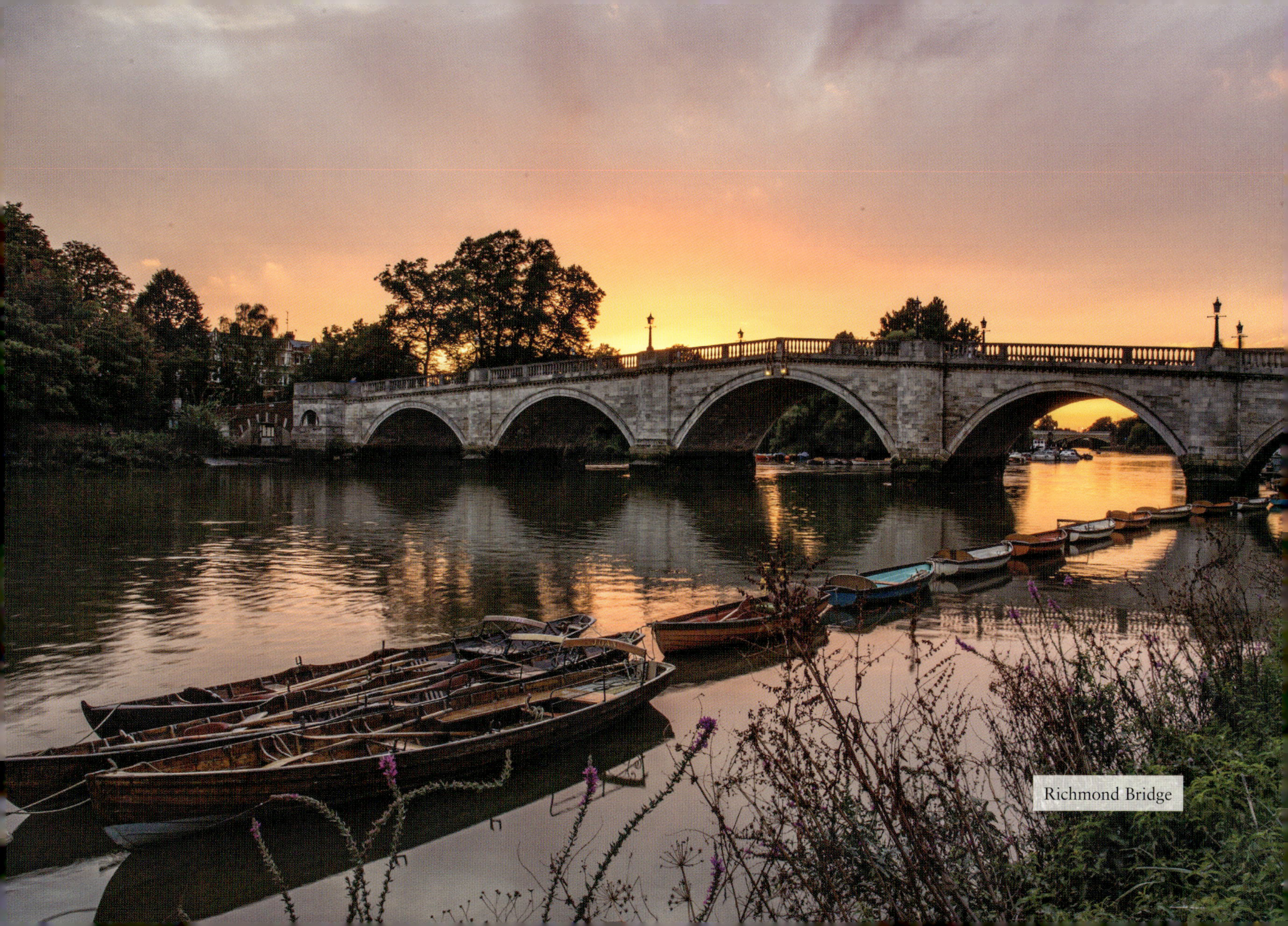

Richmond Bridge

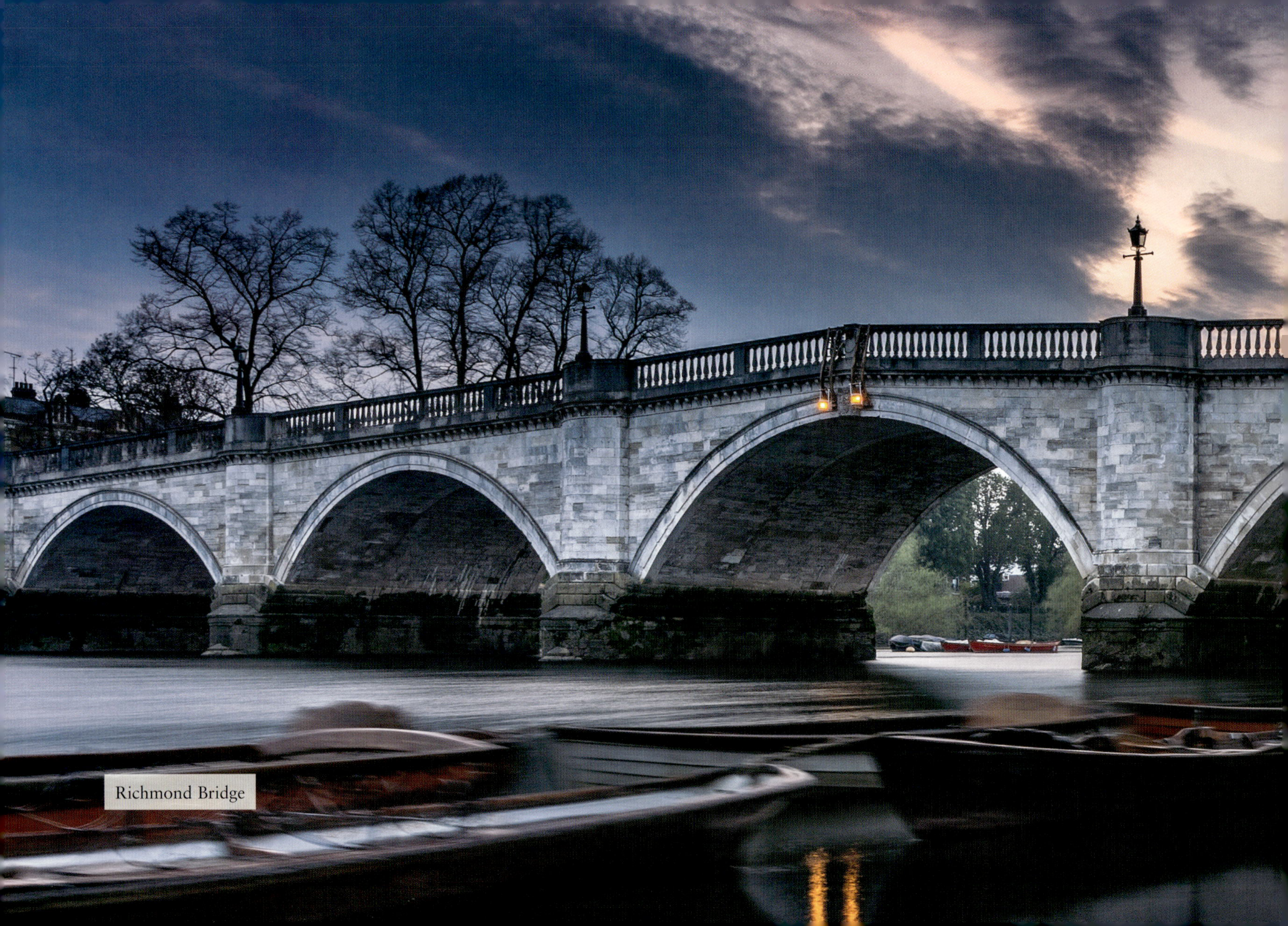

Richmond Bridge

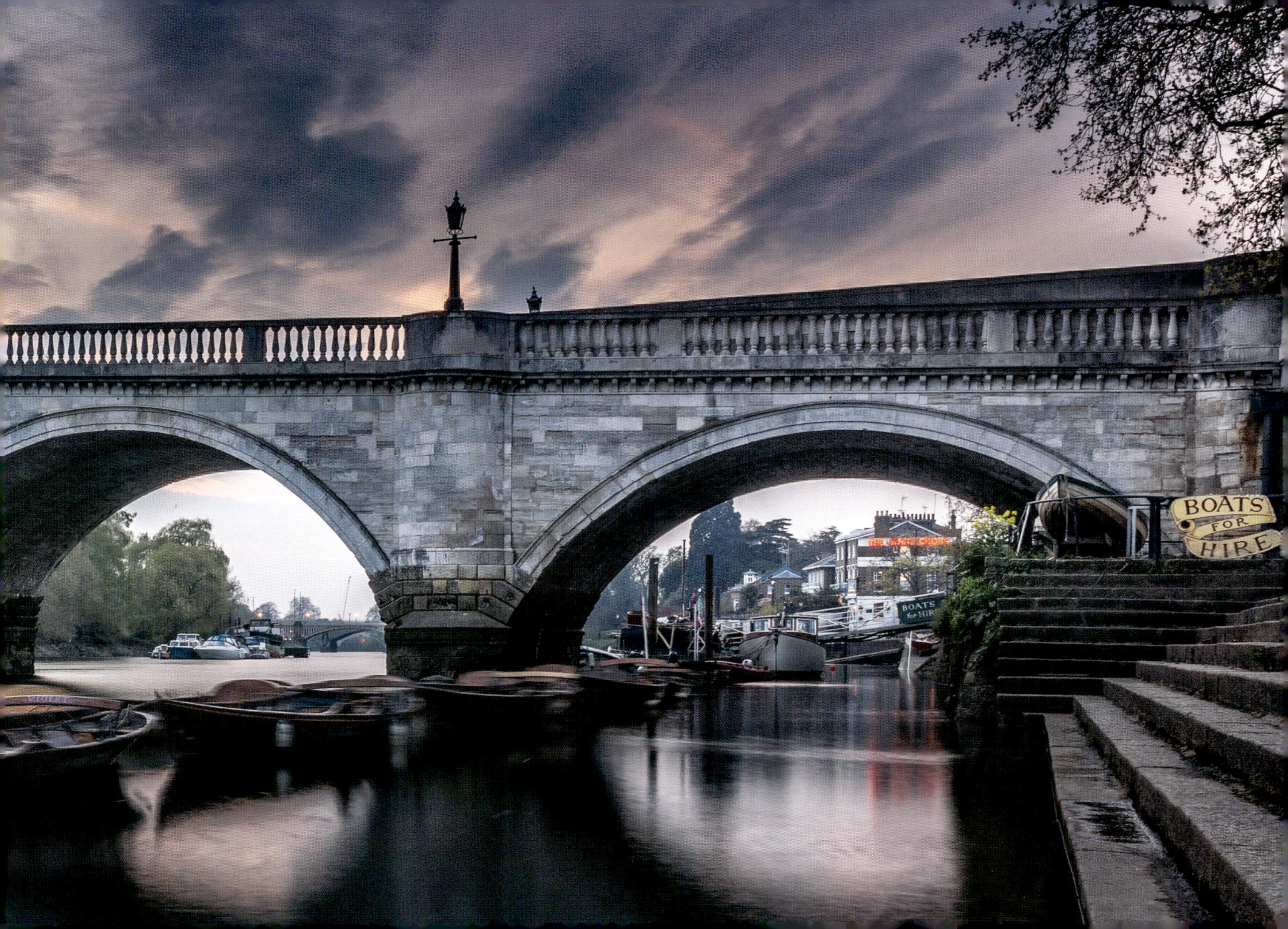
BOATS
FOR
HIRE
THE WHITE CROSS
BOATS for HIRE
VIOLET

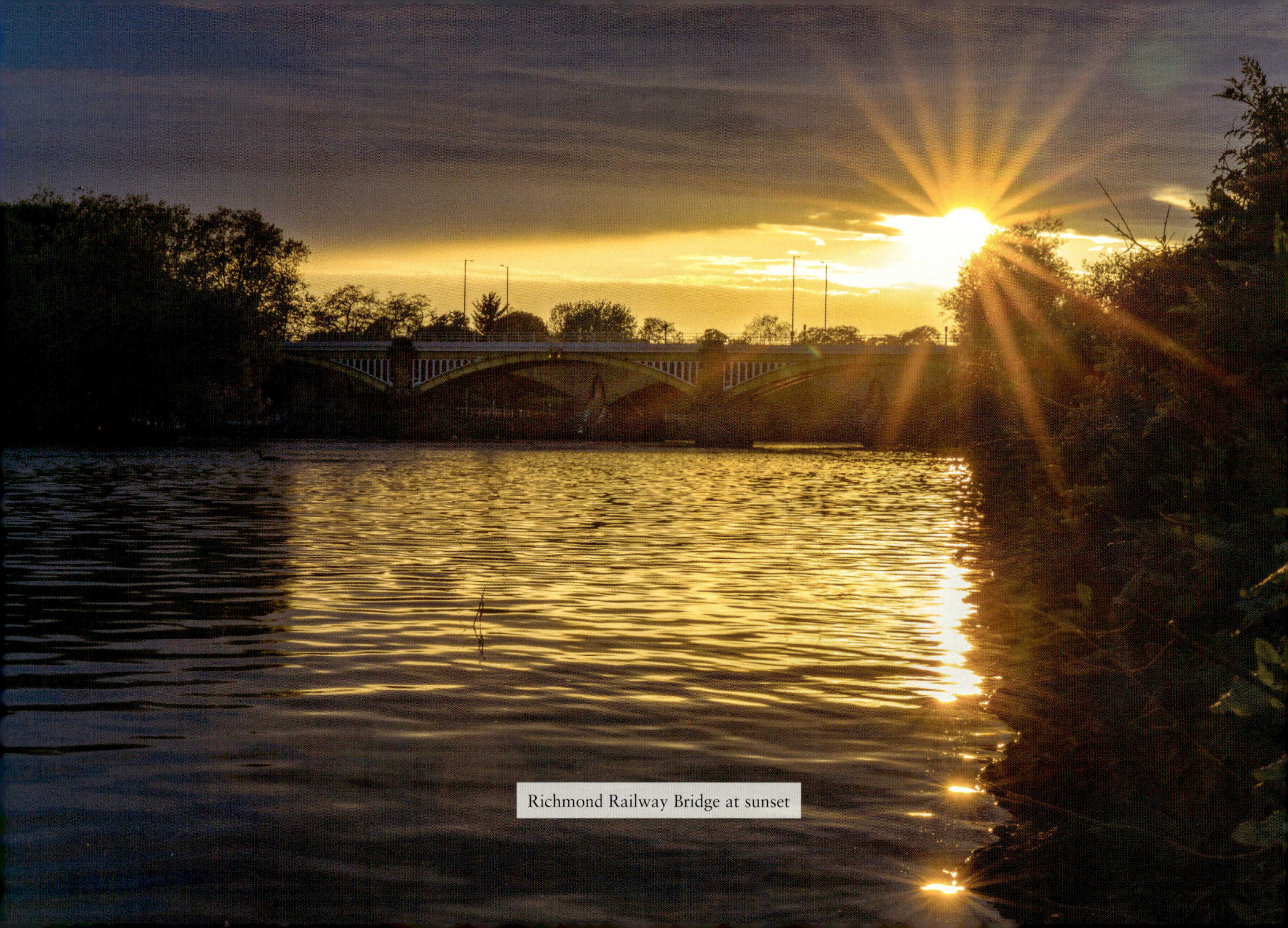

Richmond Railway Bridge at sunset

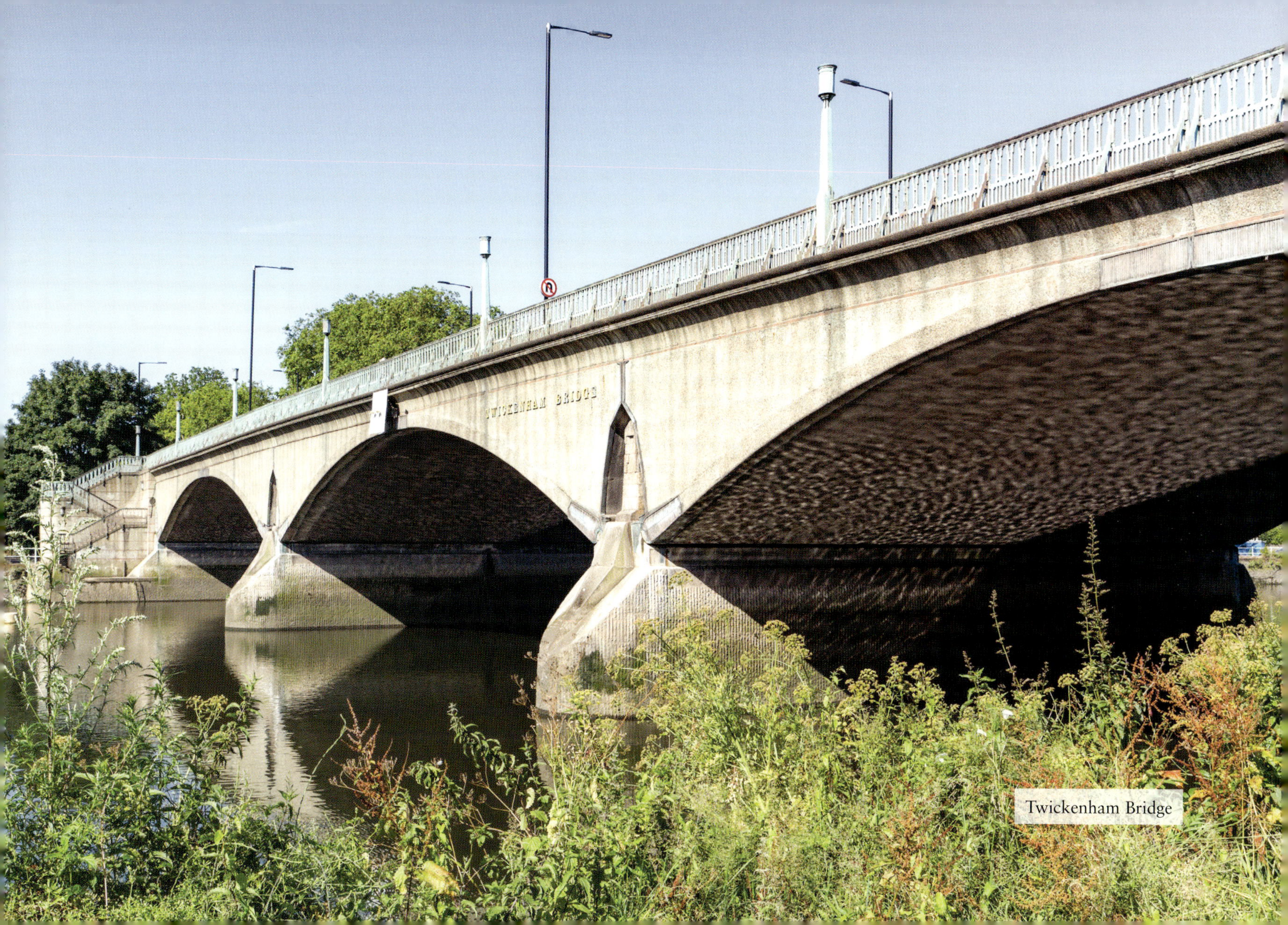

Twickenham Bridge

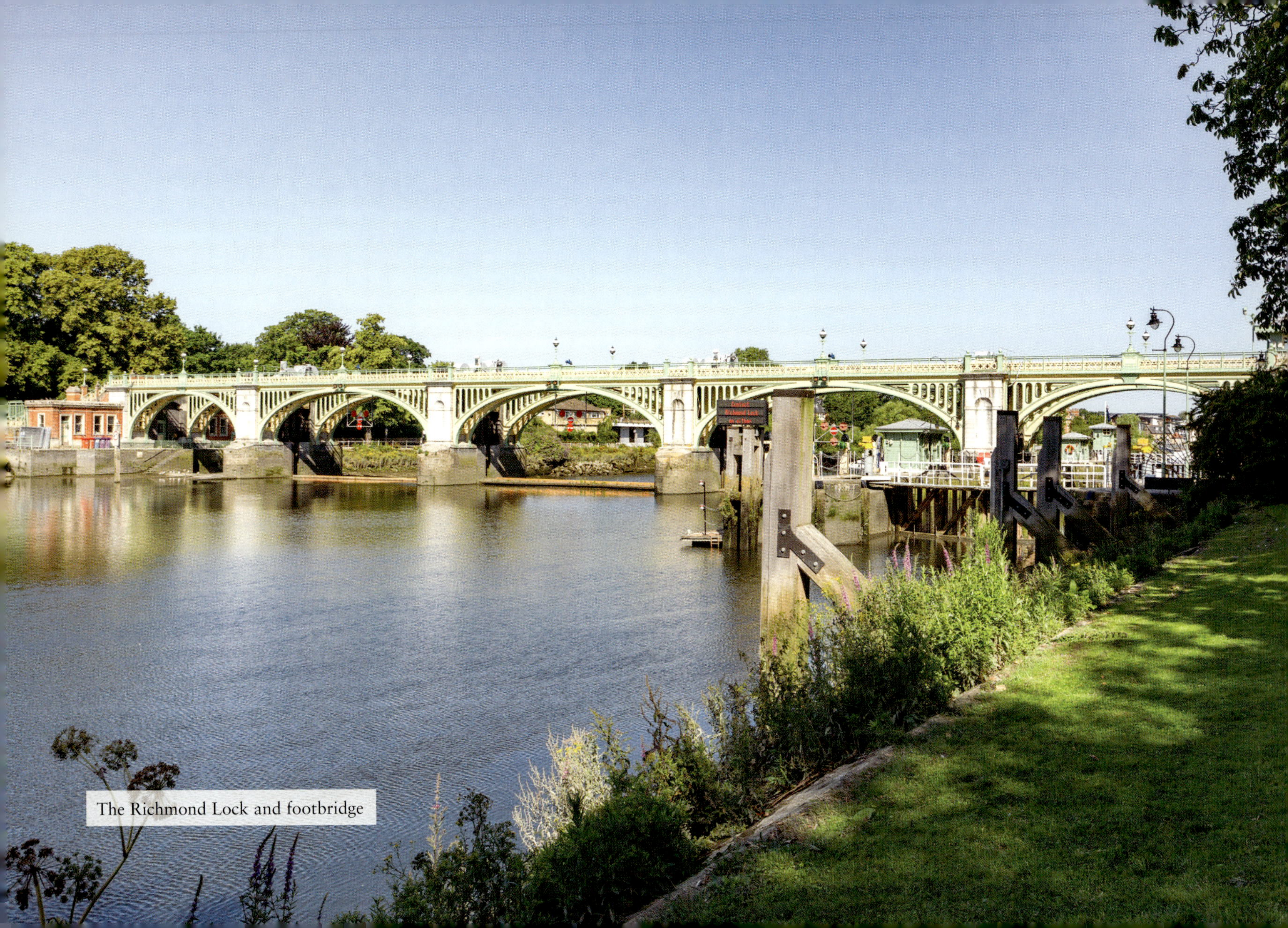

The Richmond Lock and footbridge

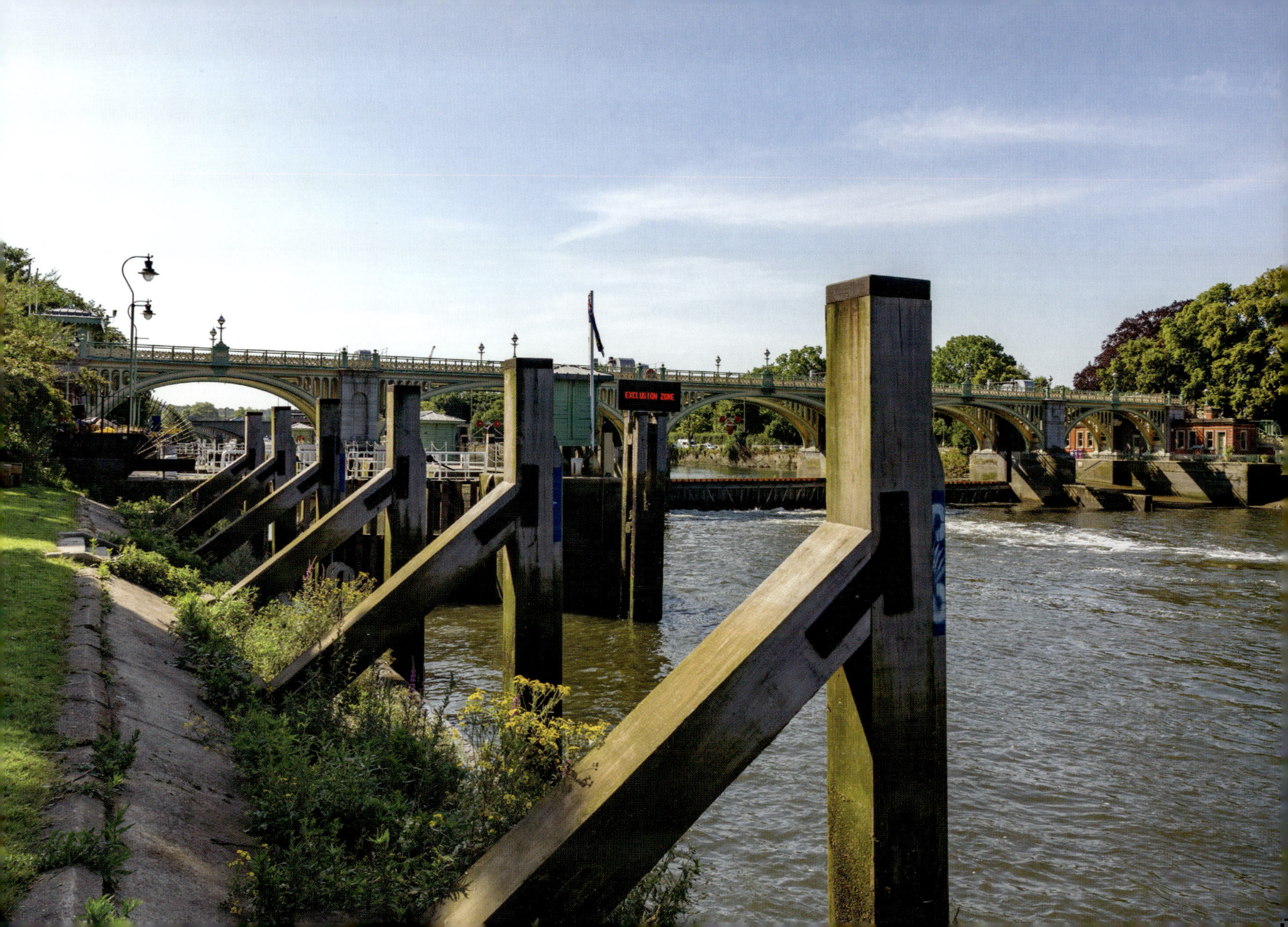
EXCLUSION ZONE

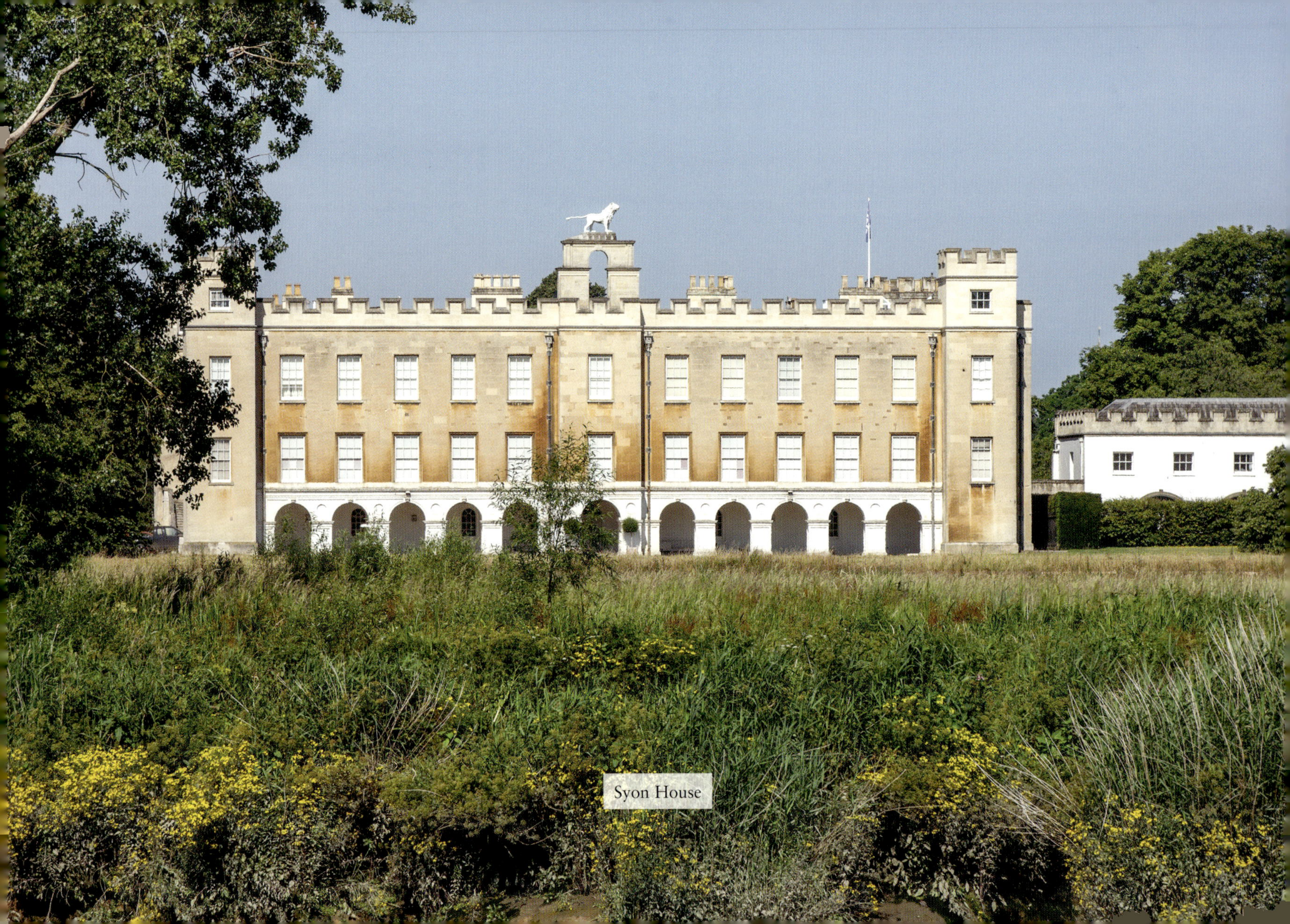

Syon House

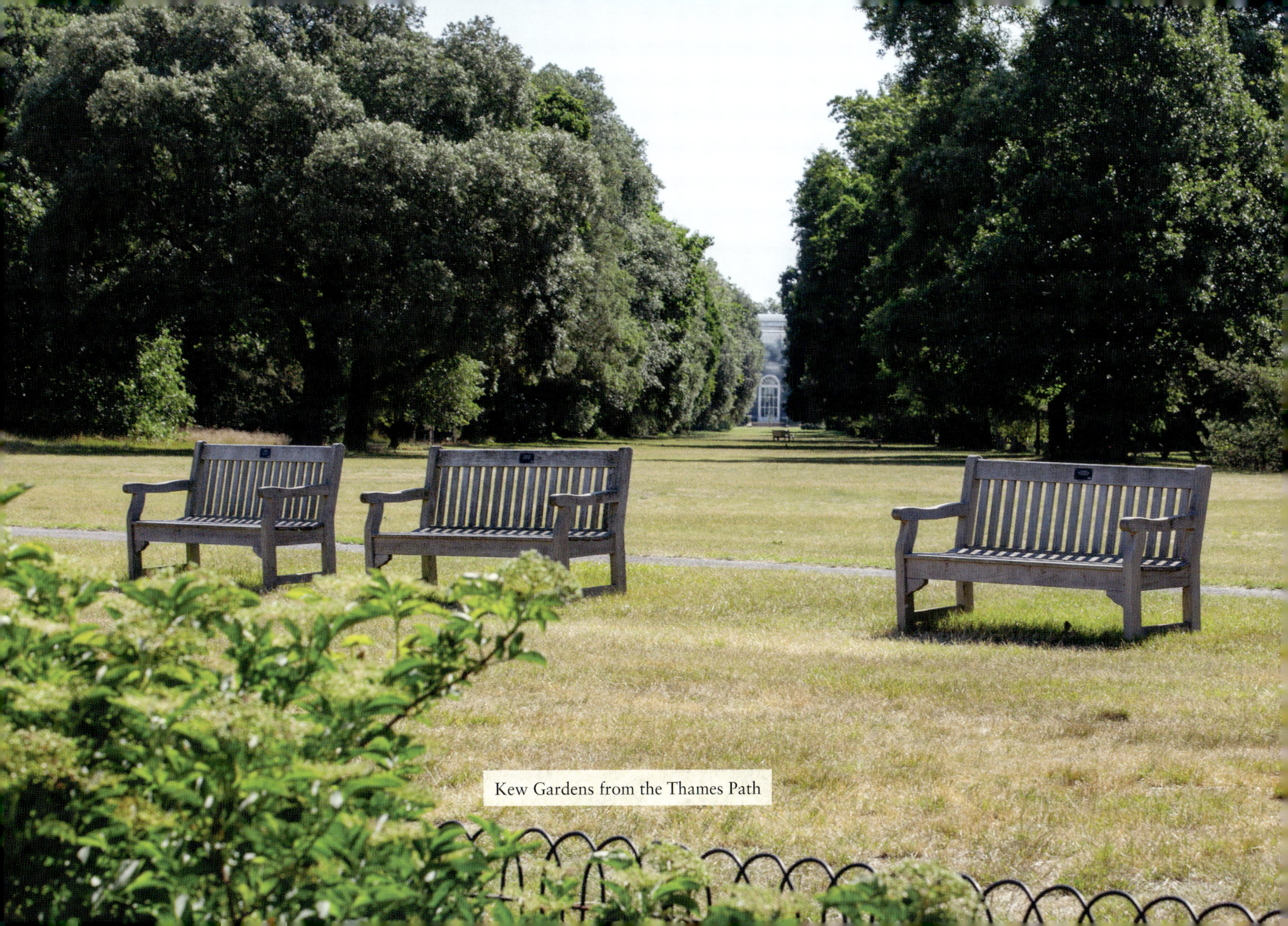

Kew Gardens from the Thames Path

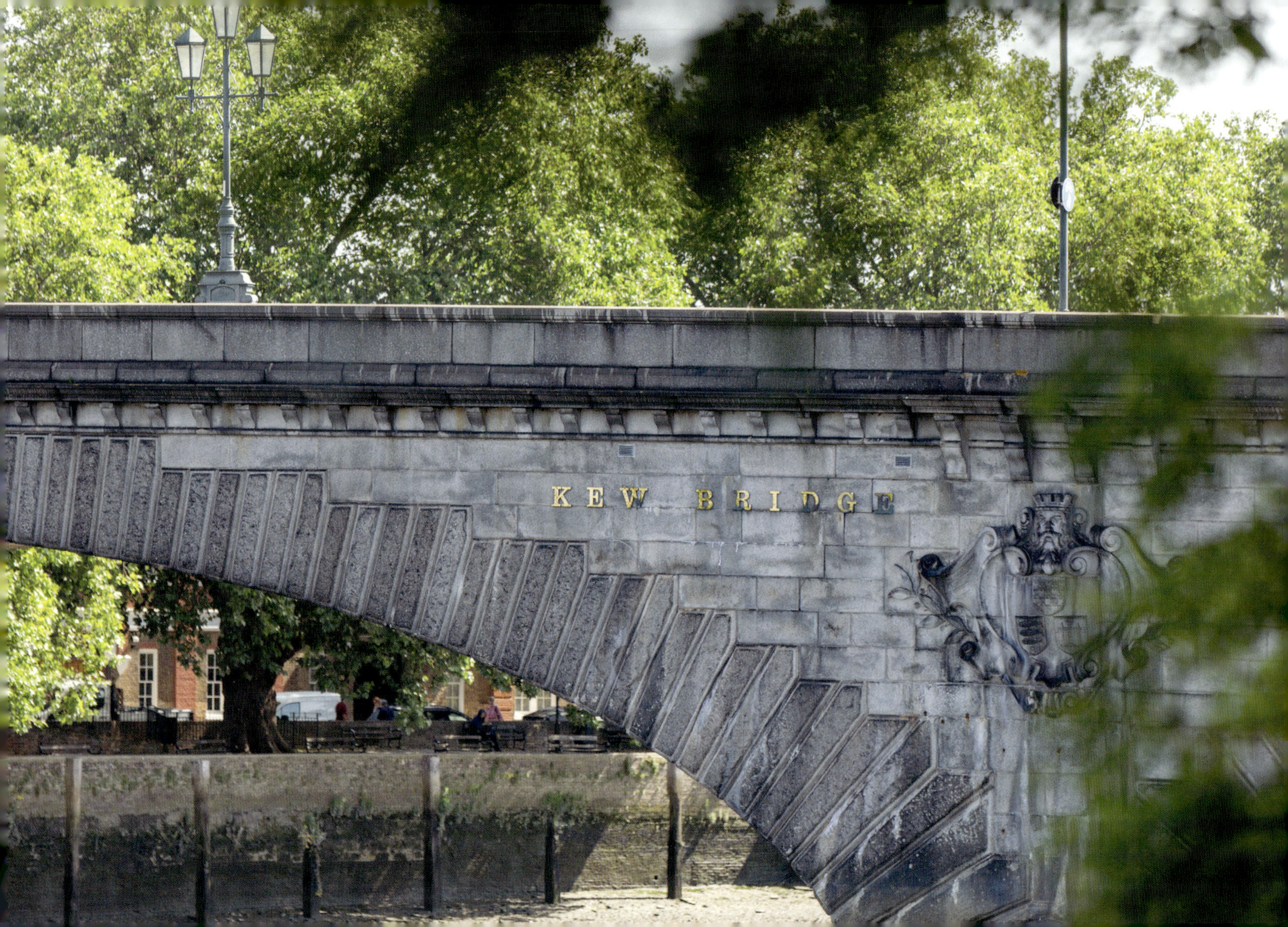

KEW BRIDGE

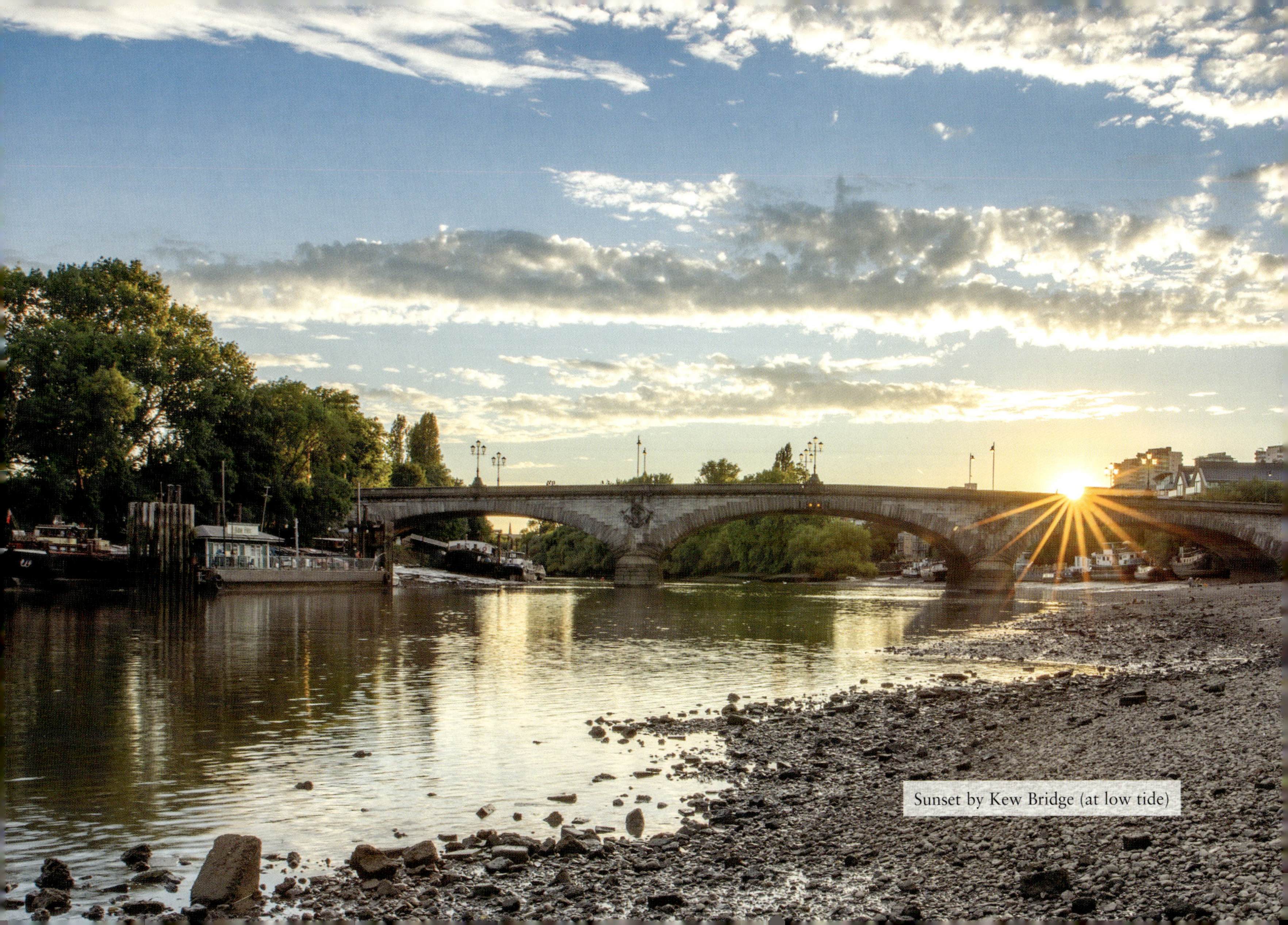

Sunset by Kew Bridge (at low tide)

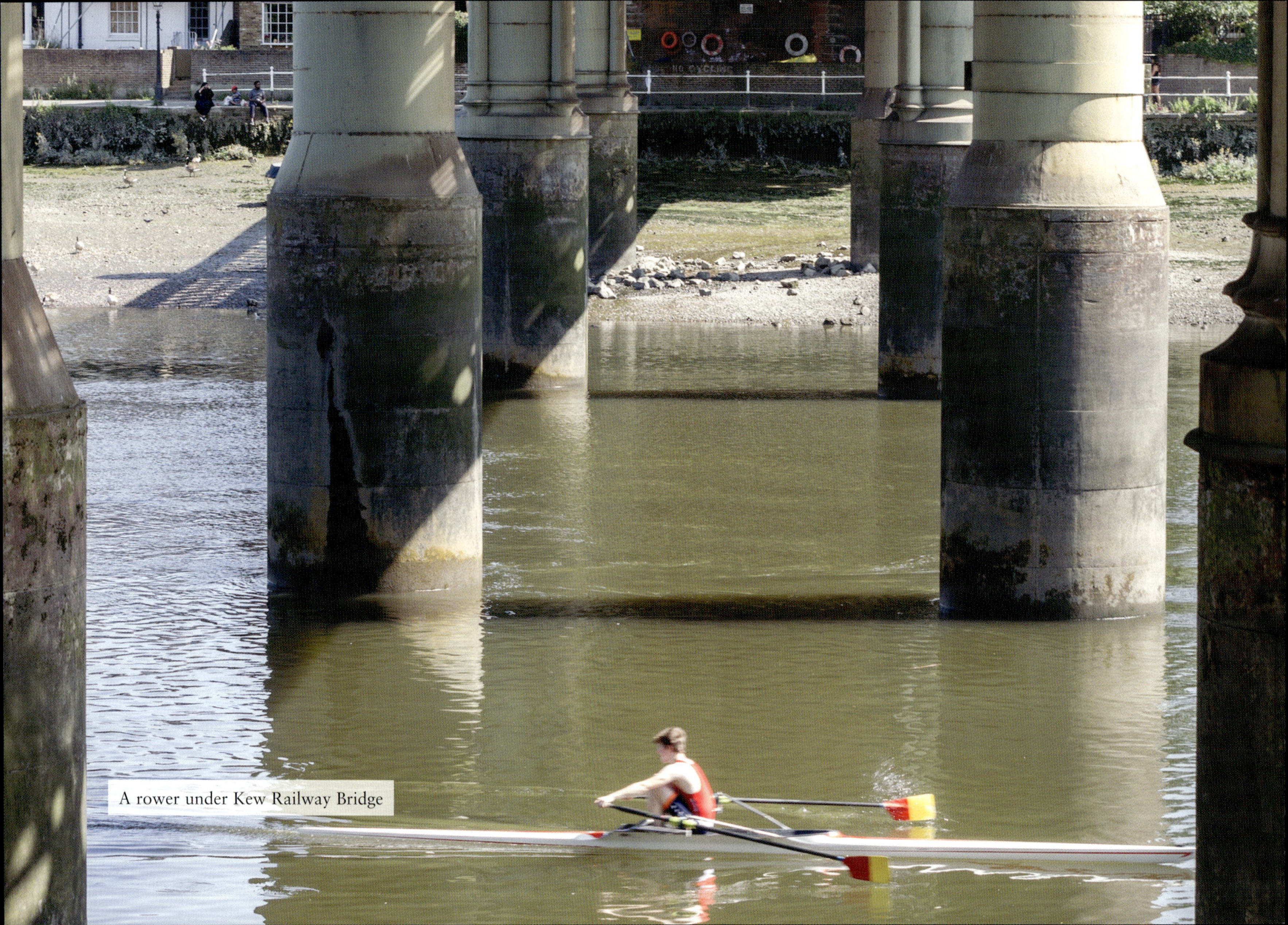

A rower under Kew Railway Bridge

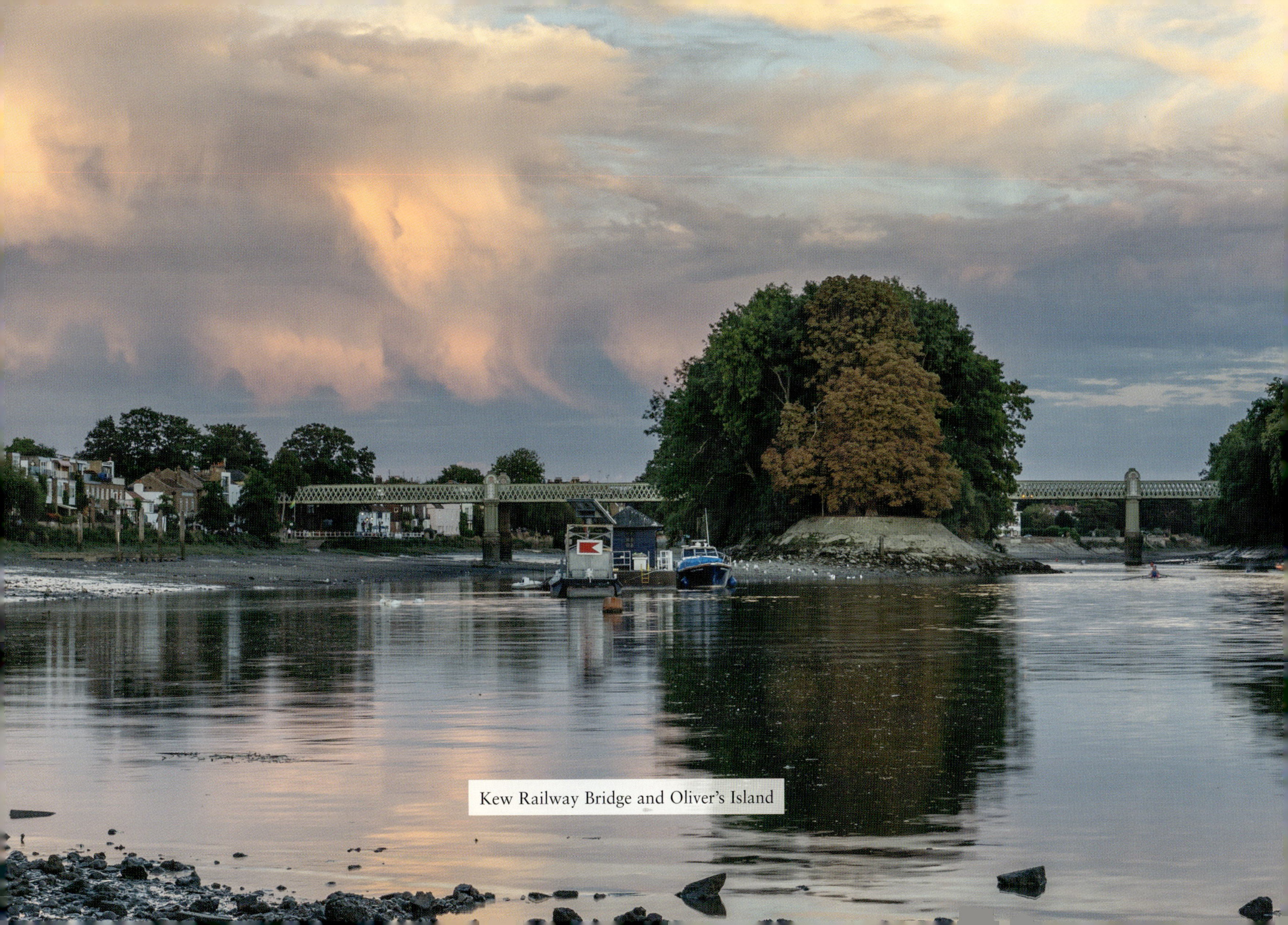

Kew Railway Bridge and Oliver's Island

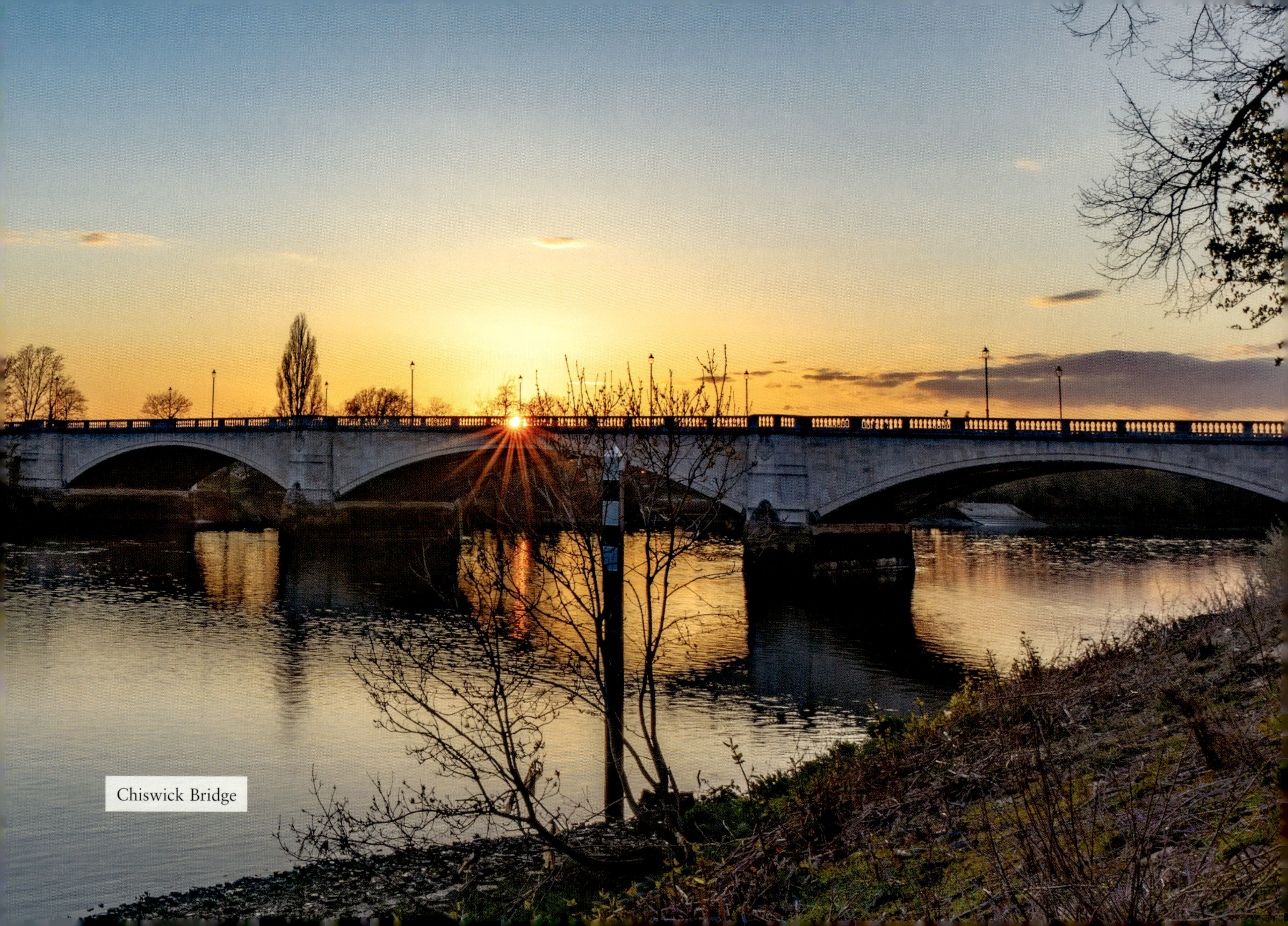
Chiswick Bridge

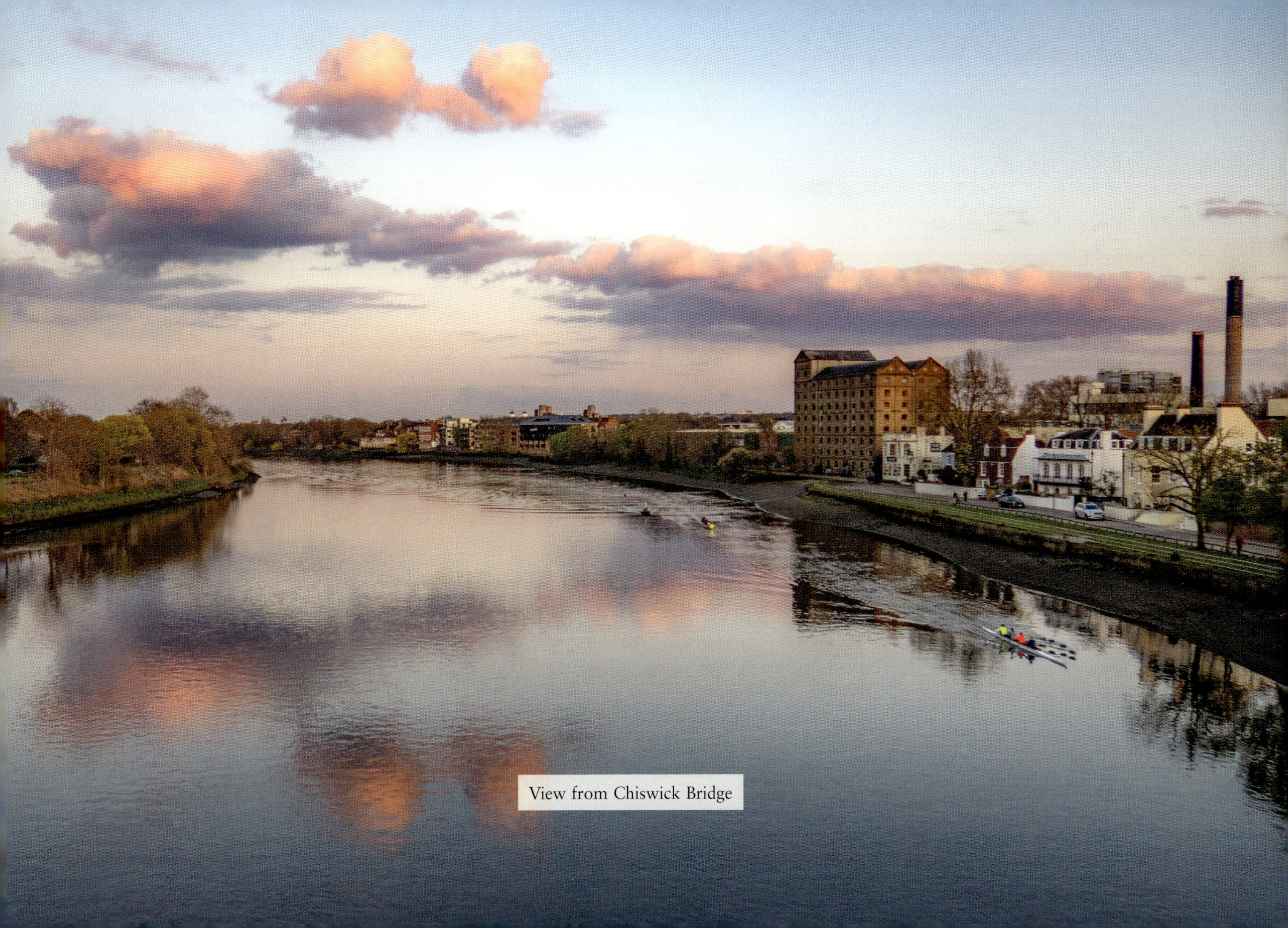

View from Chiswick Bridge

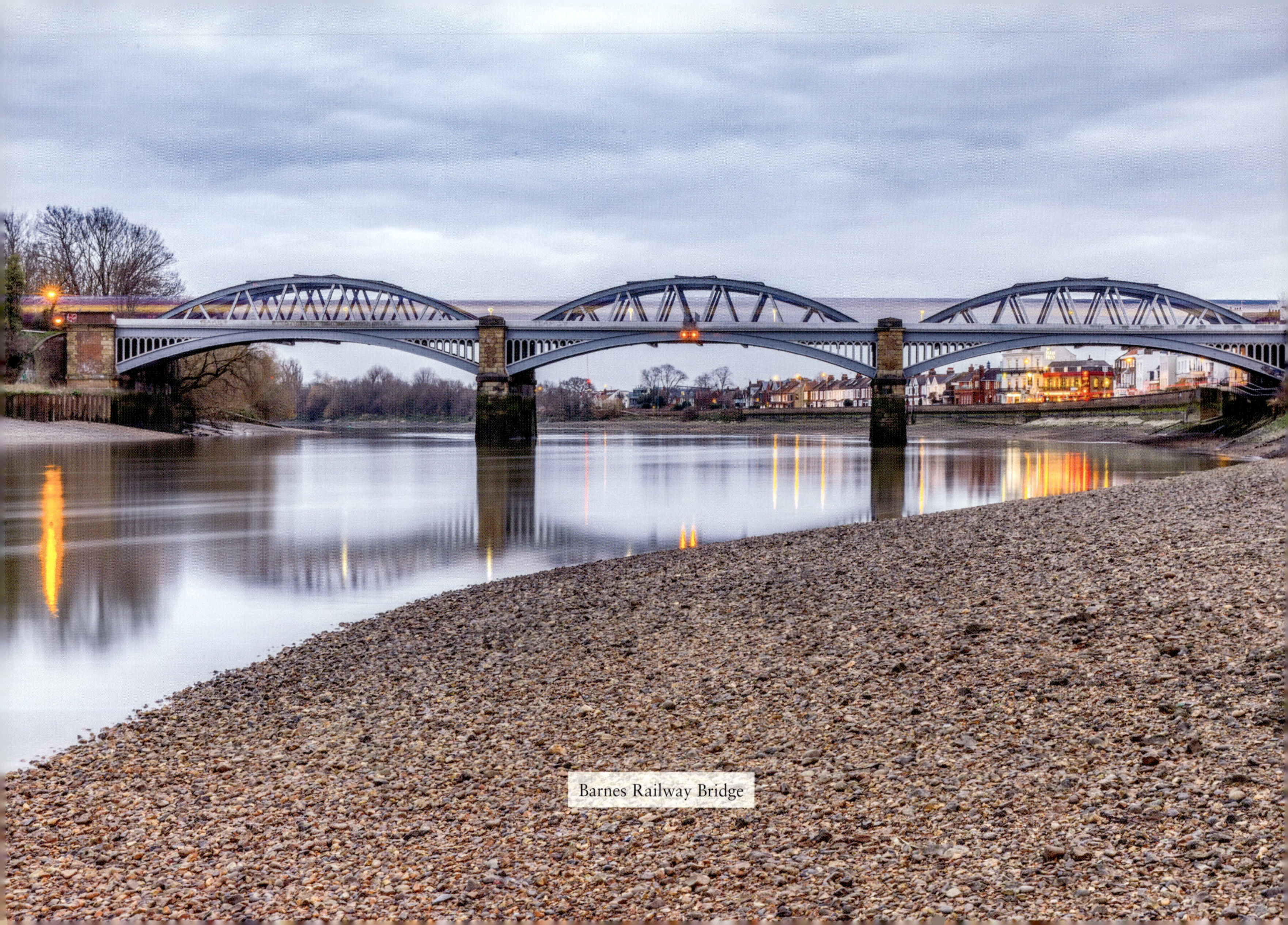

Barnes Railway Bridge

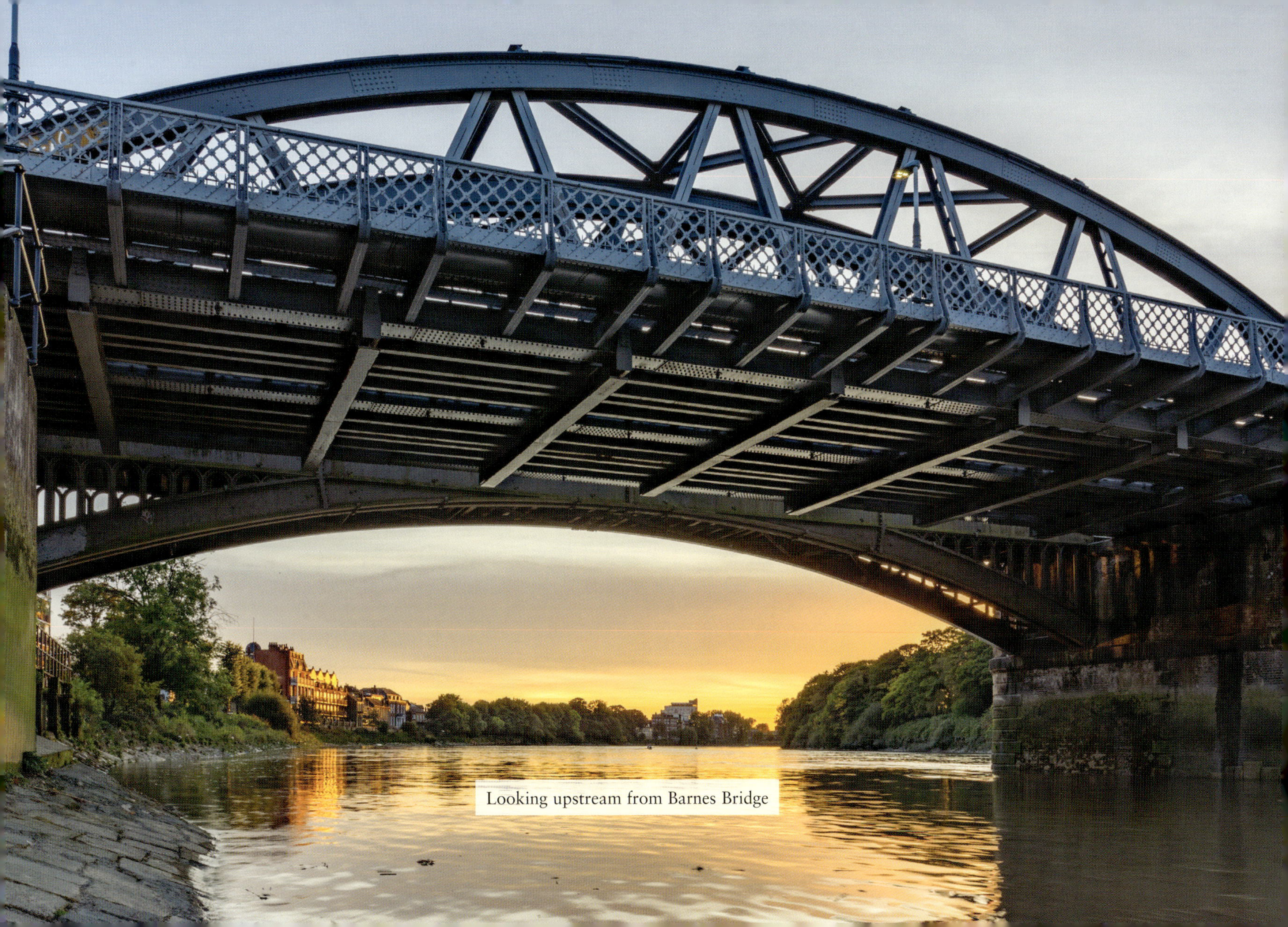

Looking upstream from Barnes Bridge

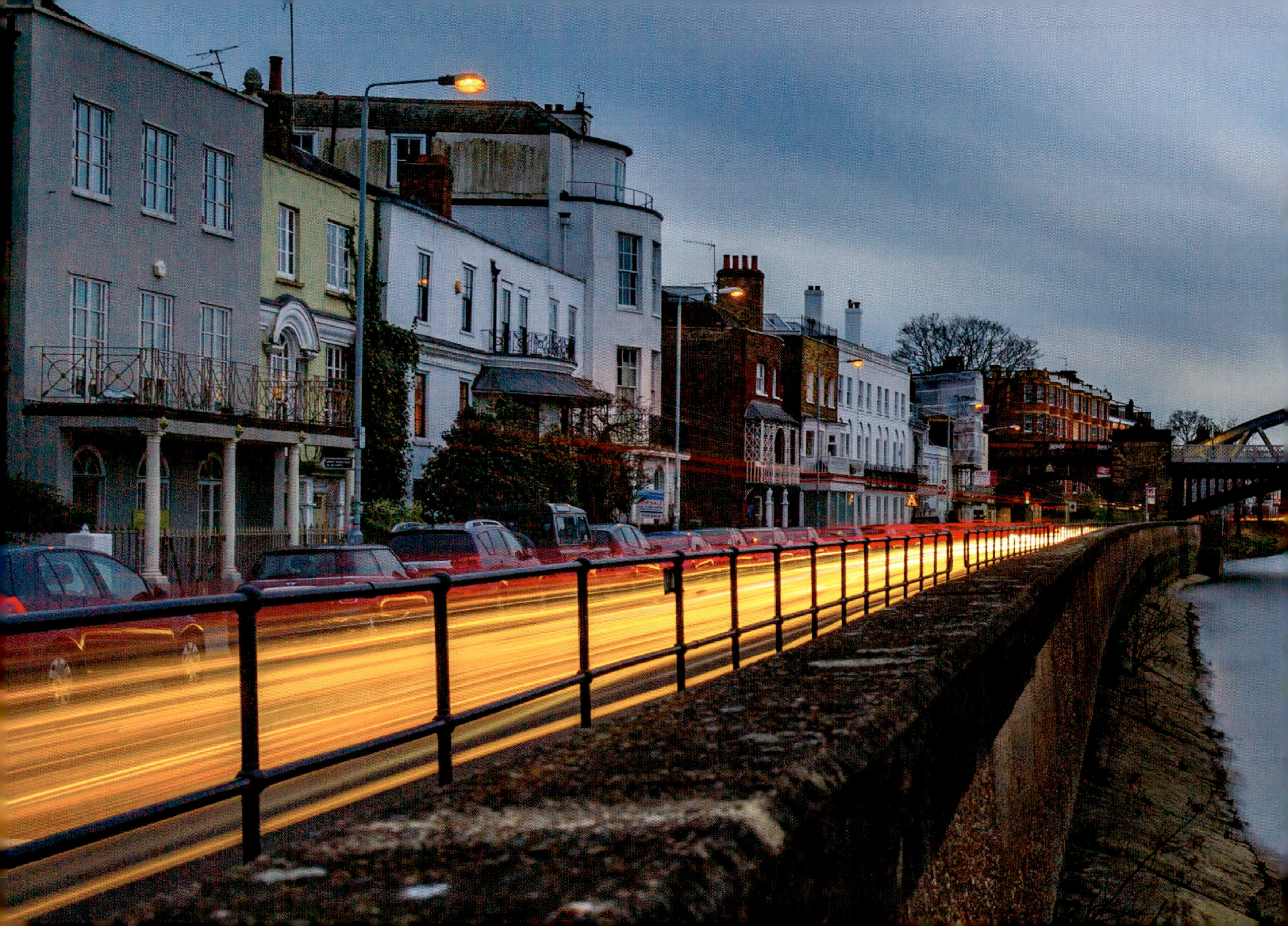

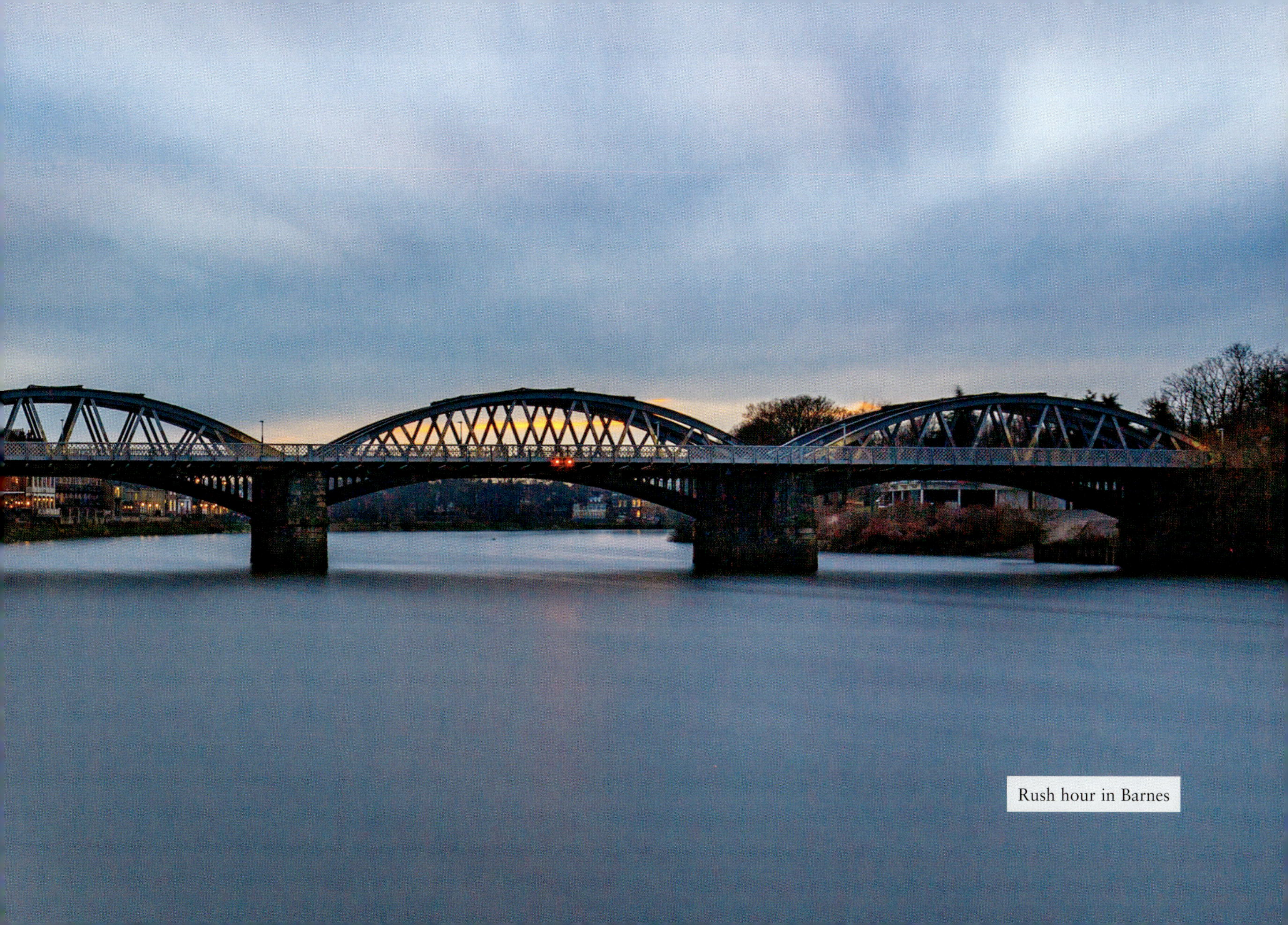

Rush hour in Barnes

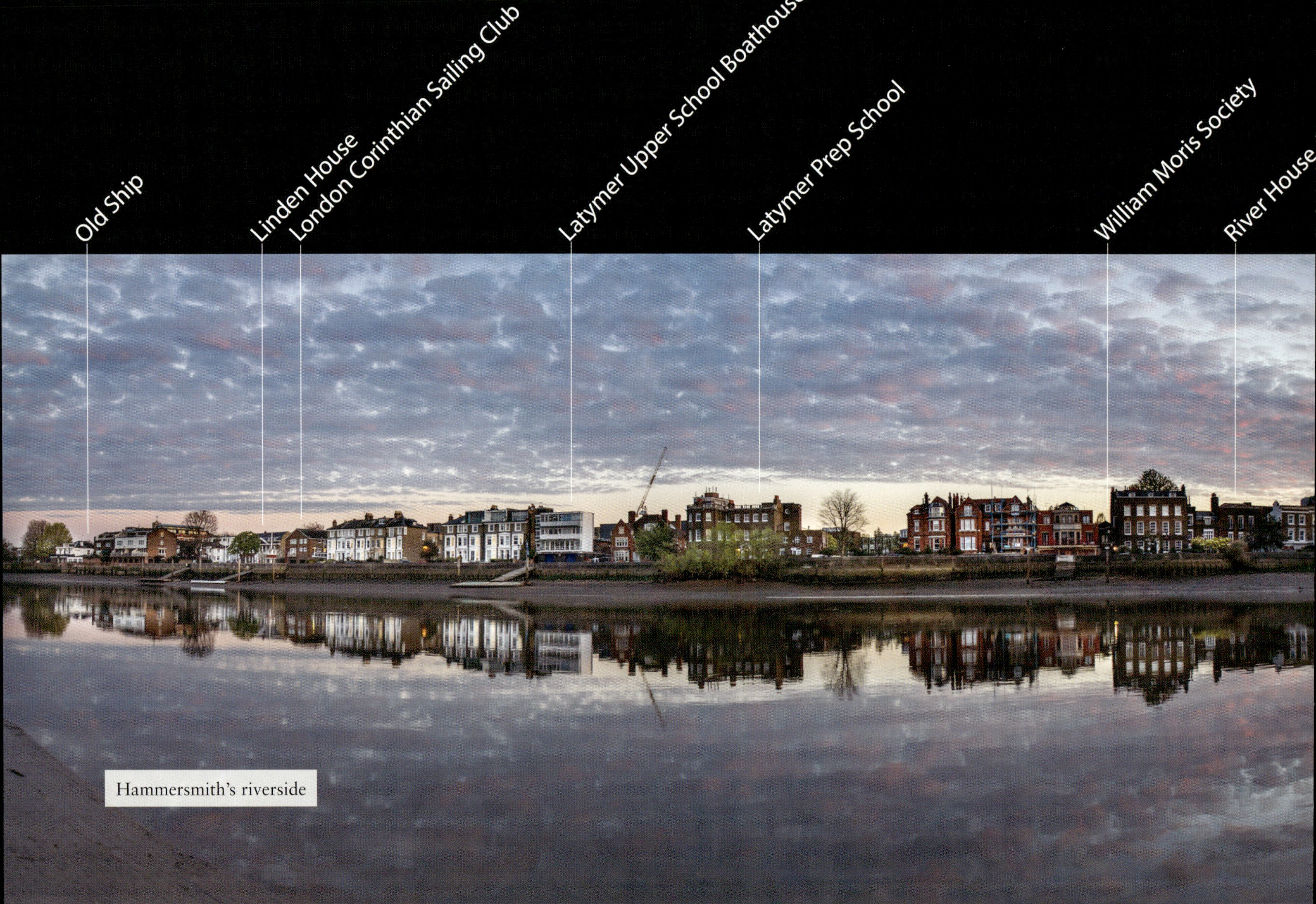

Hammersmith's riverside

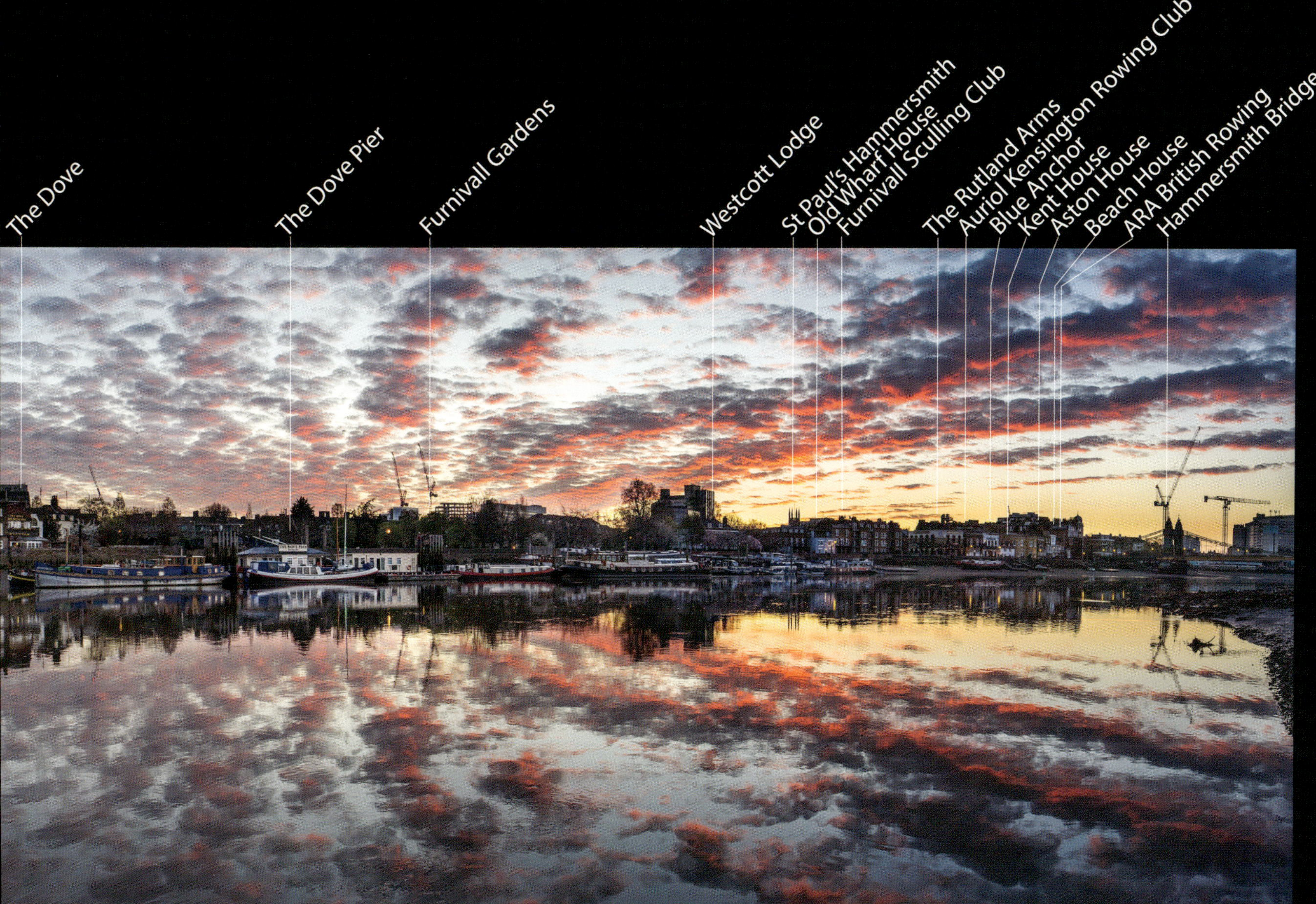

The Dove
The Dove Pier
Furnivall Gardens
Westcott Lodge
St Paul's Hammersmith
Old Wharf House
Furnivall Sculling Club
The Rutland Arms
Auriol Kensington Rowing Club
Blue Anchor
Kent House
Aston House
Beach House
ARA British Rowing
Hammersmith Bridge

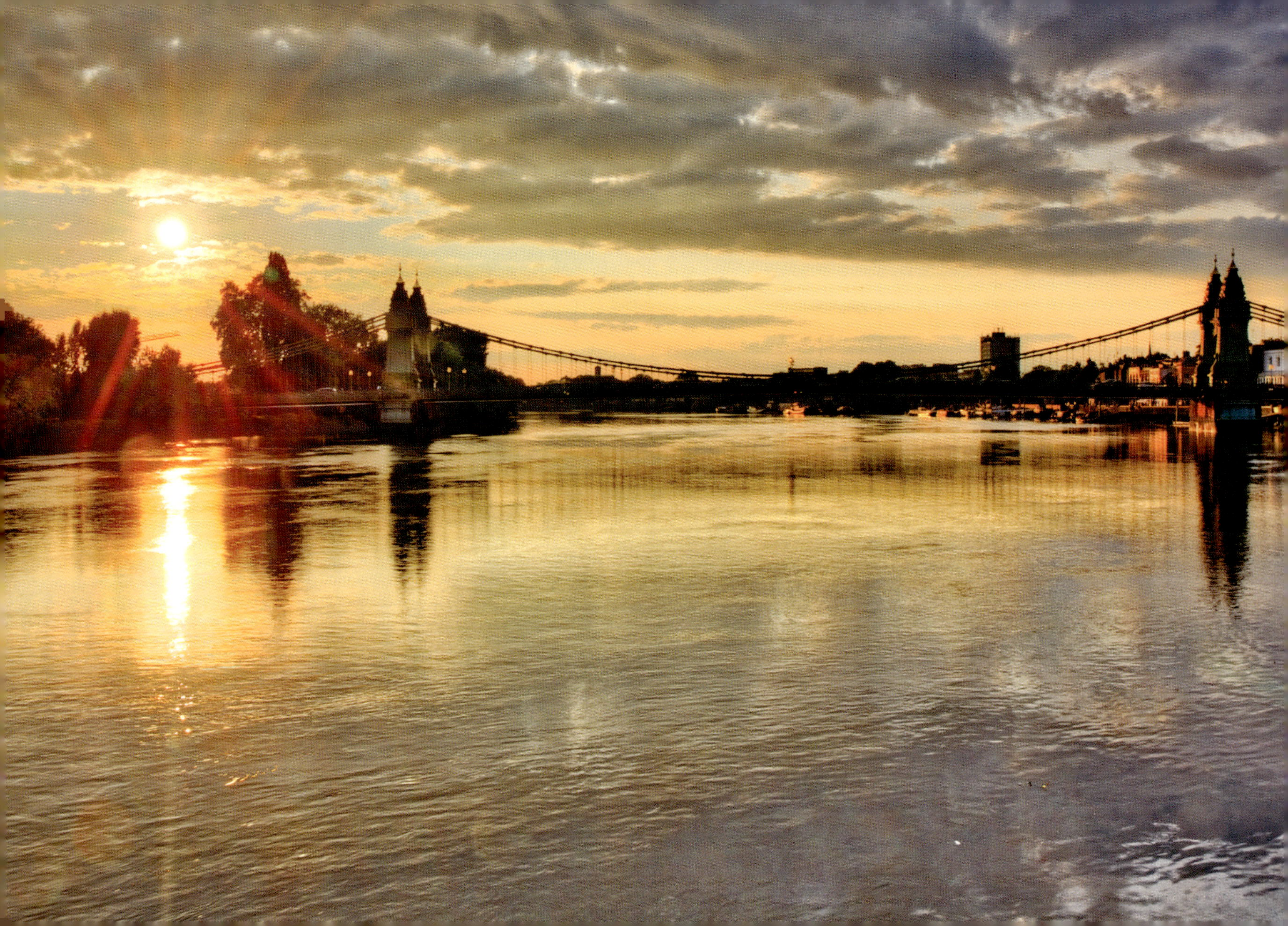

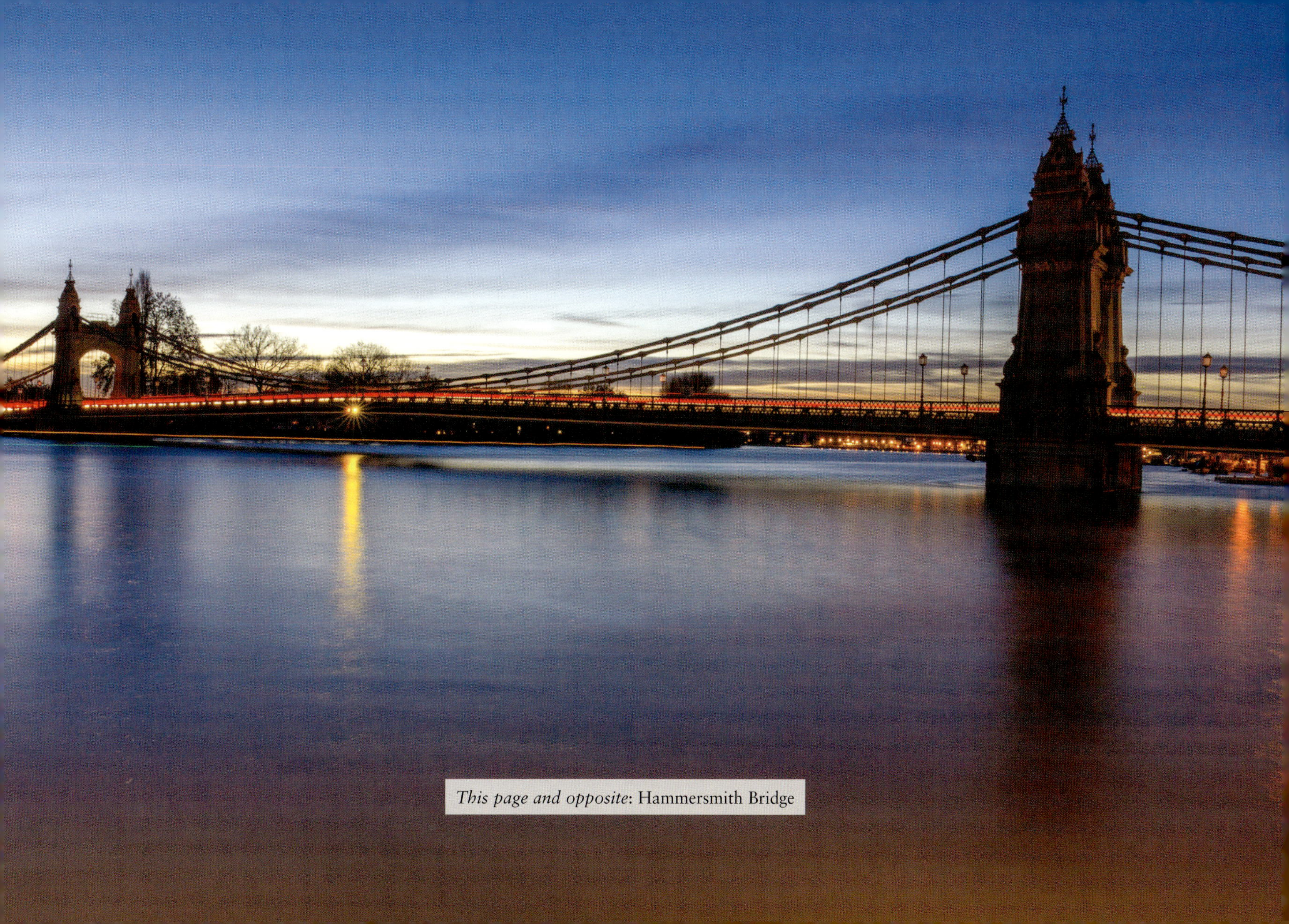

This page and opposite: Hammersmith Bridge

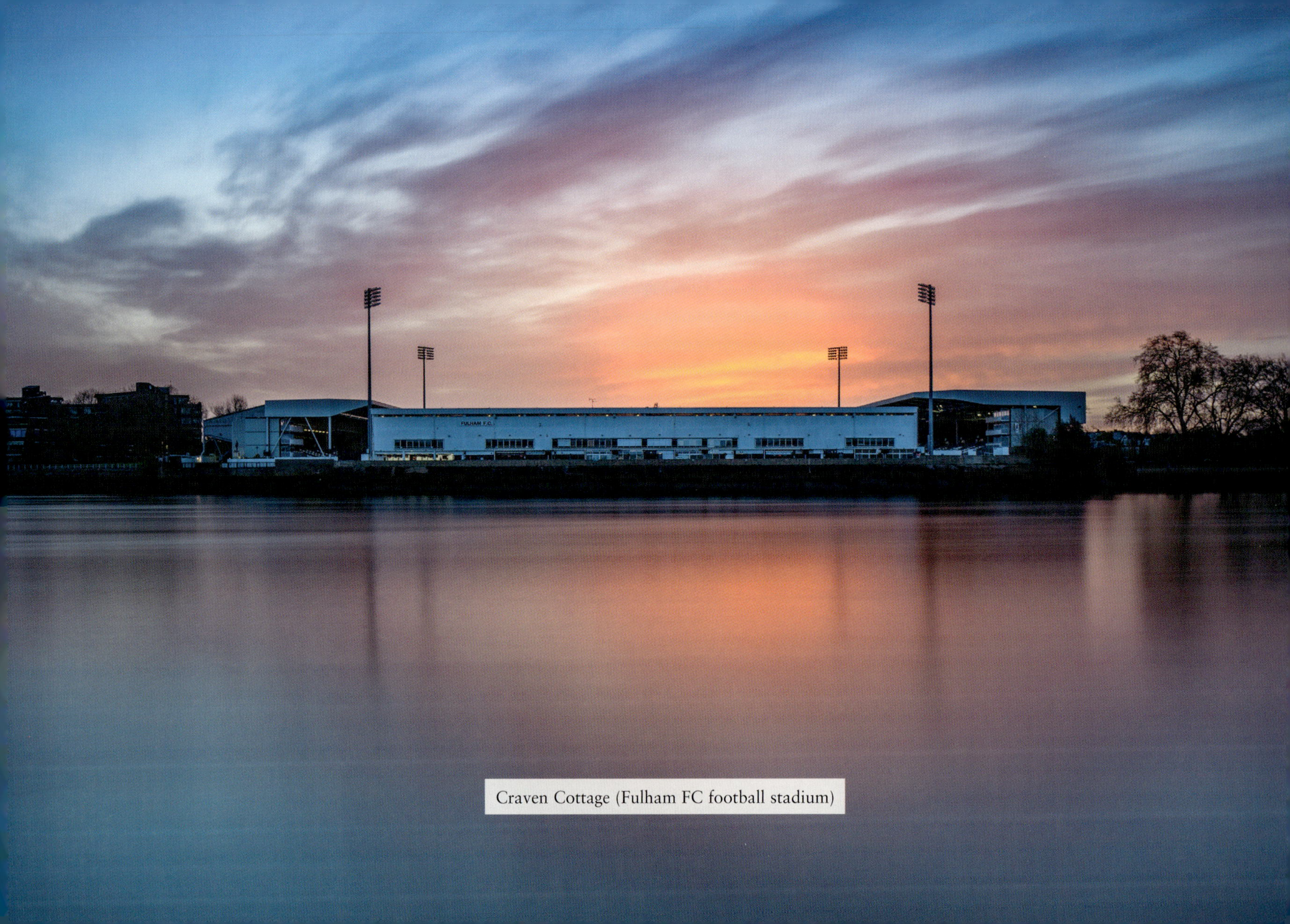

Craven Cottage (Fulham FC football stadium)

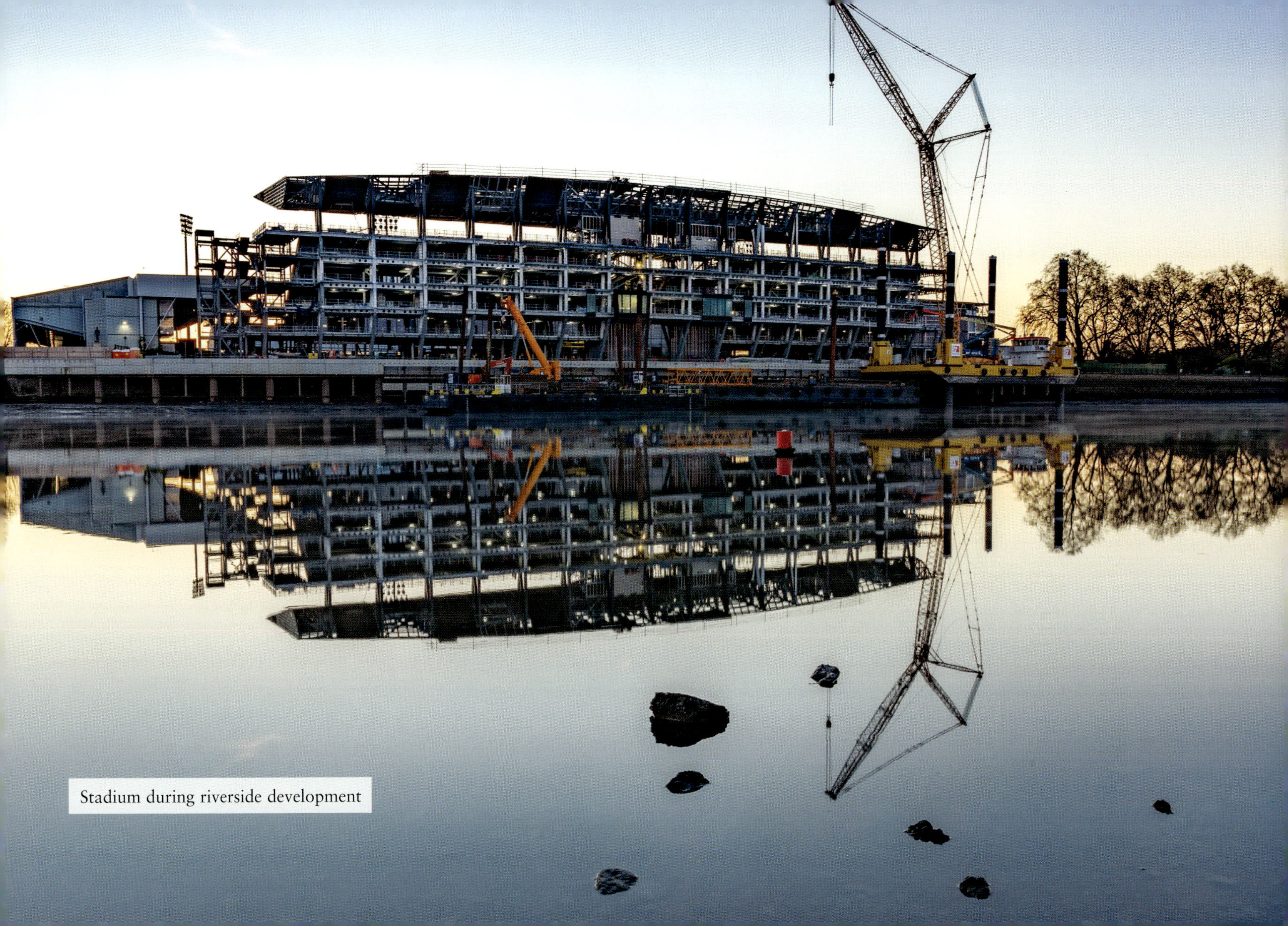

Stadium during riverside development

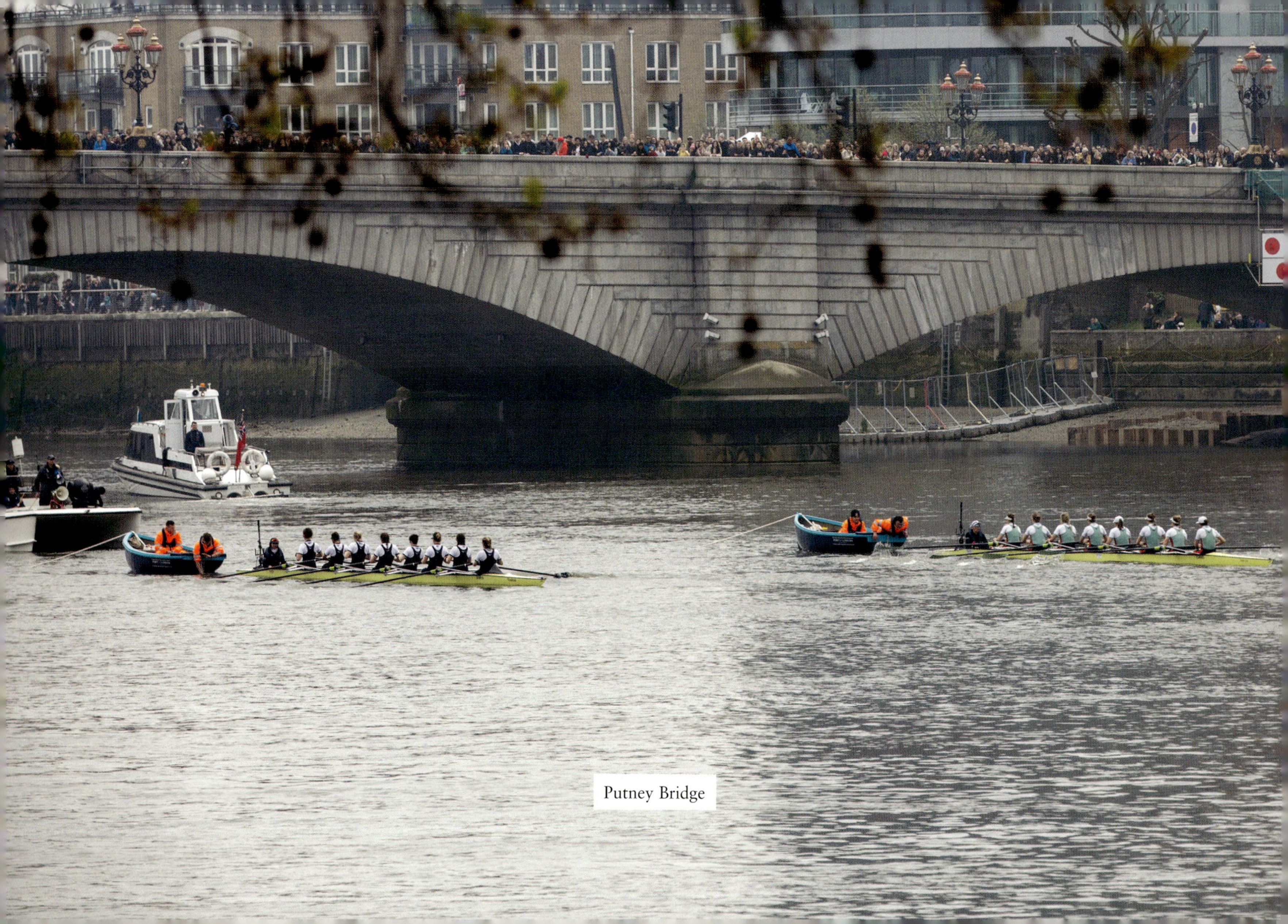

Putney Bridge

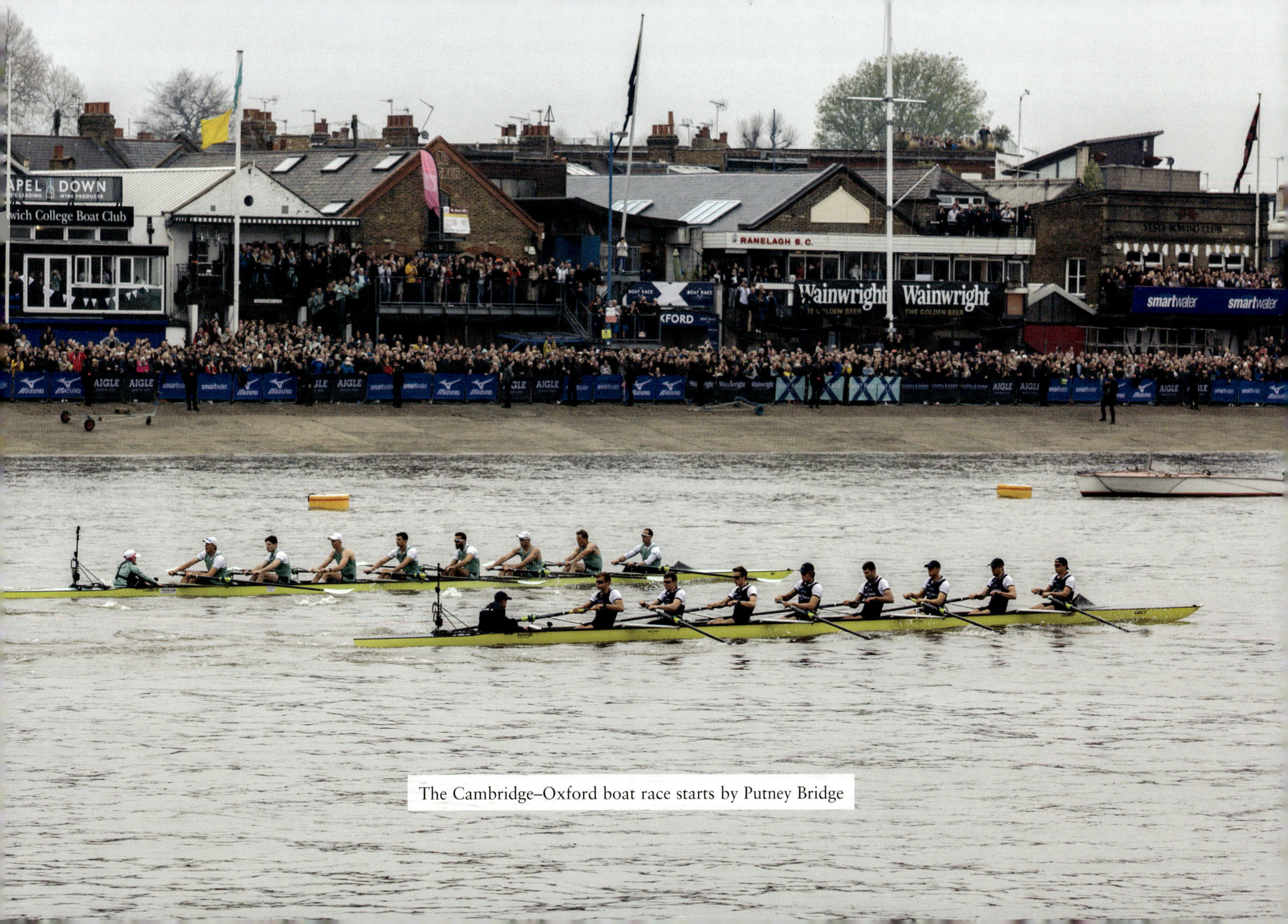

The Cambridge–Oxford boat race starts by Putney Bridge

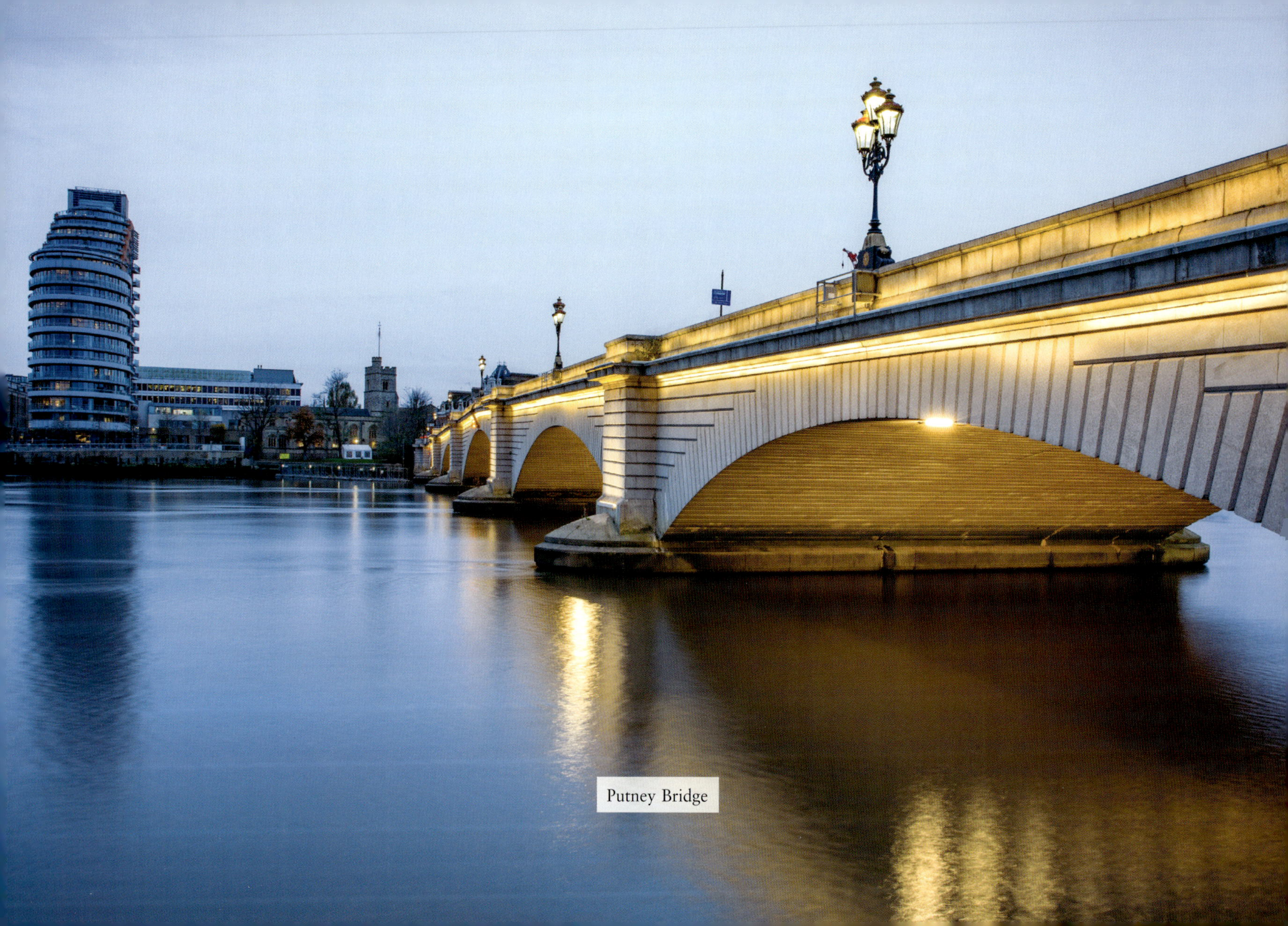

Putney Bridge

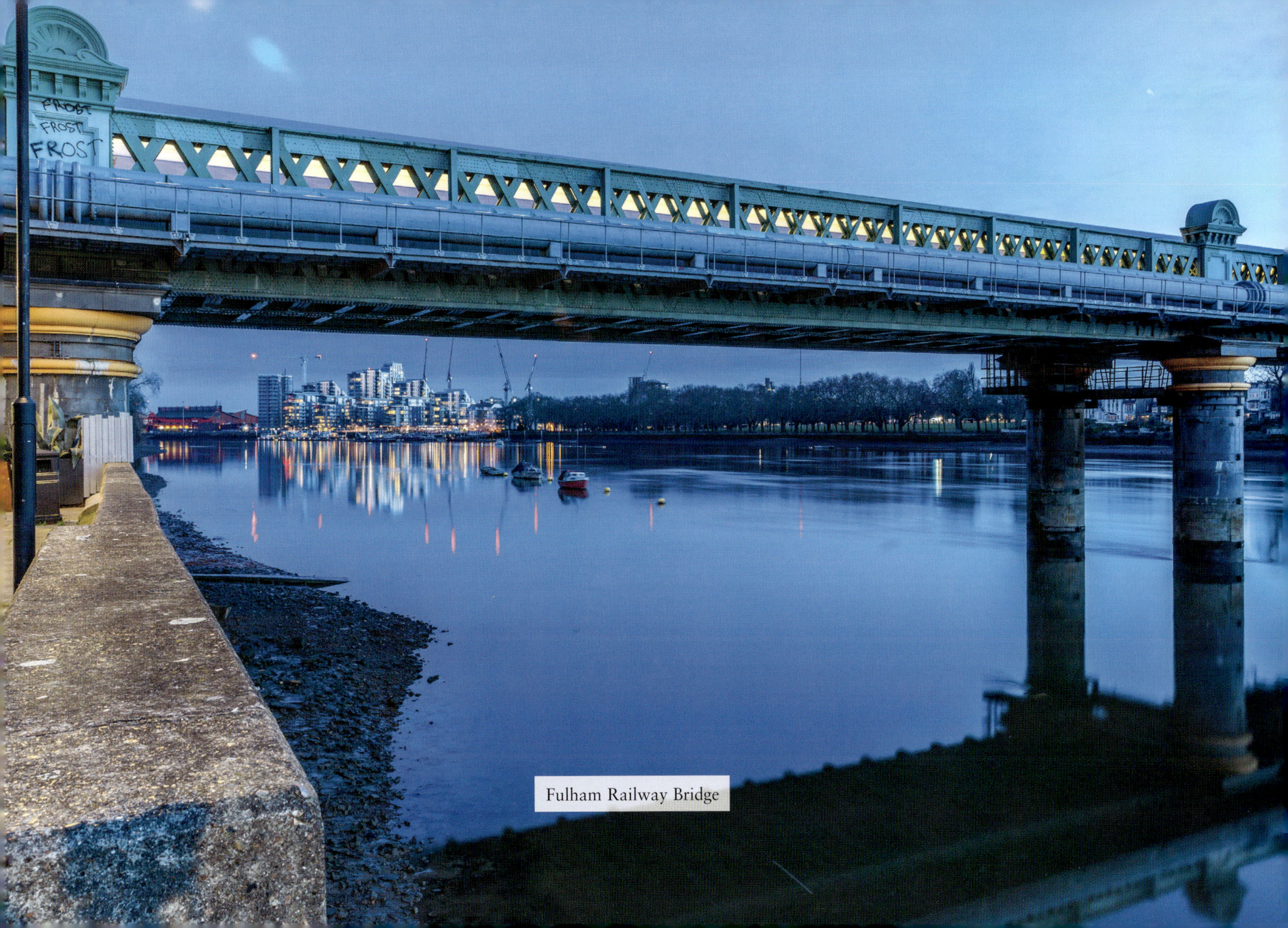

Fulham Railway Bridge

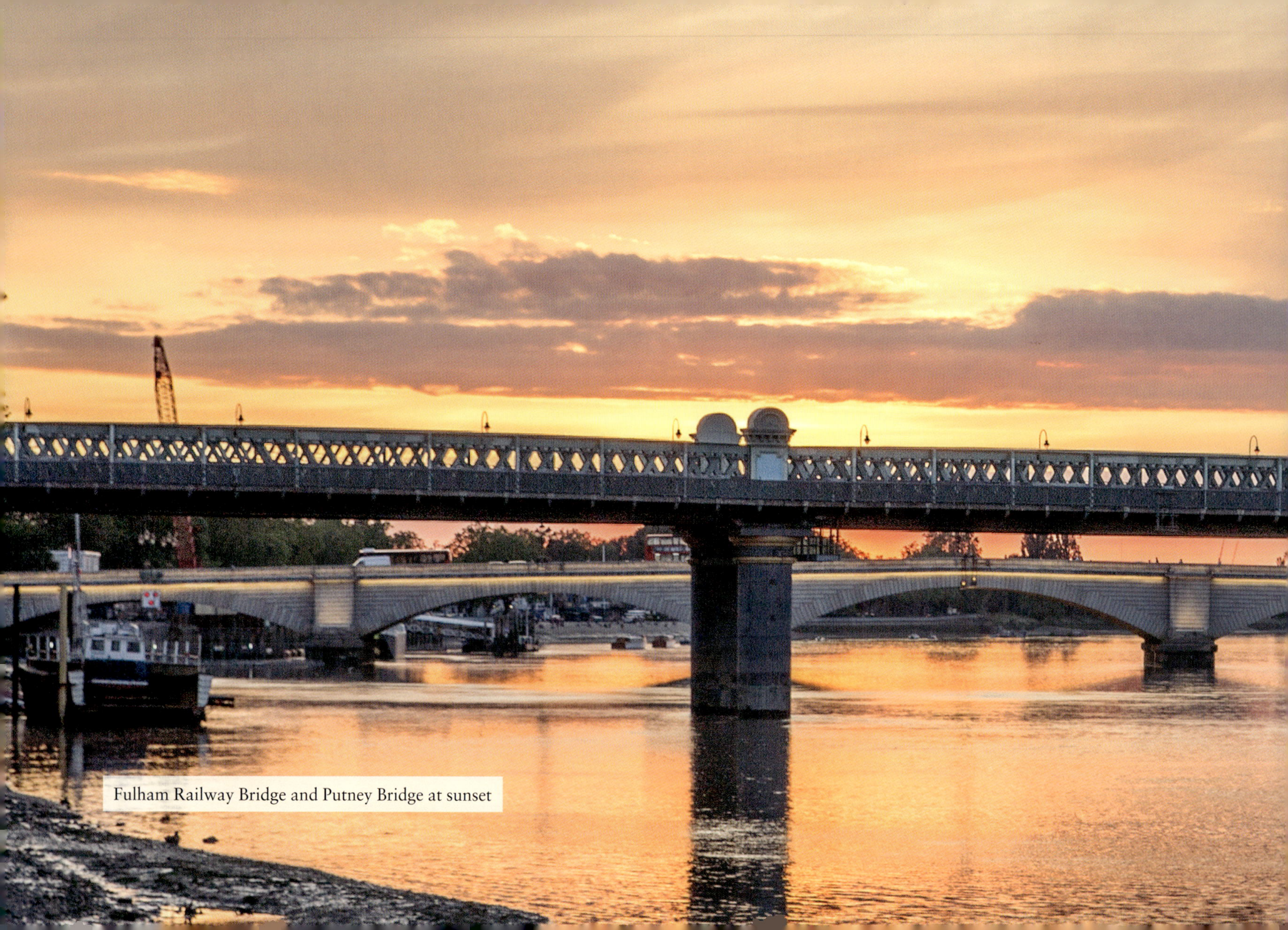

Fulham Railway Bridge and Putney Bridge at sunset

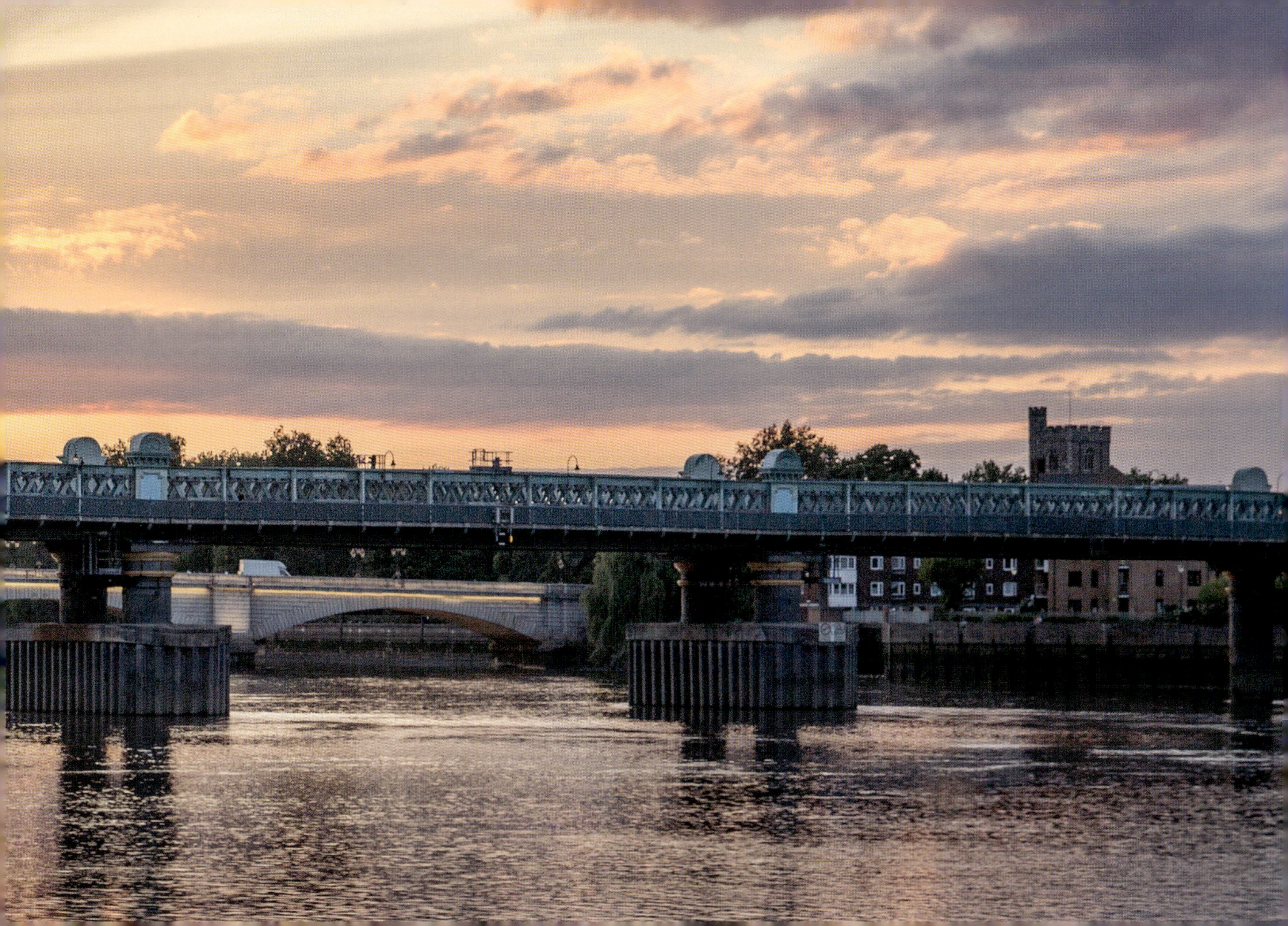

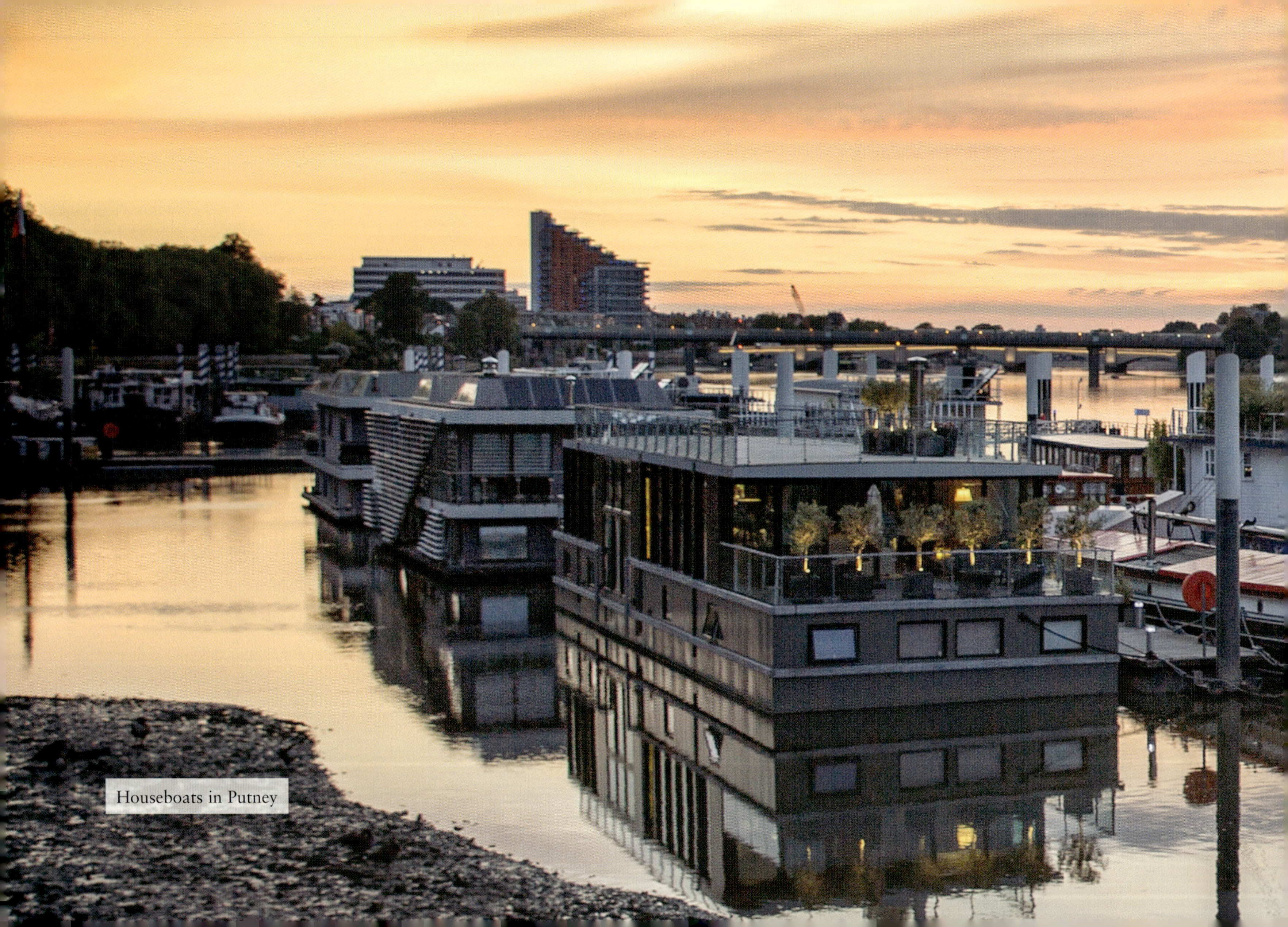

Houseboats in Putney

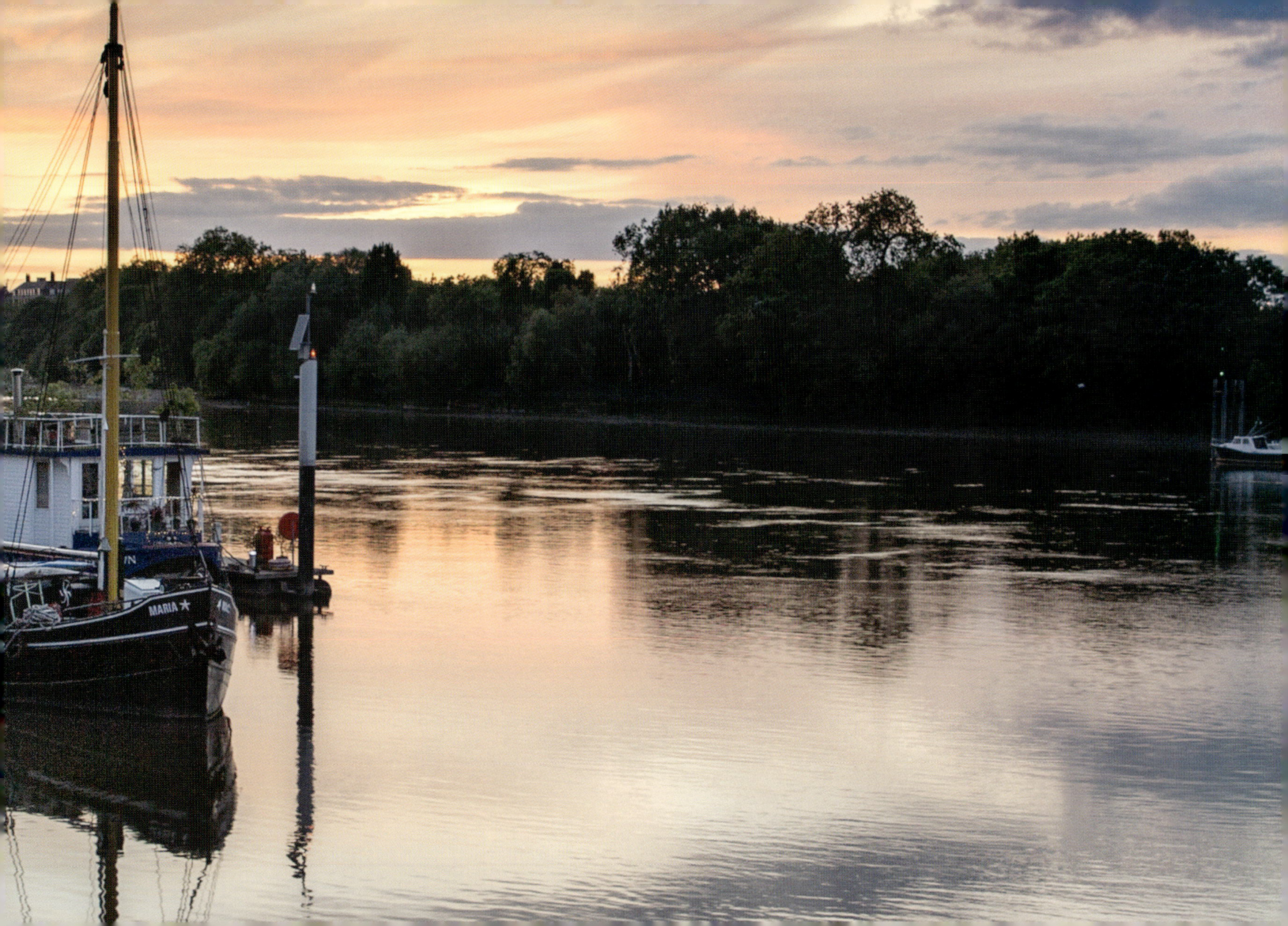
MARIA

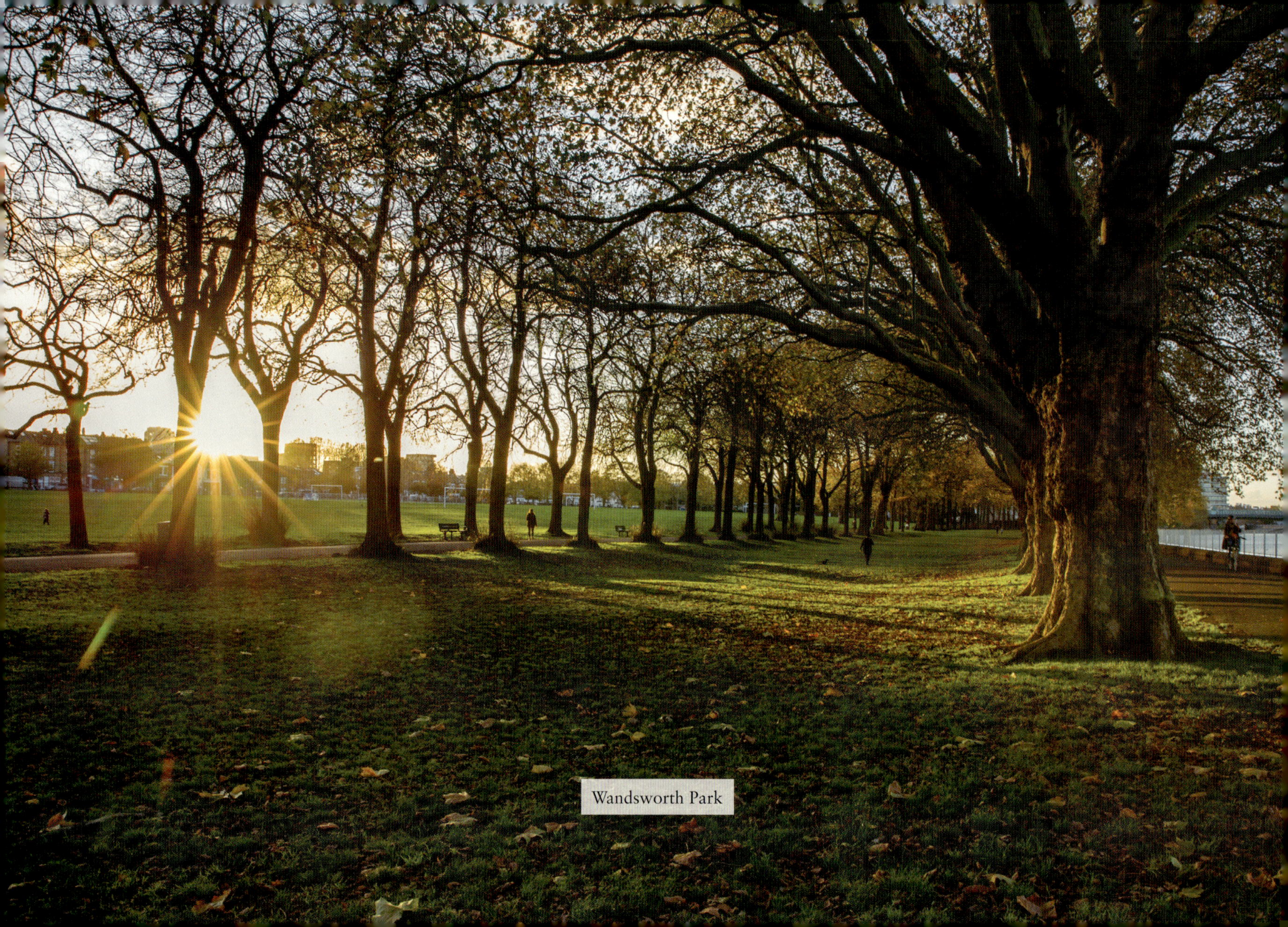
Wandsworth Park

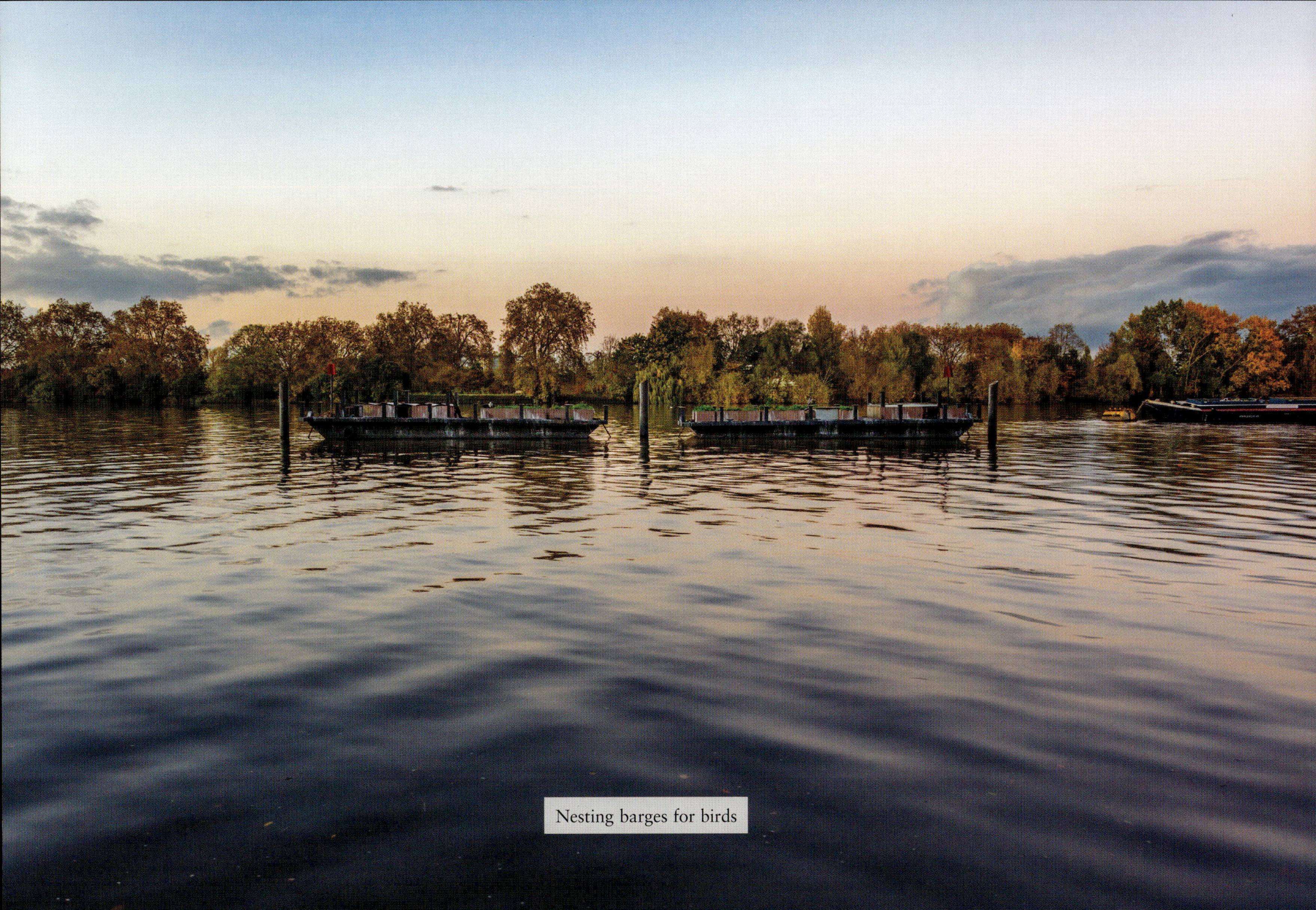

Nesting barges for birds

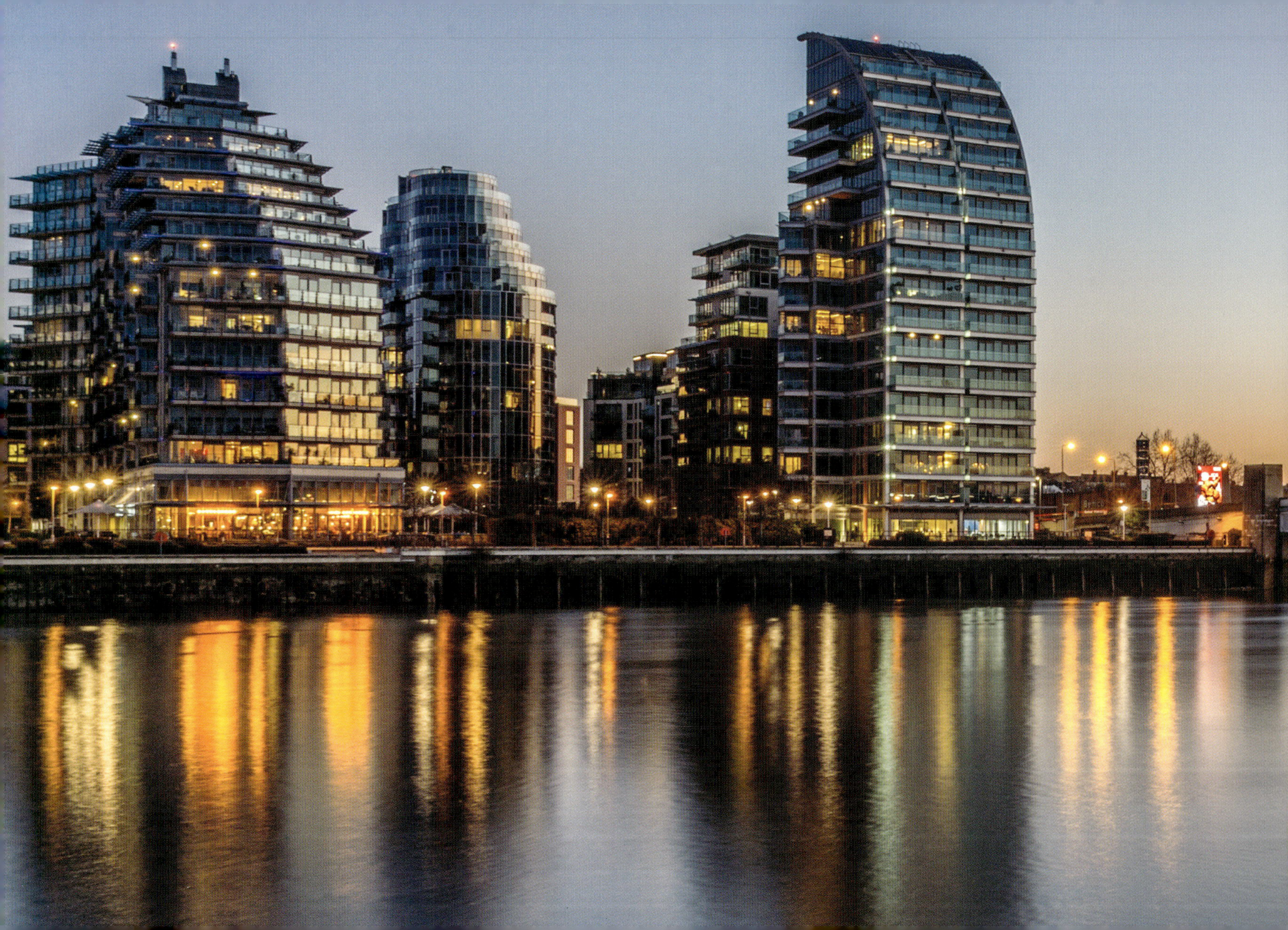

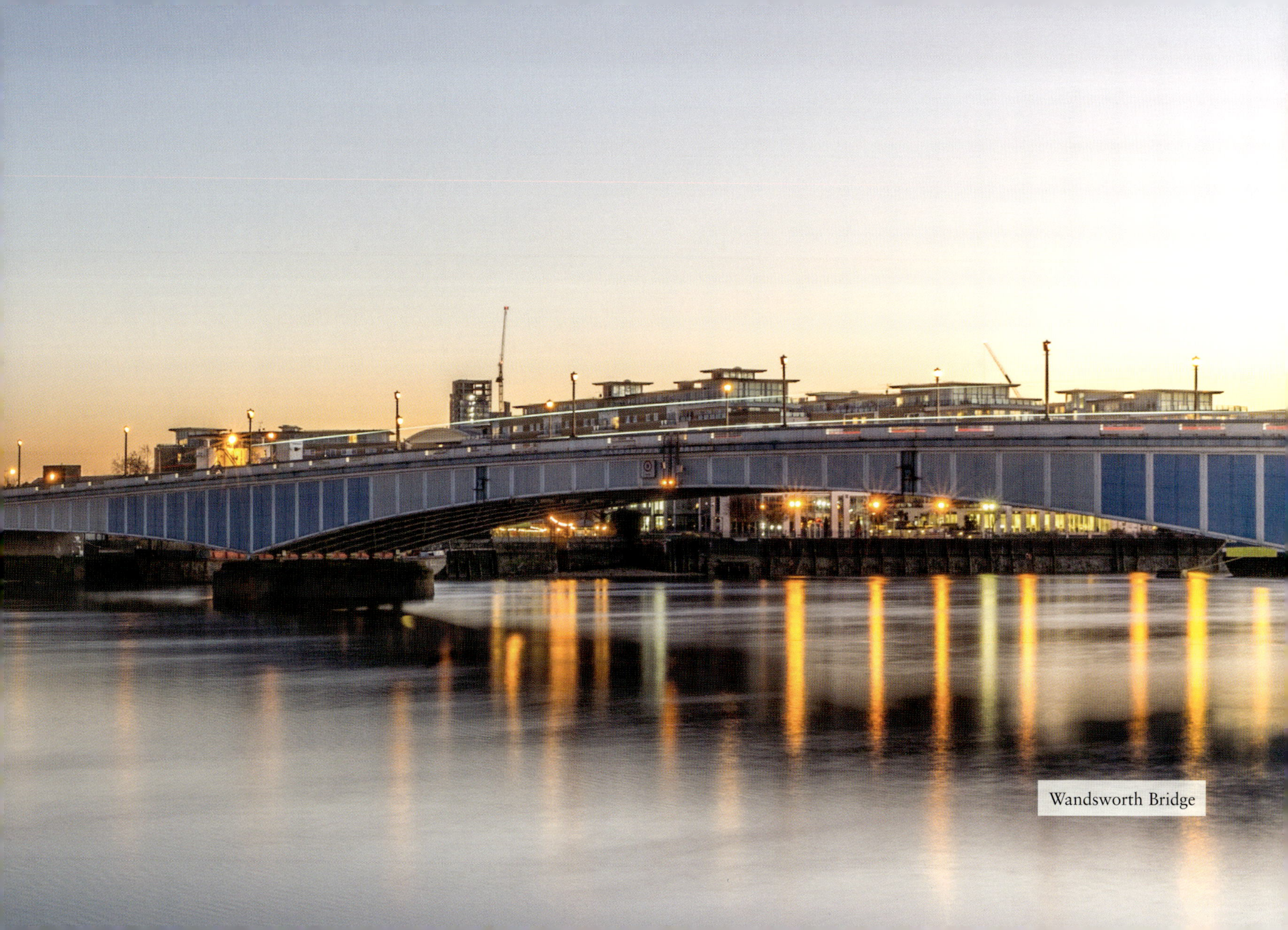
Wandsworth Bridge

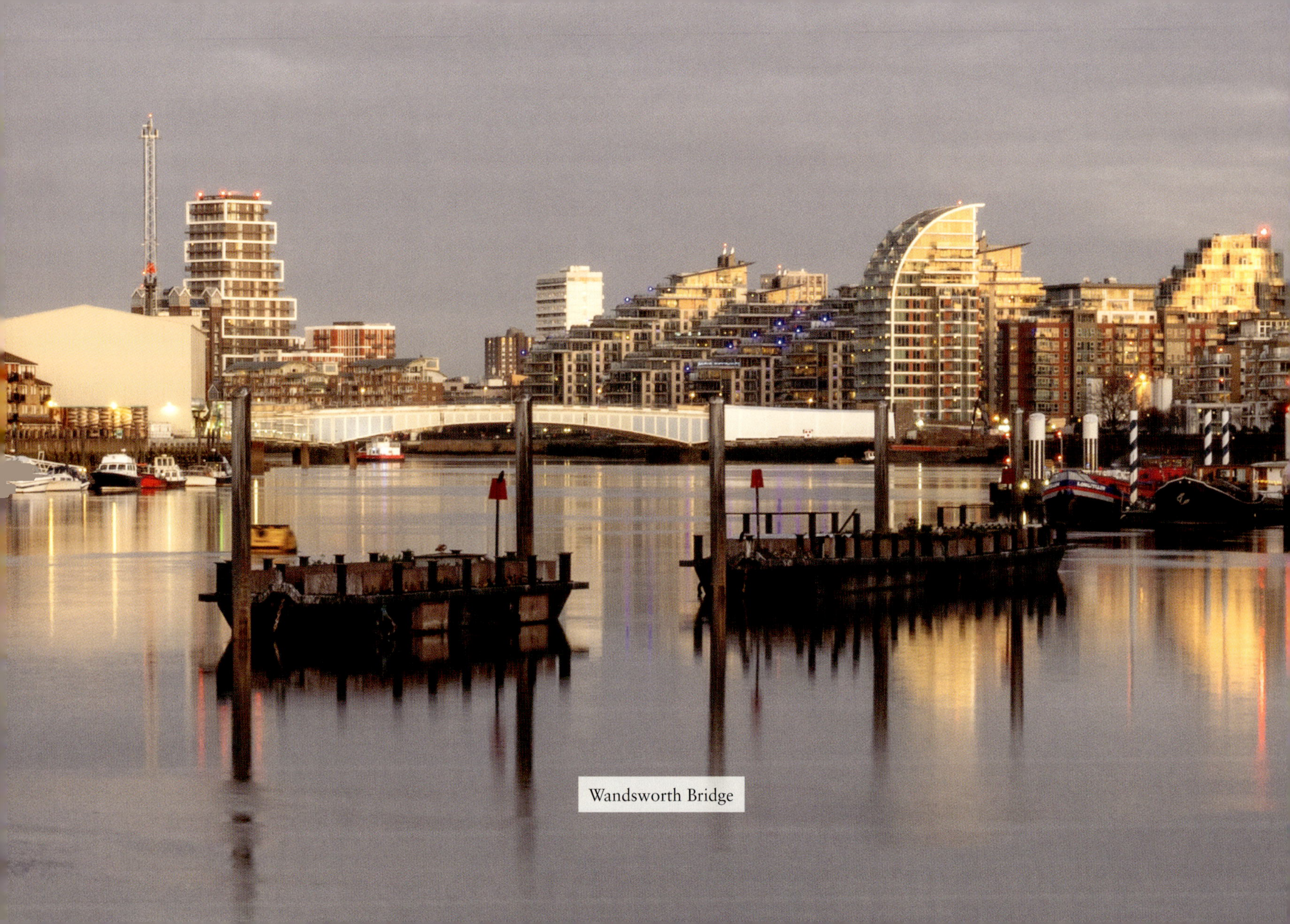

Wandsworth Bridge

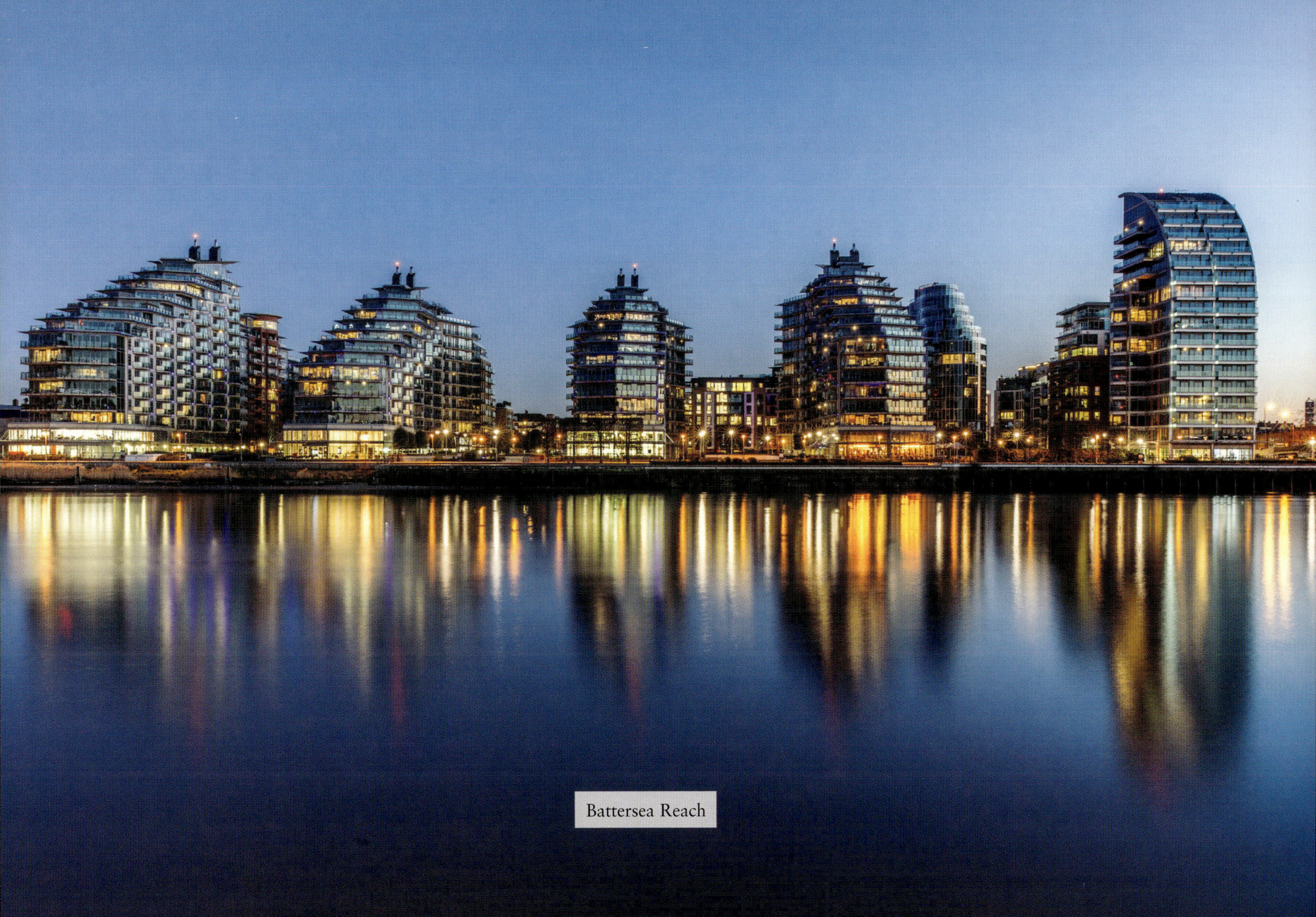

Battersea Reach

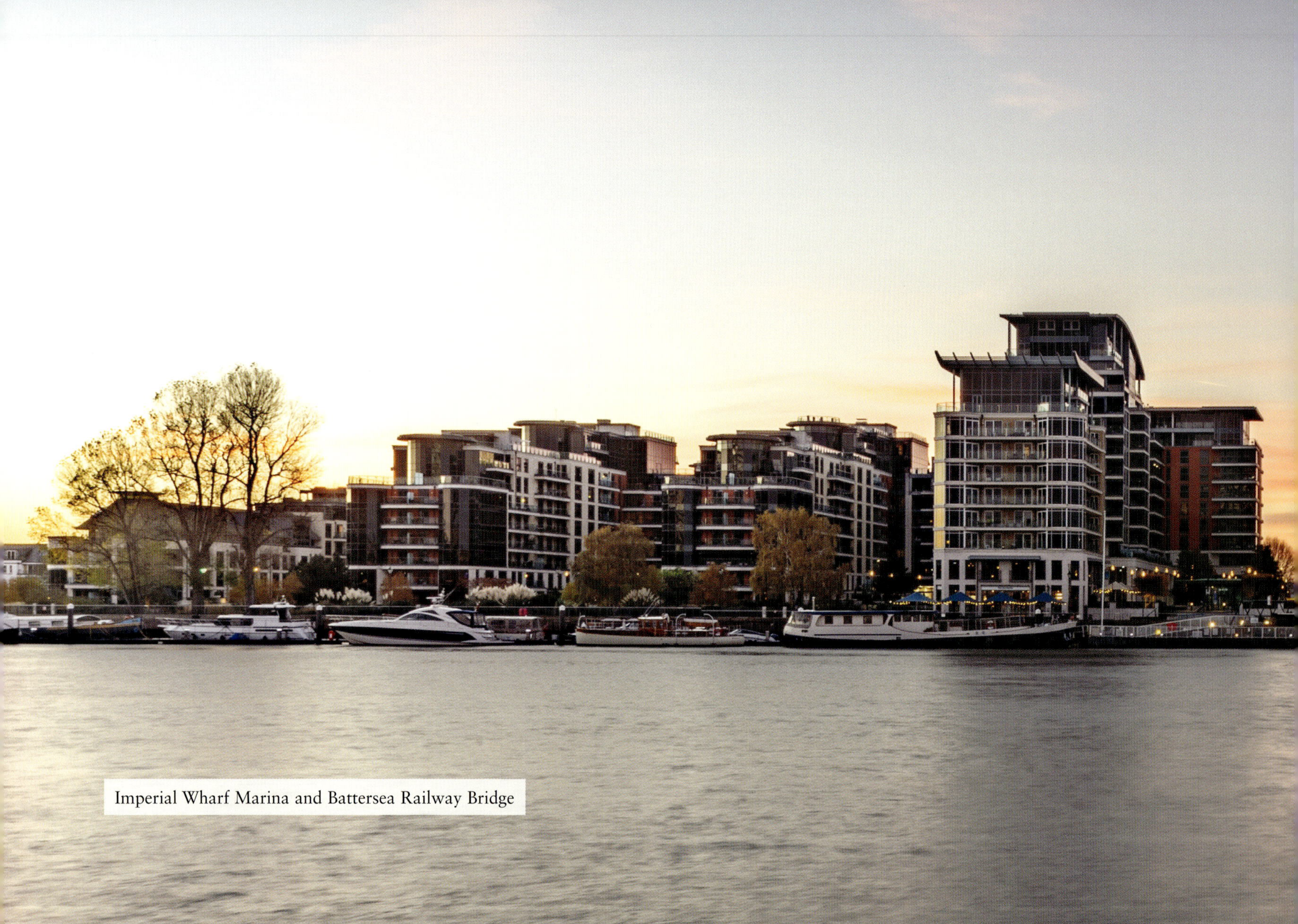

Imperial Wharf Marina and Battersea Railway Bridge

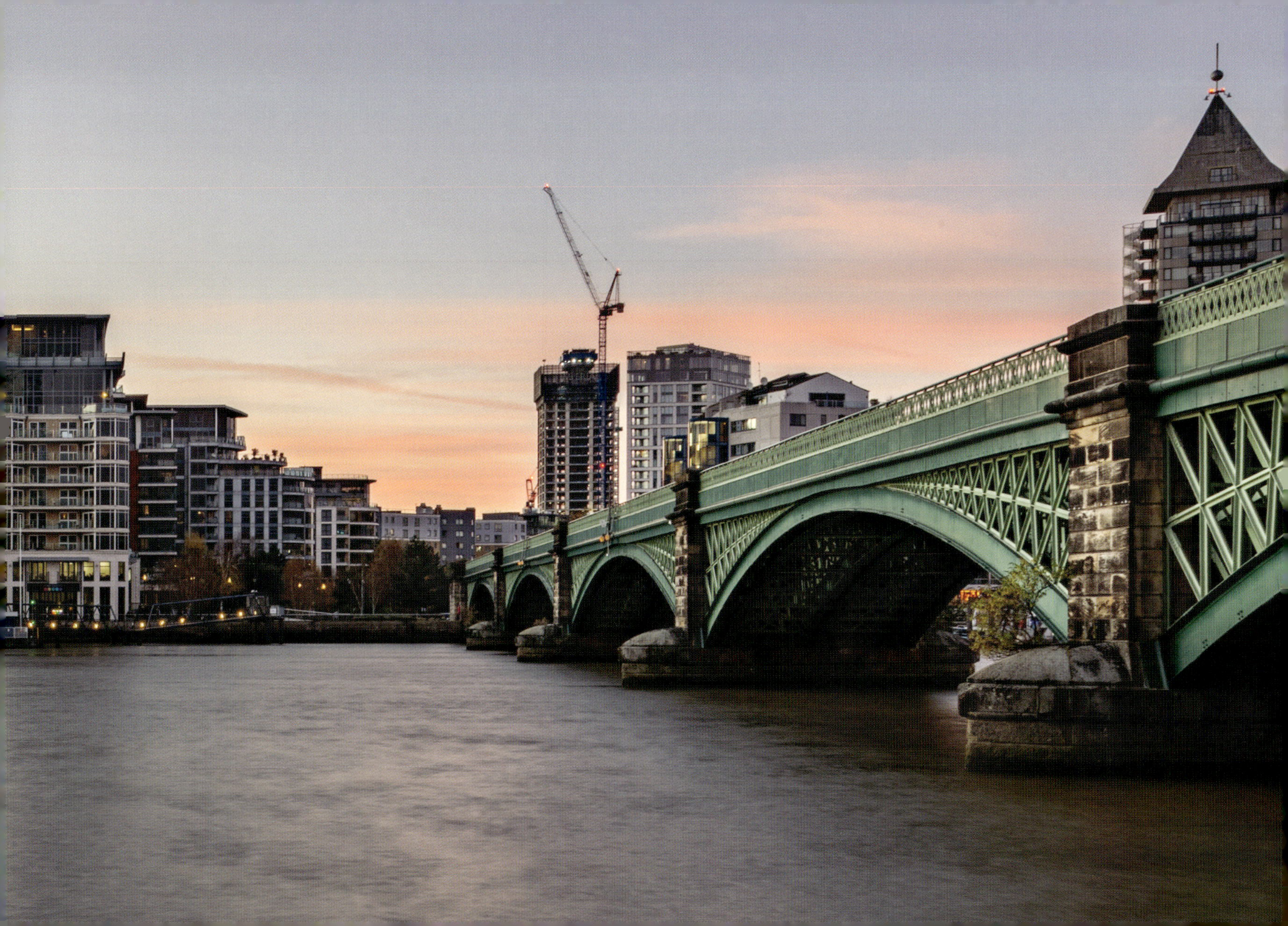

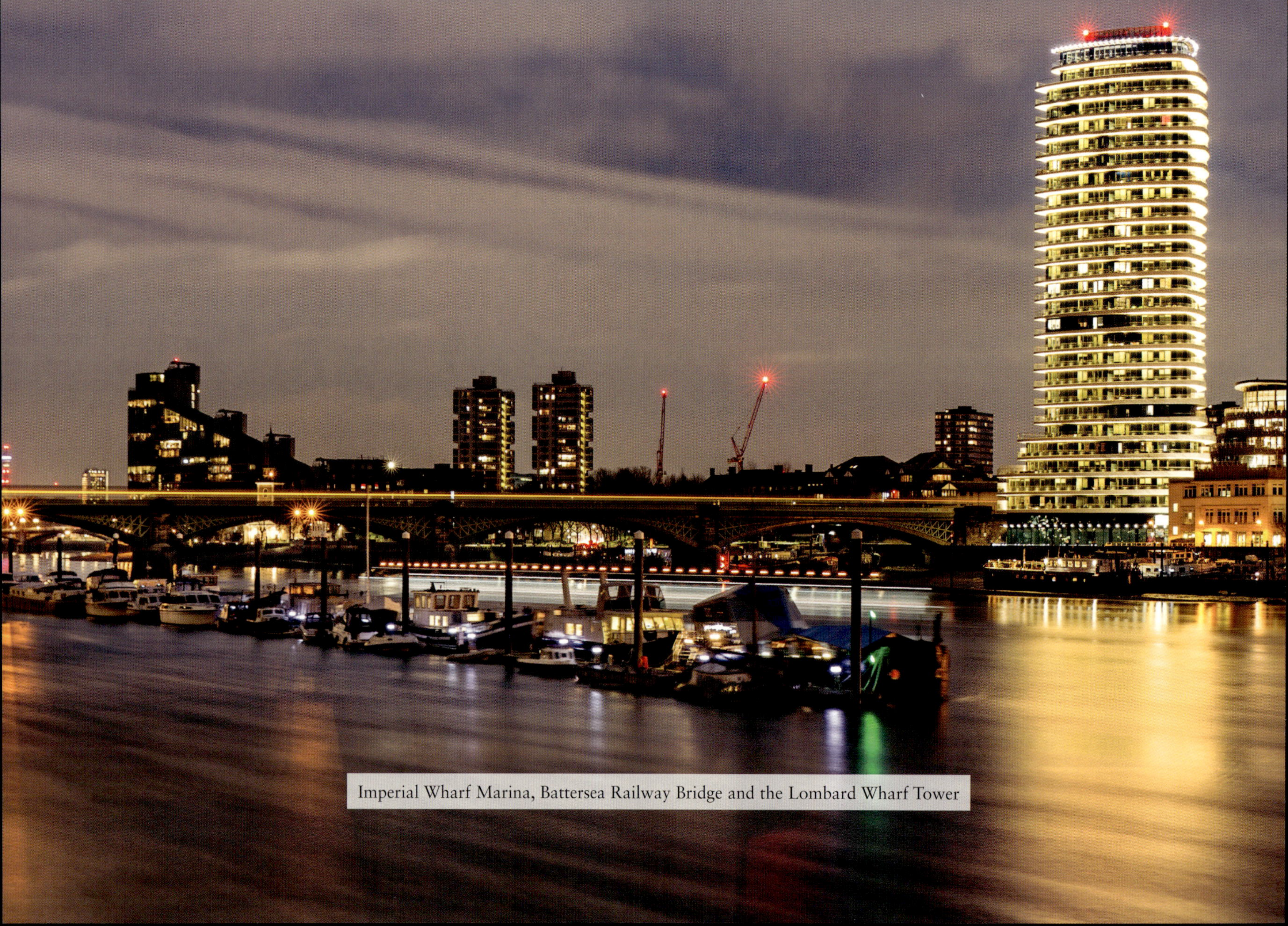

Imperial Wharf Marina, Battersea Railway Bridge and the Lombard Wharf Tower

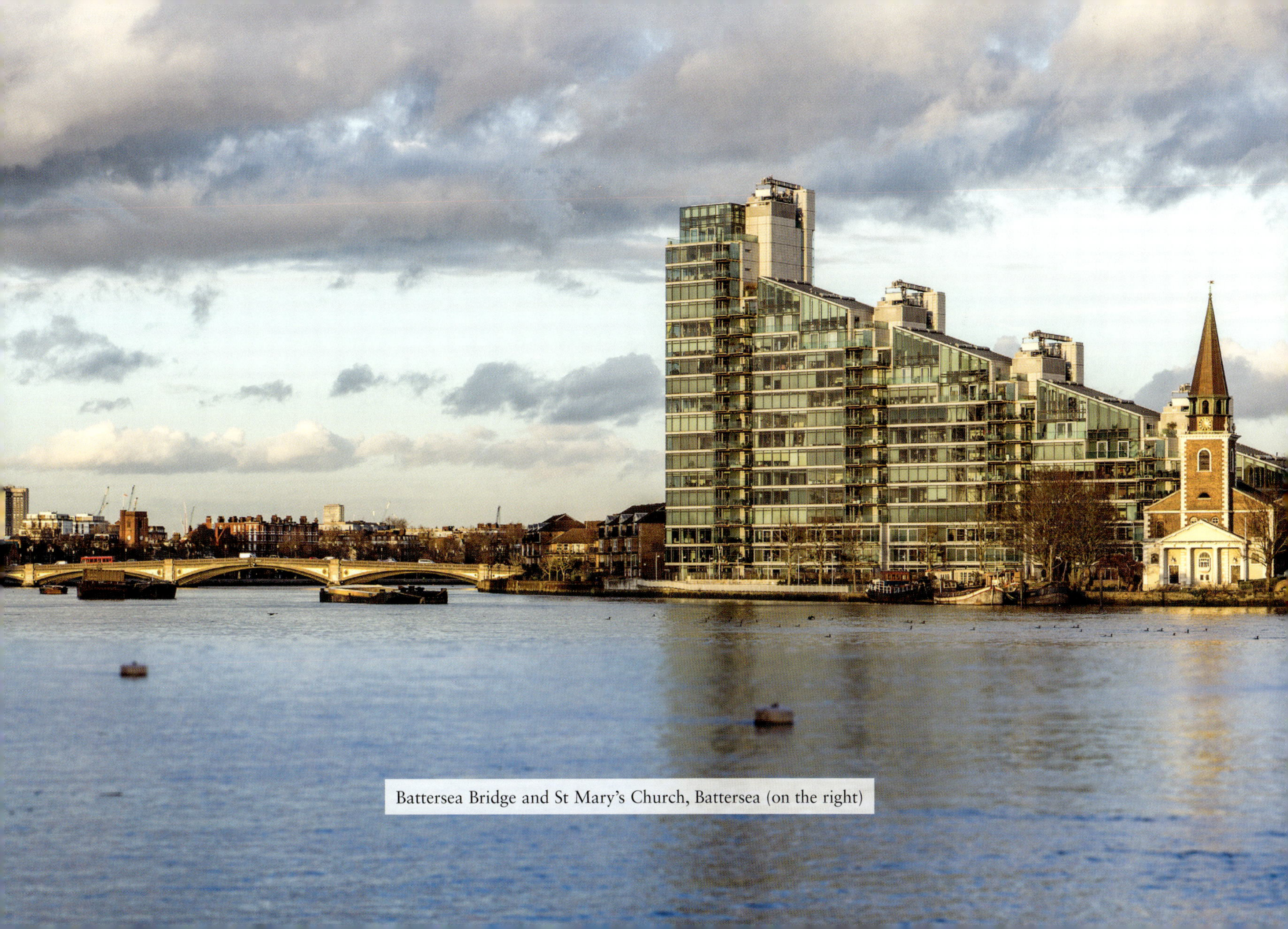

Battersea Bridge and St Mary's Church, Battersea (on the right)

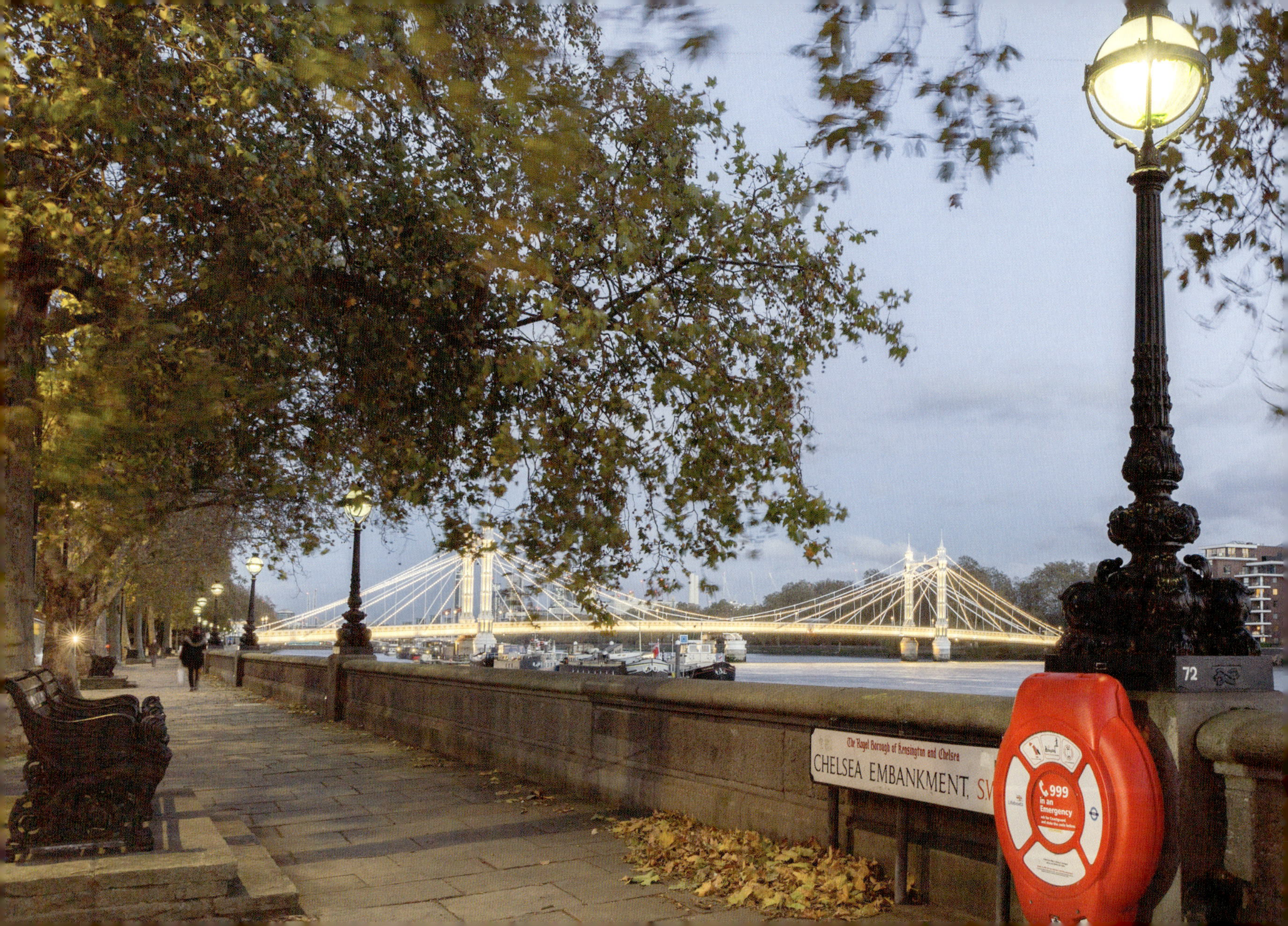

The Royal Borough of Kensington and Chelsea
CHELSEA EMBANKMENT, S.W.
72
999
In an
Emergency

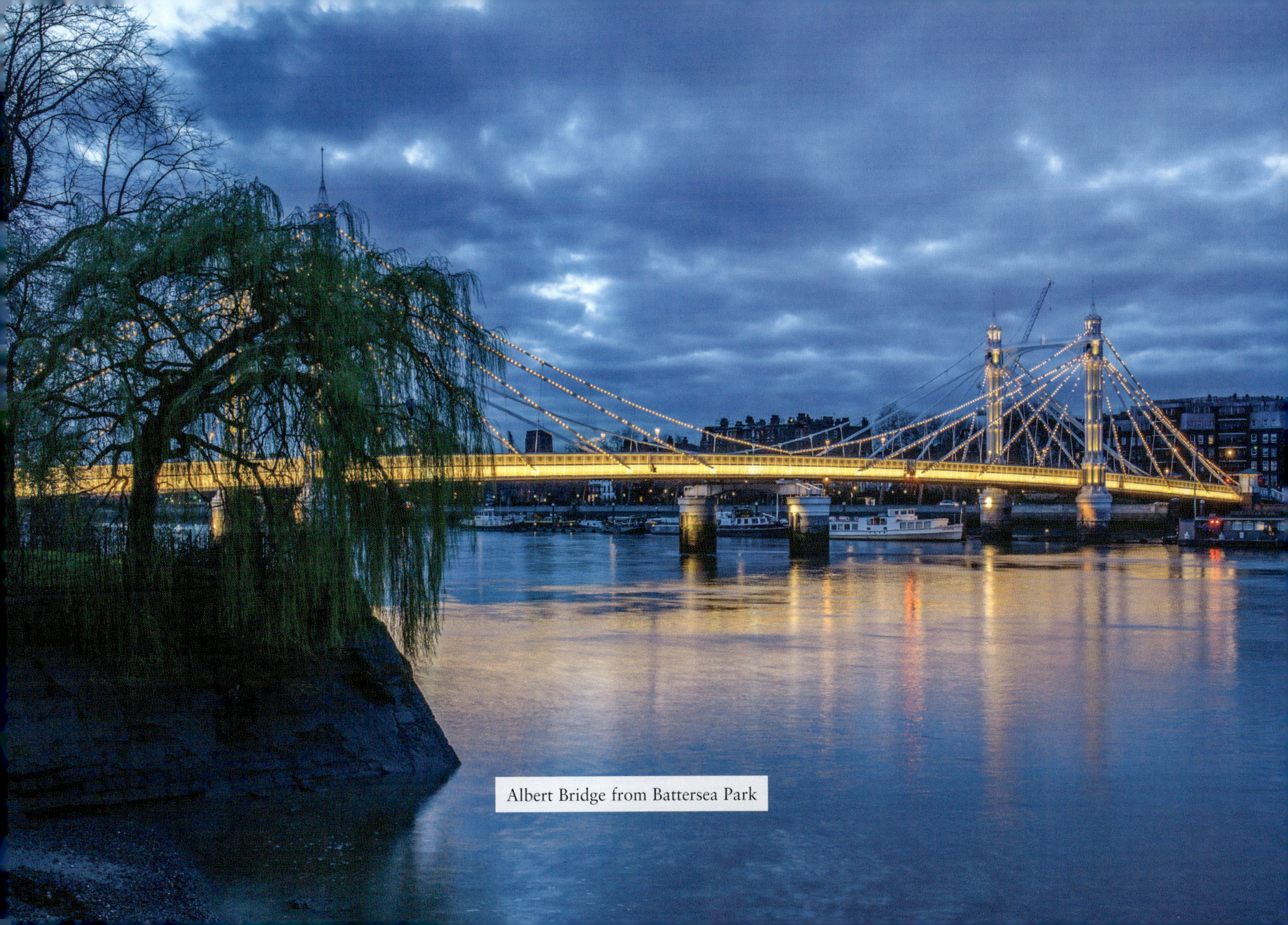

Albert Bridge from Battersea Park

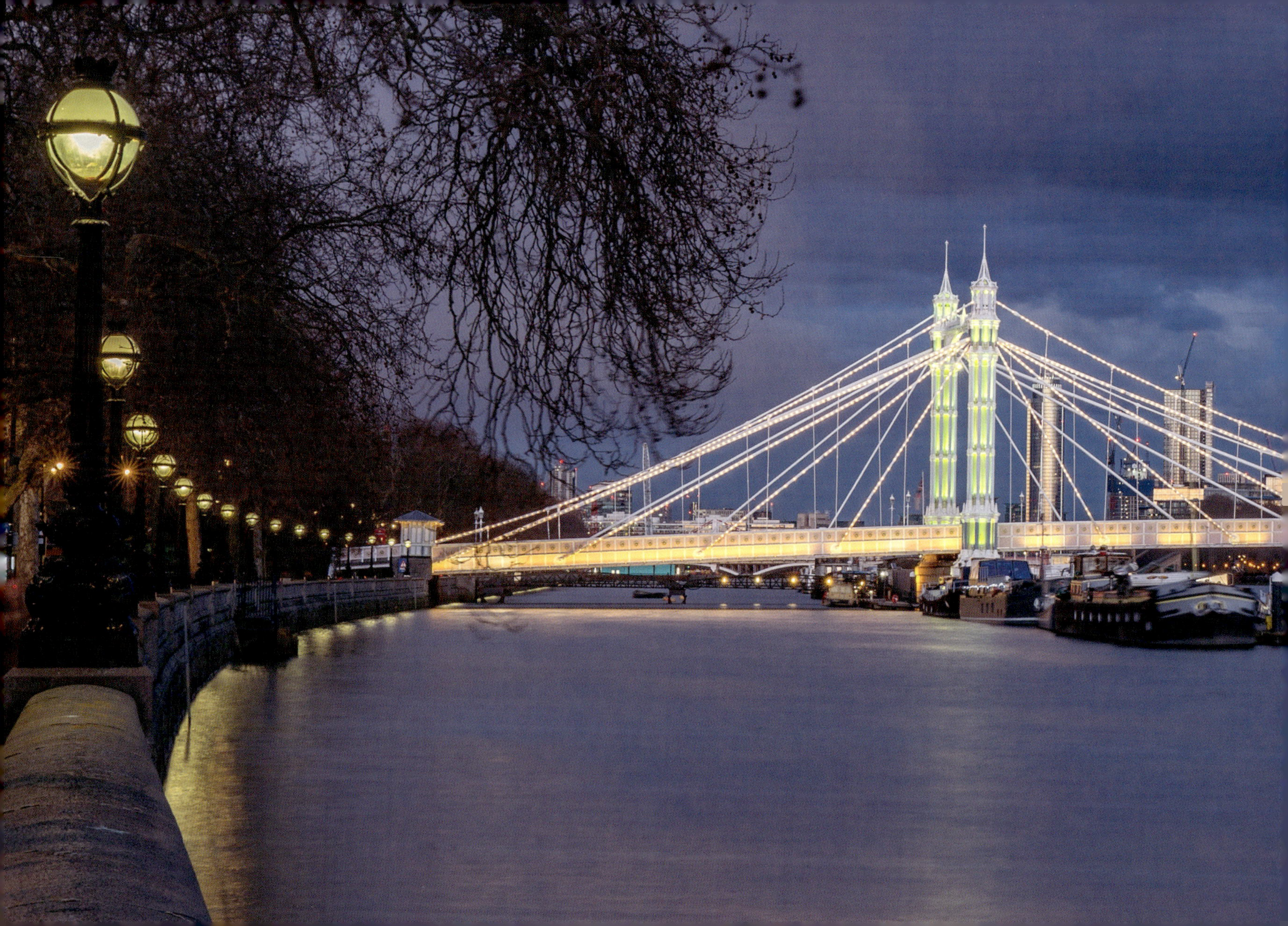

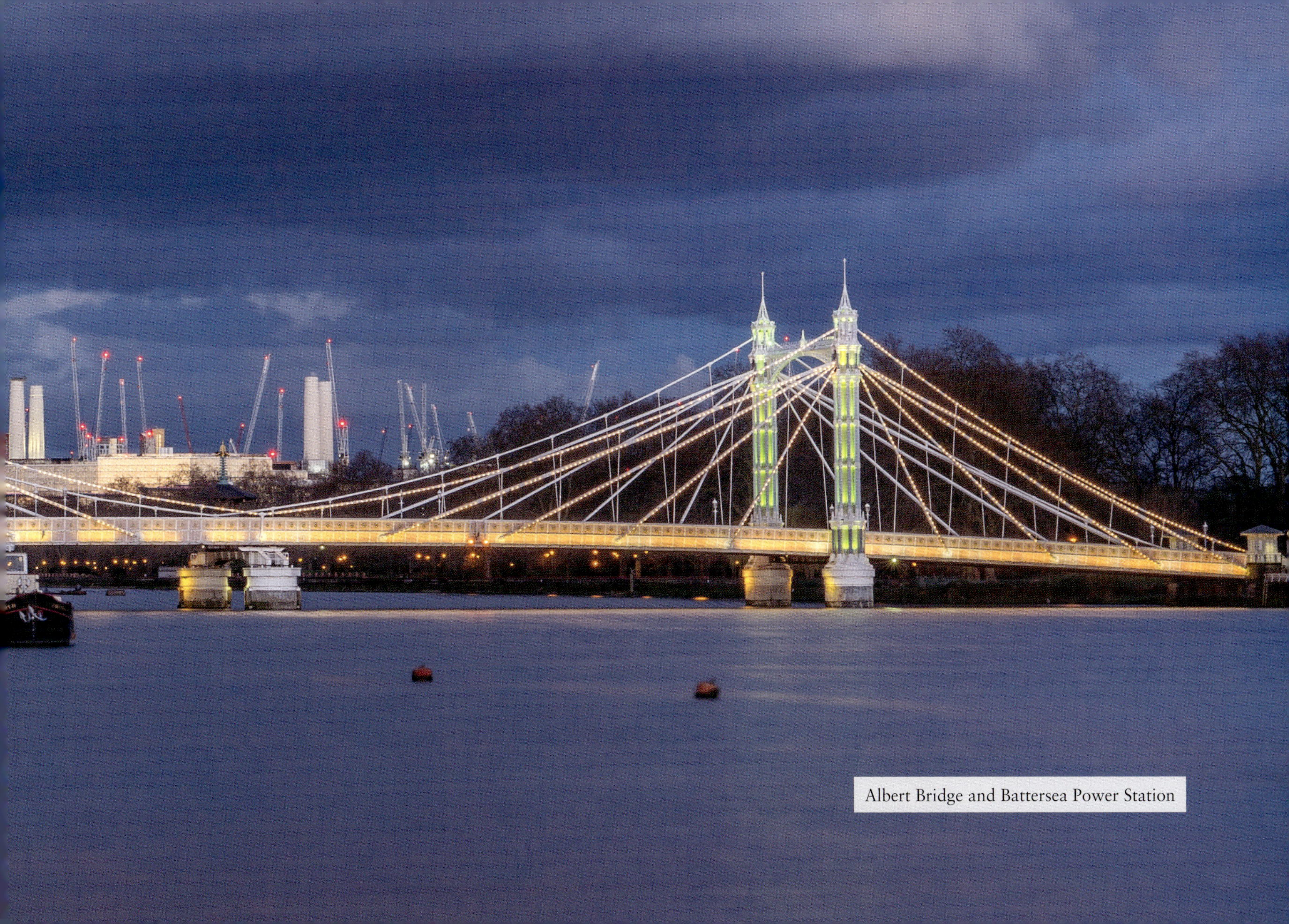

Albert Bridge and Battersea Power Station

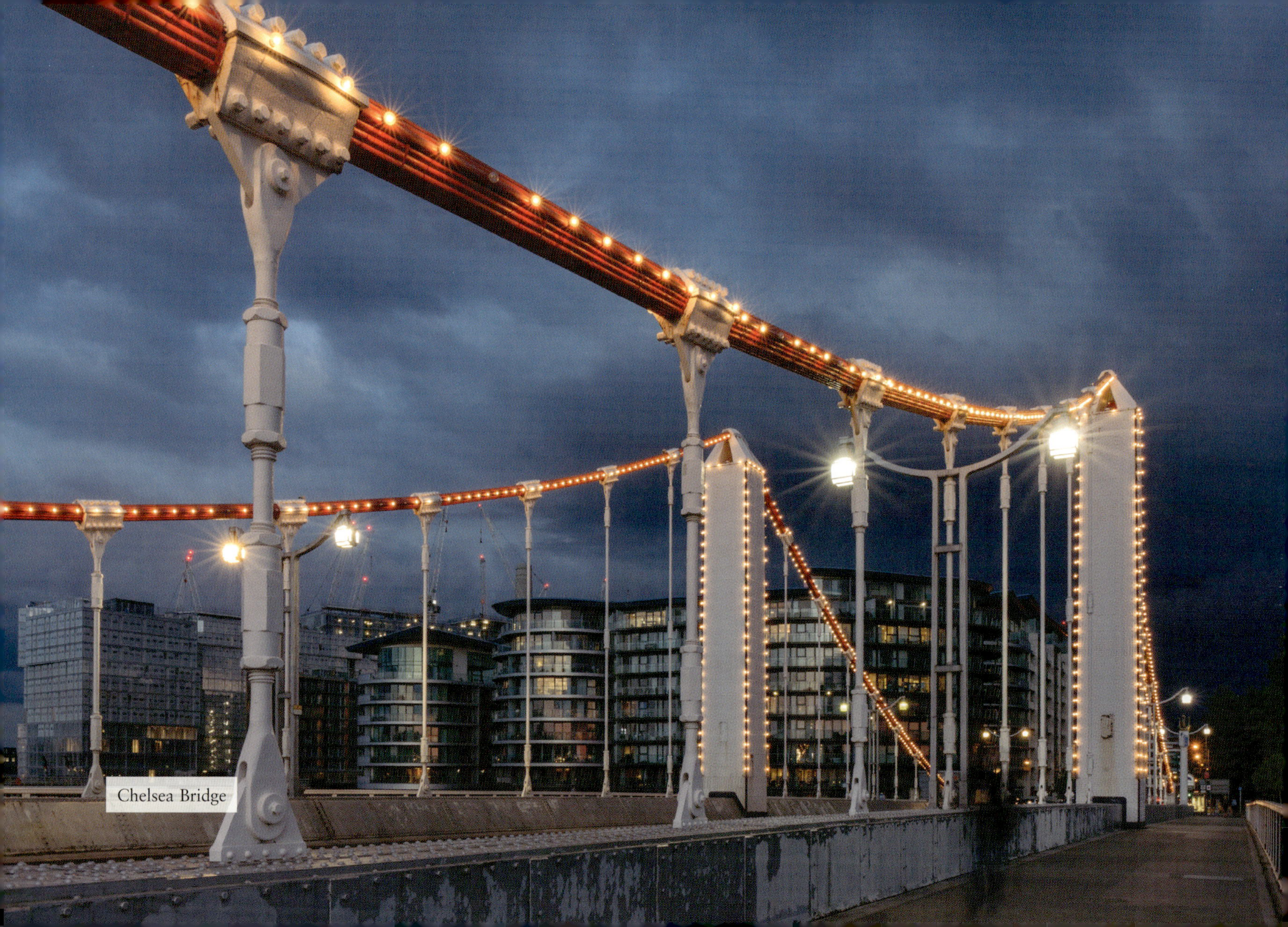
Chelsea Bridge

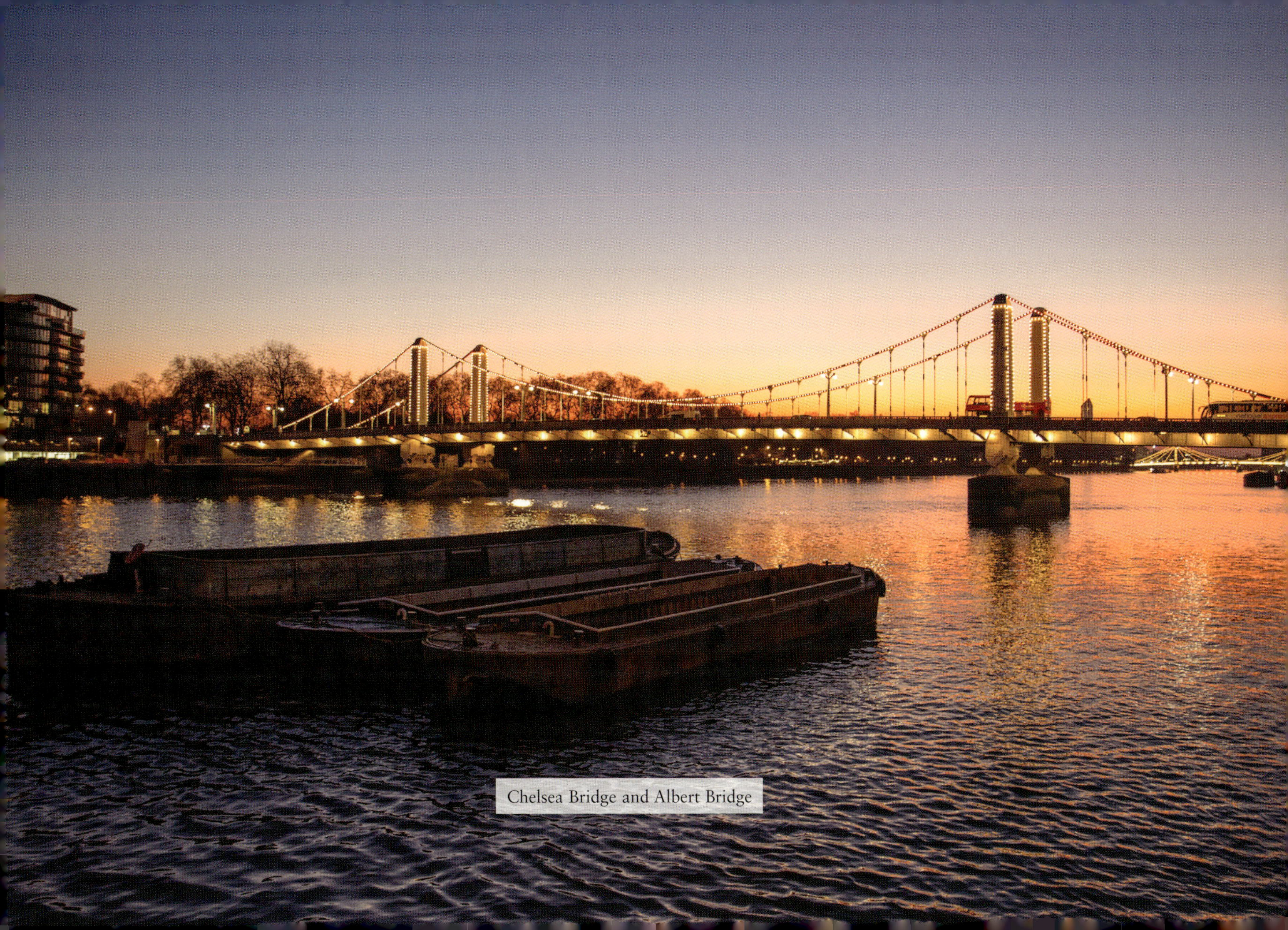

Chelsea Bridge and Albert Bridge

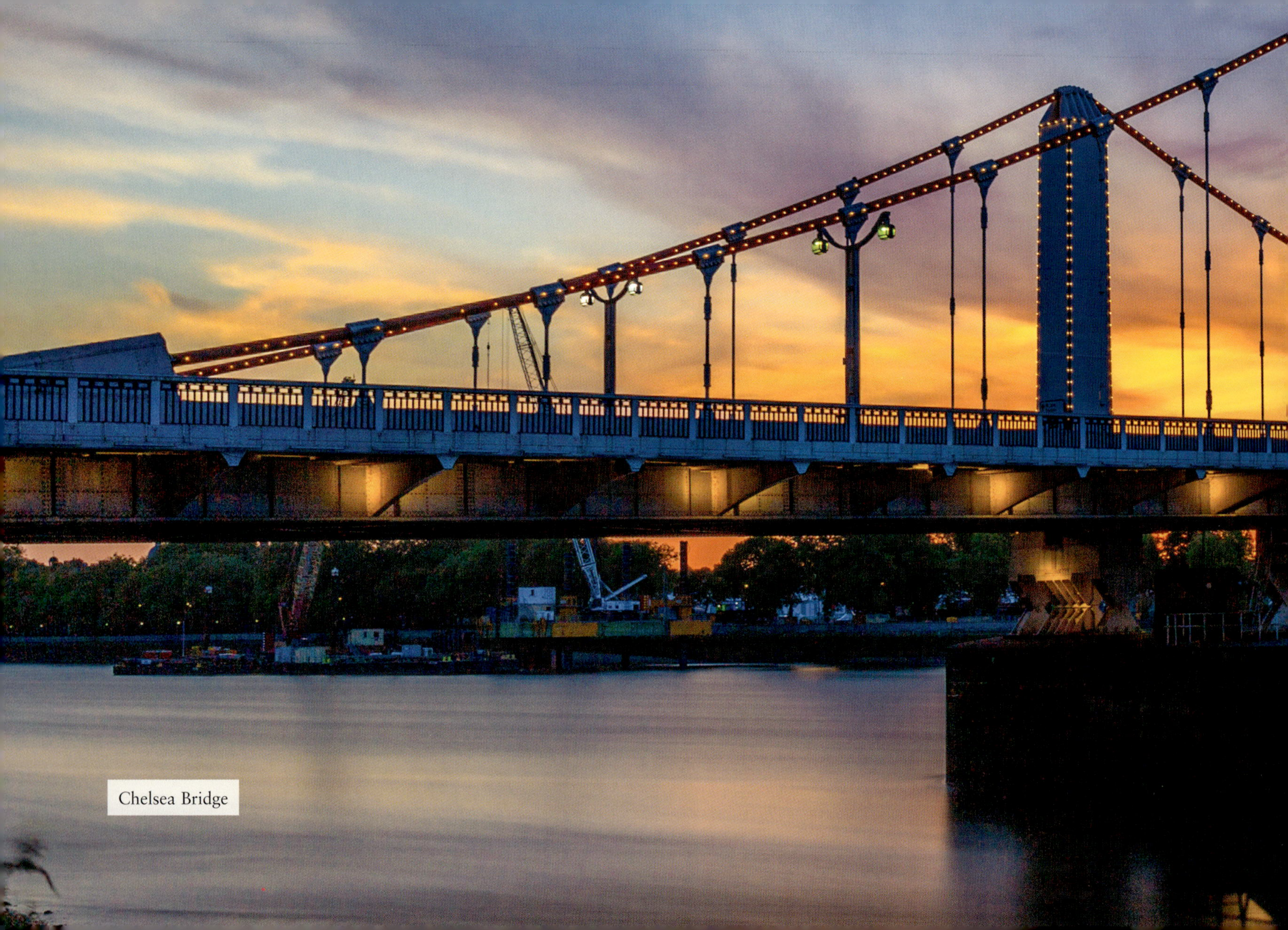

Chelsea Bridge

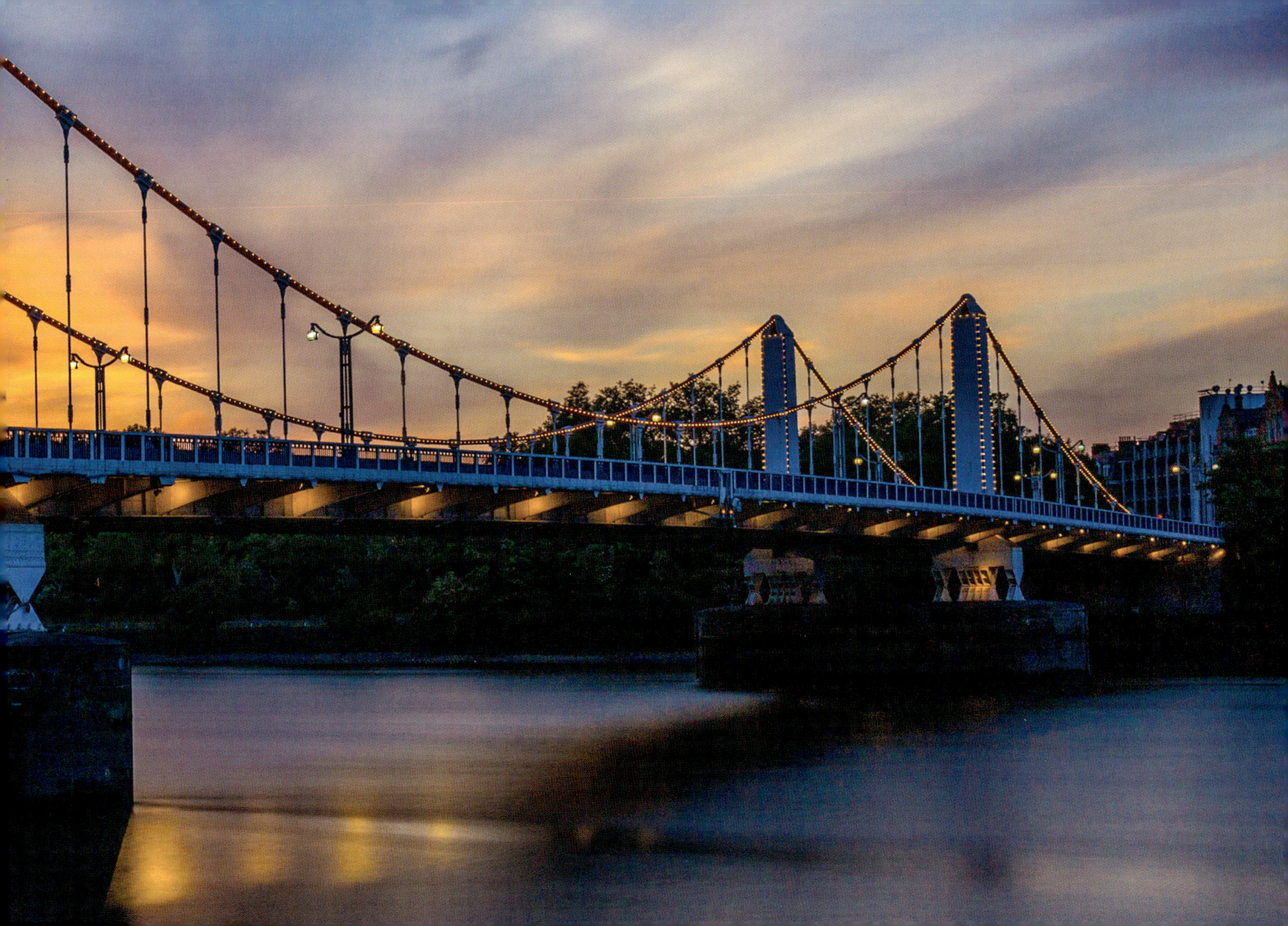

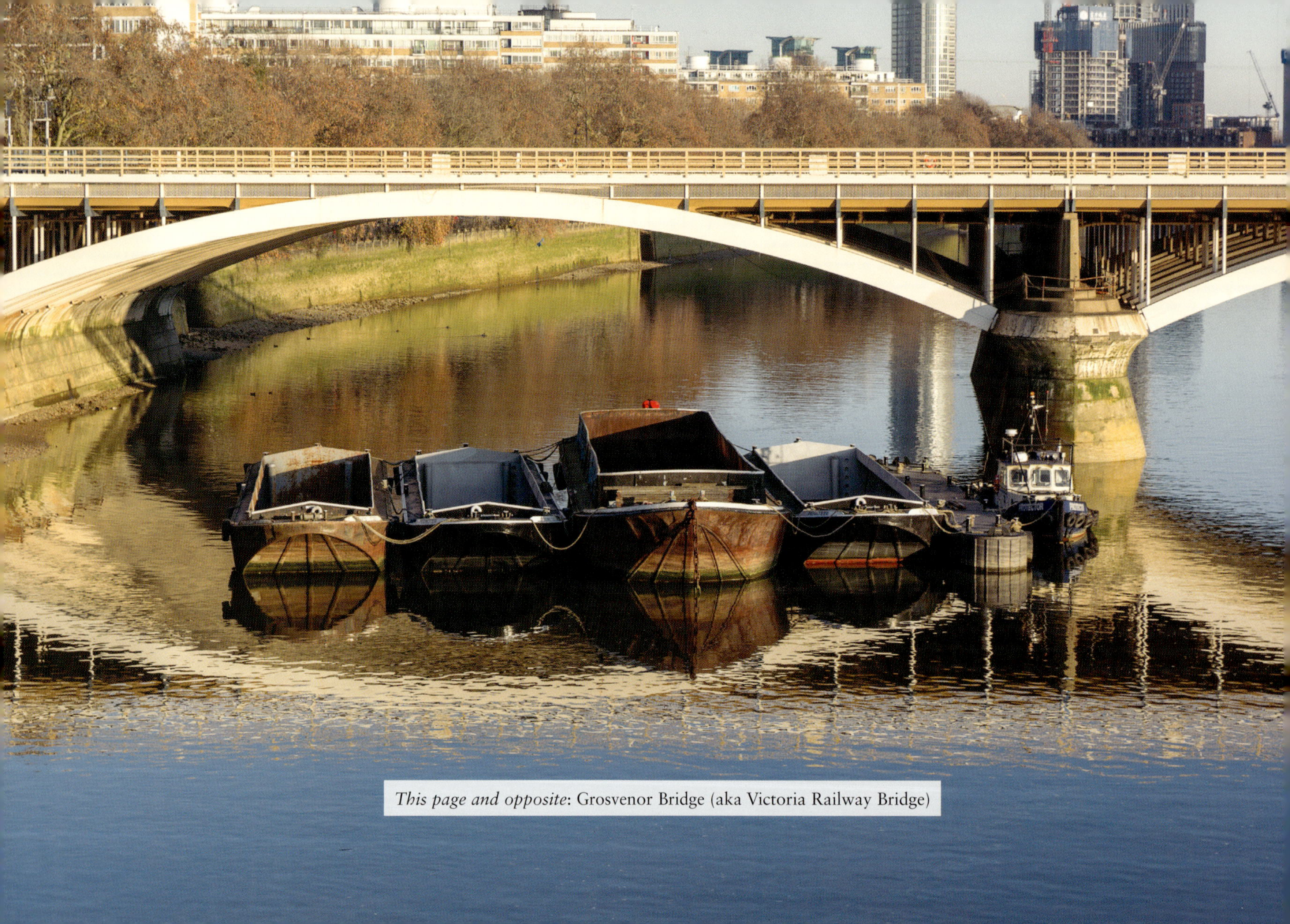

This page and opposite: Grosvenor Bridge (aka Victoria Railway Bridge)

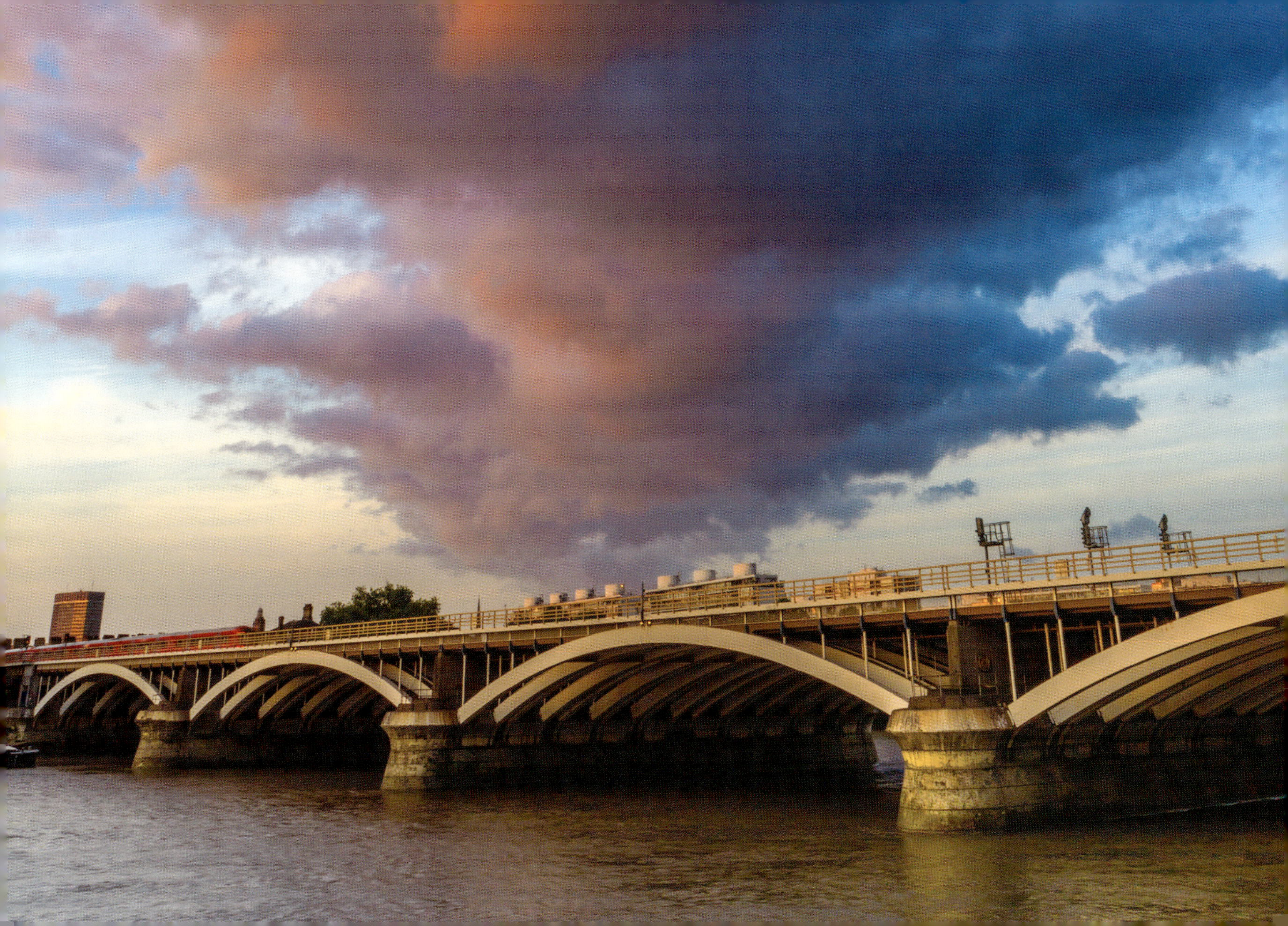

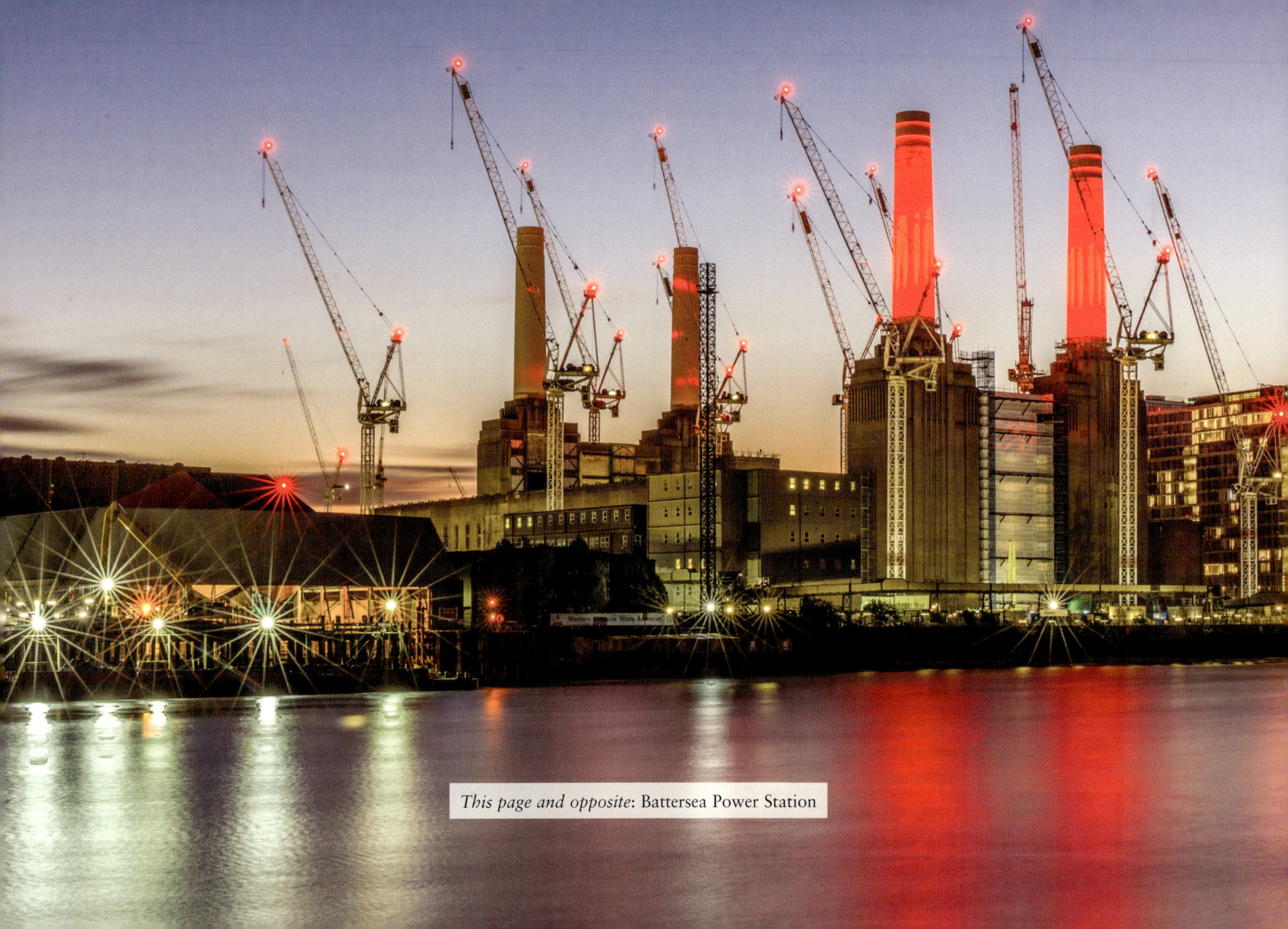

This page and opposite: Battersea Power Station

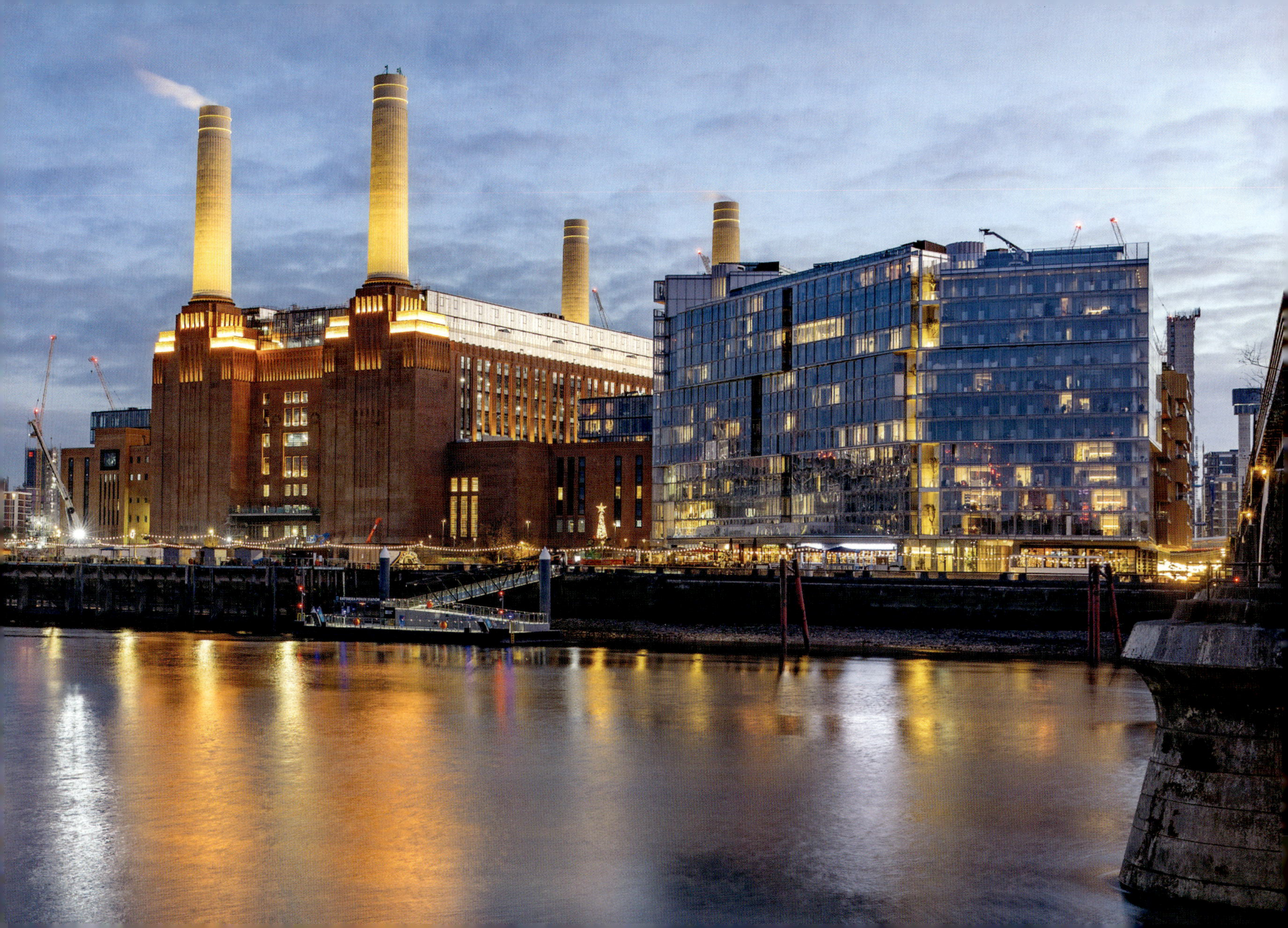

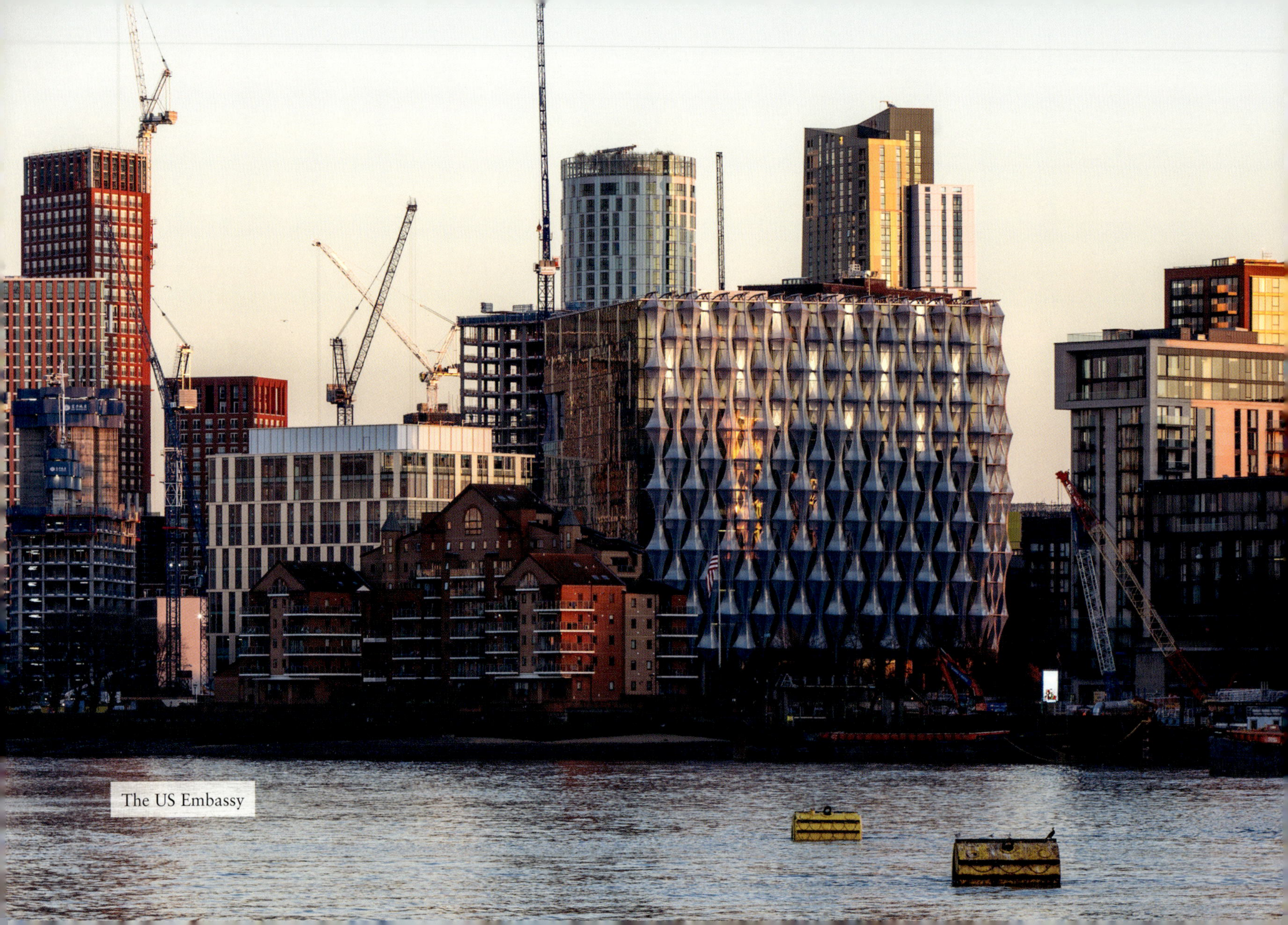

The US Embassy

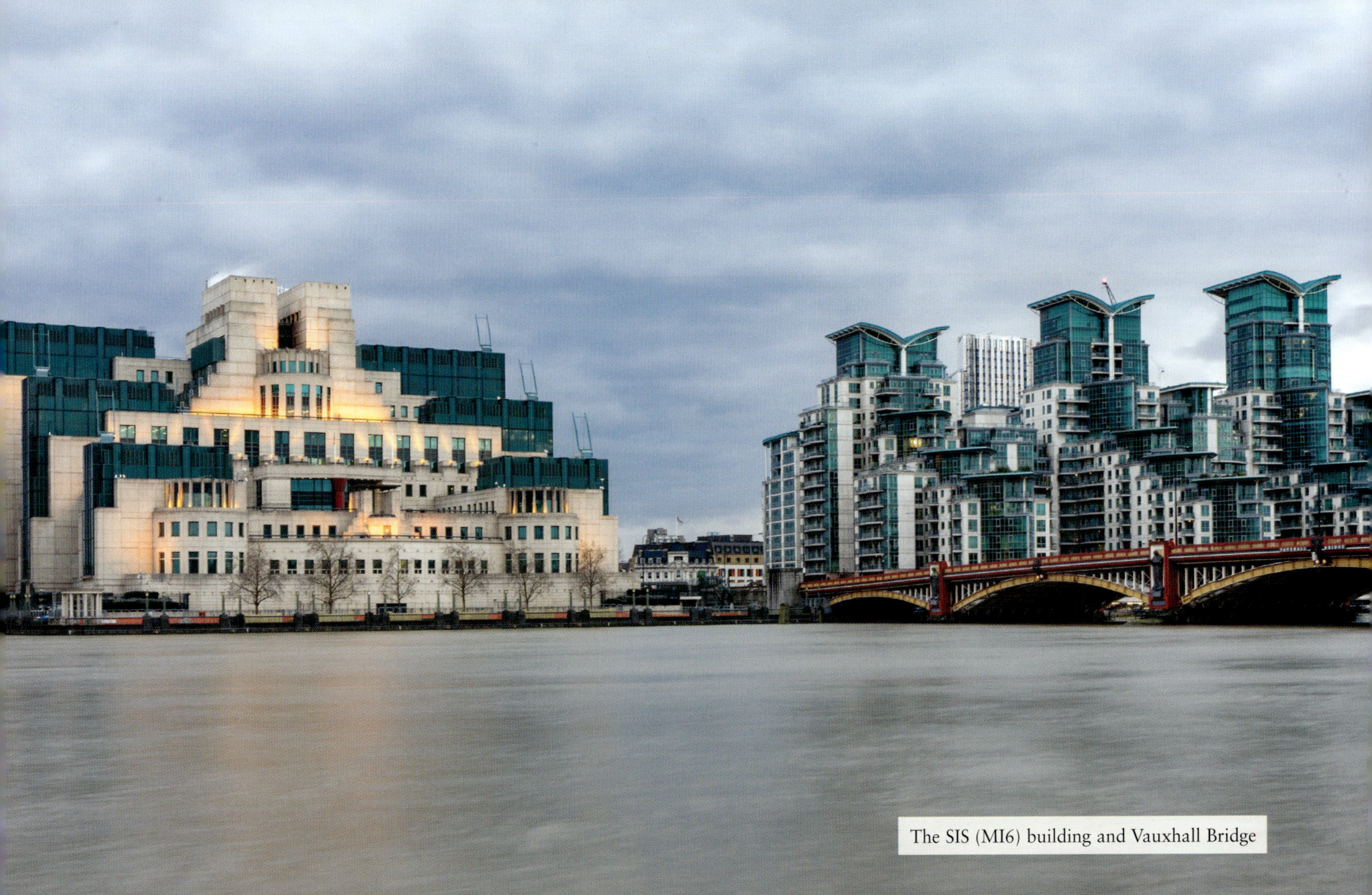

The SIS (MI6) building and Vauxhall Bridge

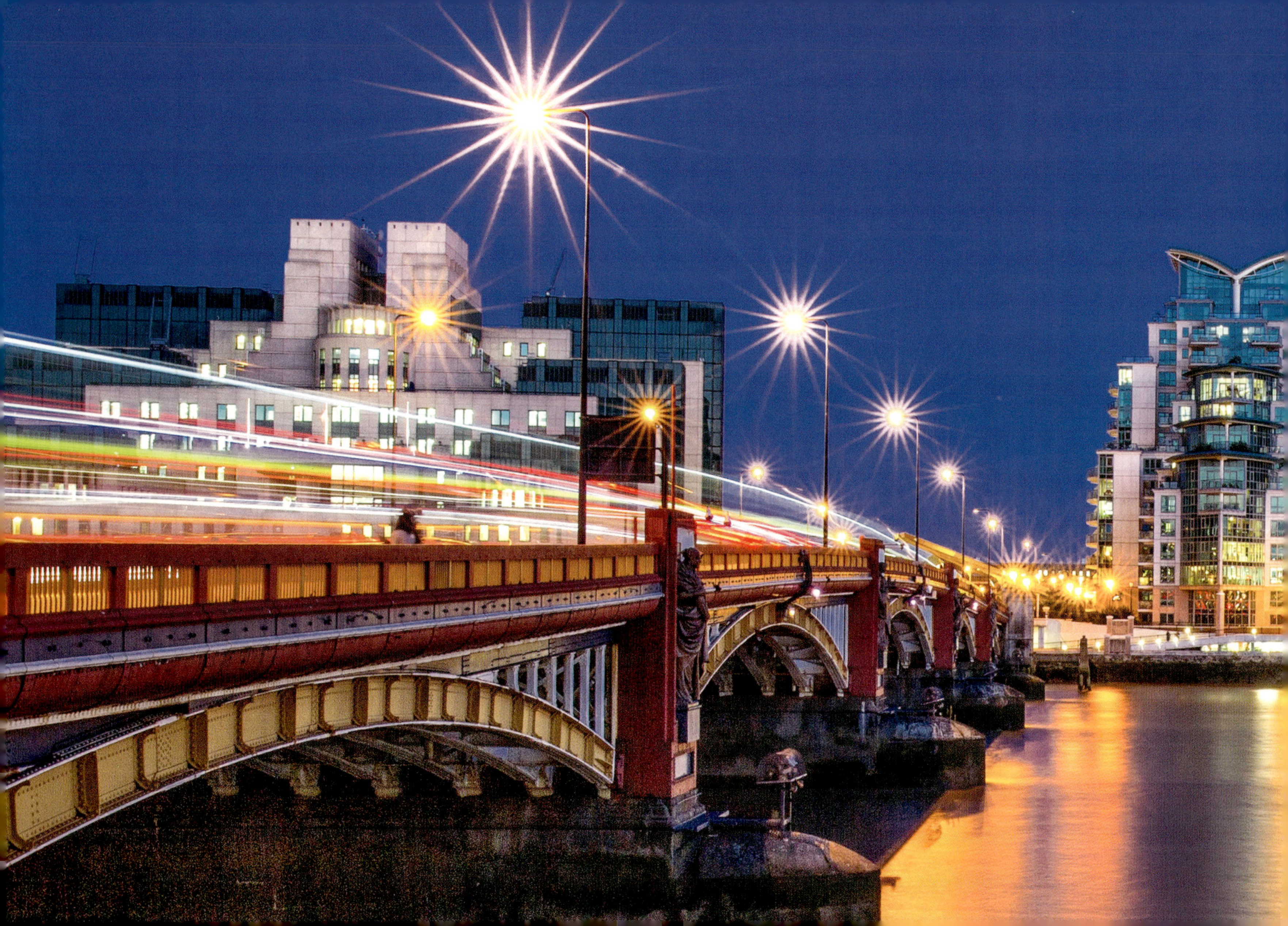

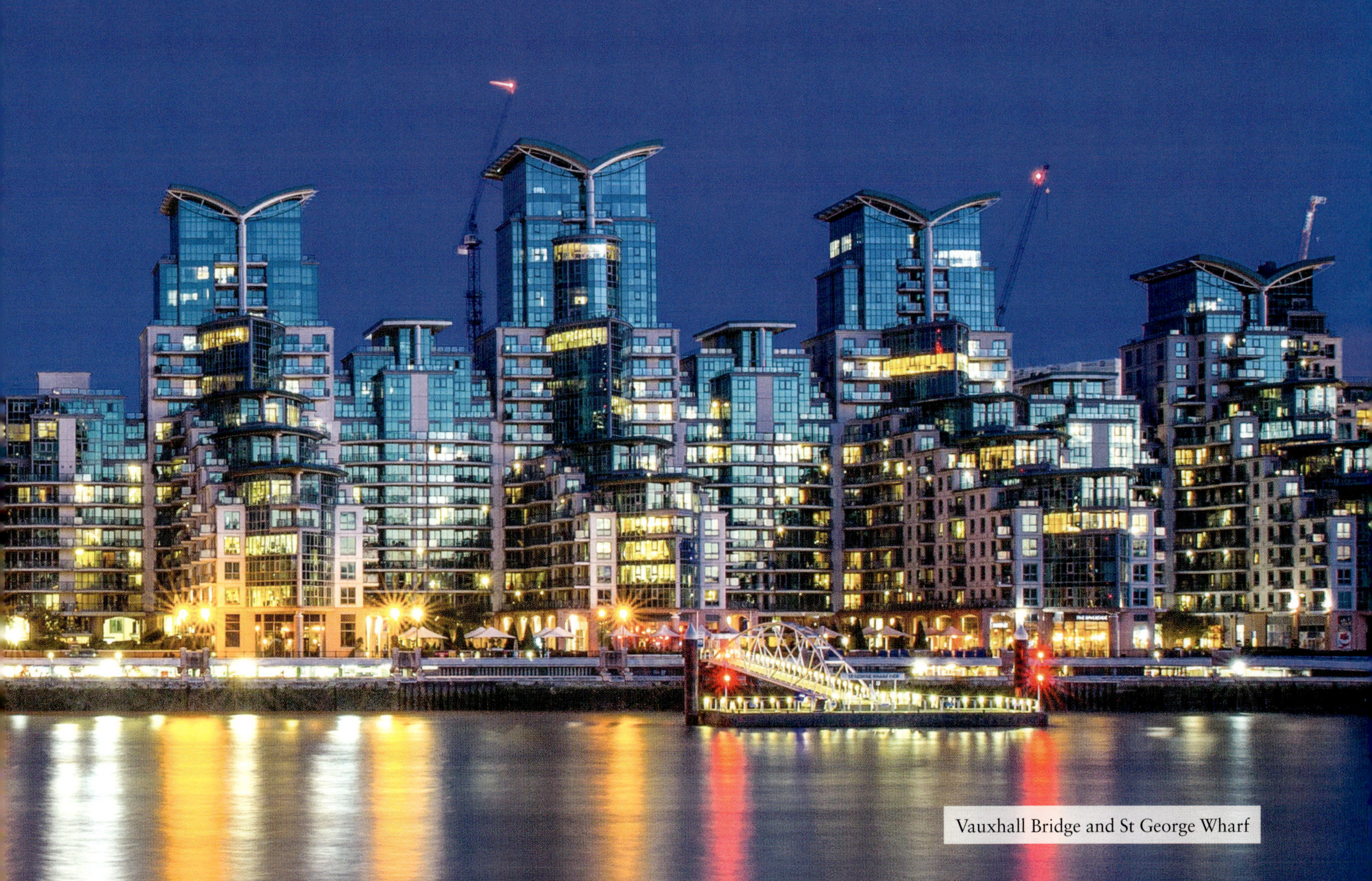

Vauxhall Bridge and St George Wharf

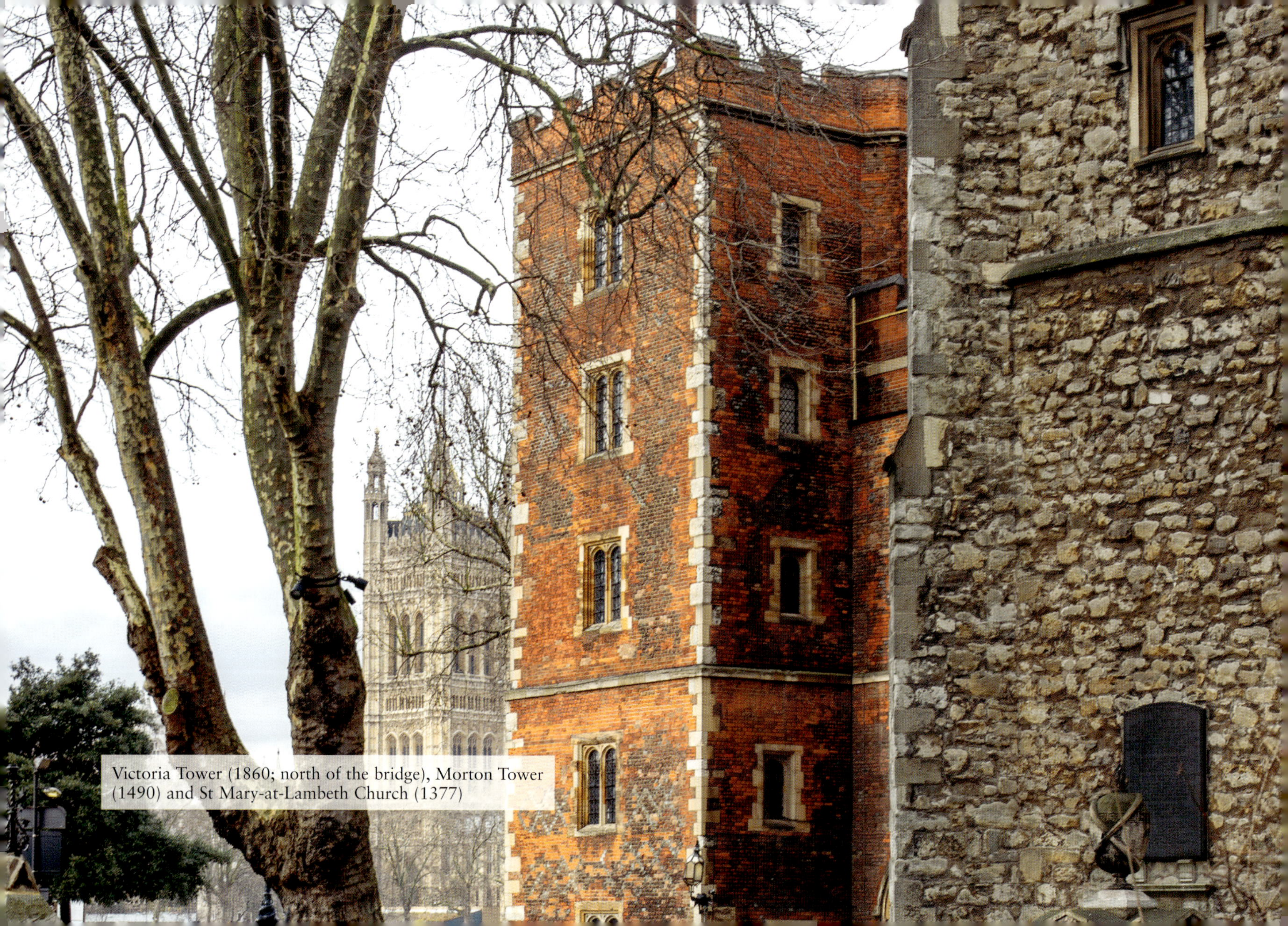

Victoria Tower (1860; north of the bridge), Morton Tower (1490) and St Mary-at-Lambeth Church (1377)

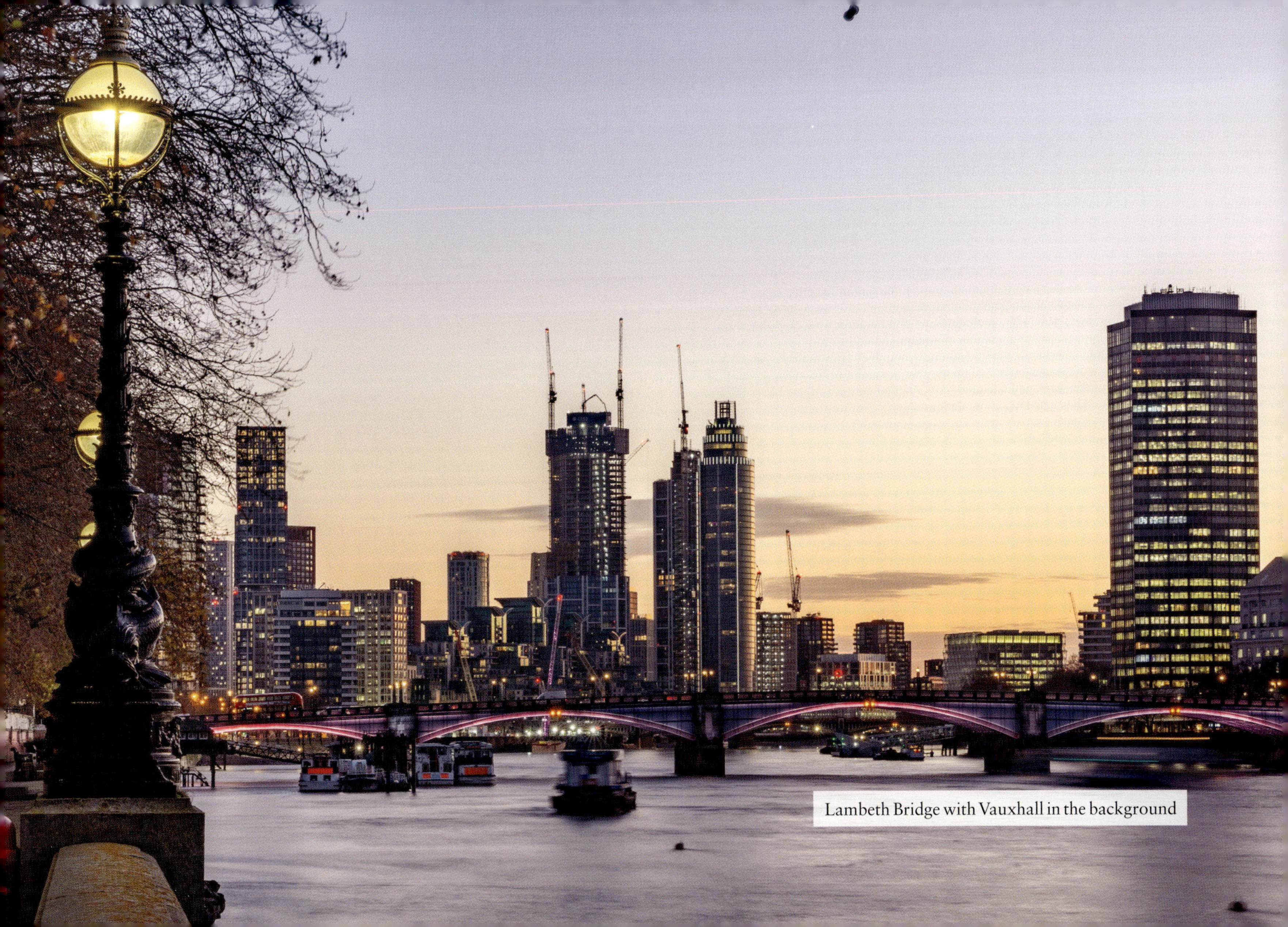

Lambeth Bridge with Vauxhall in the background

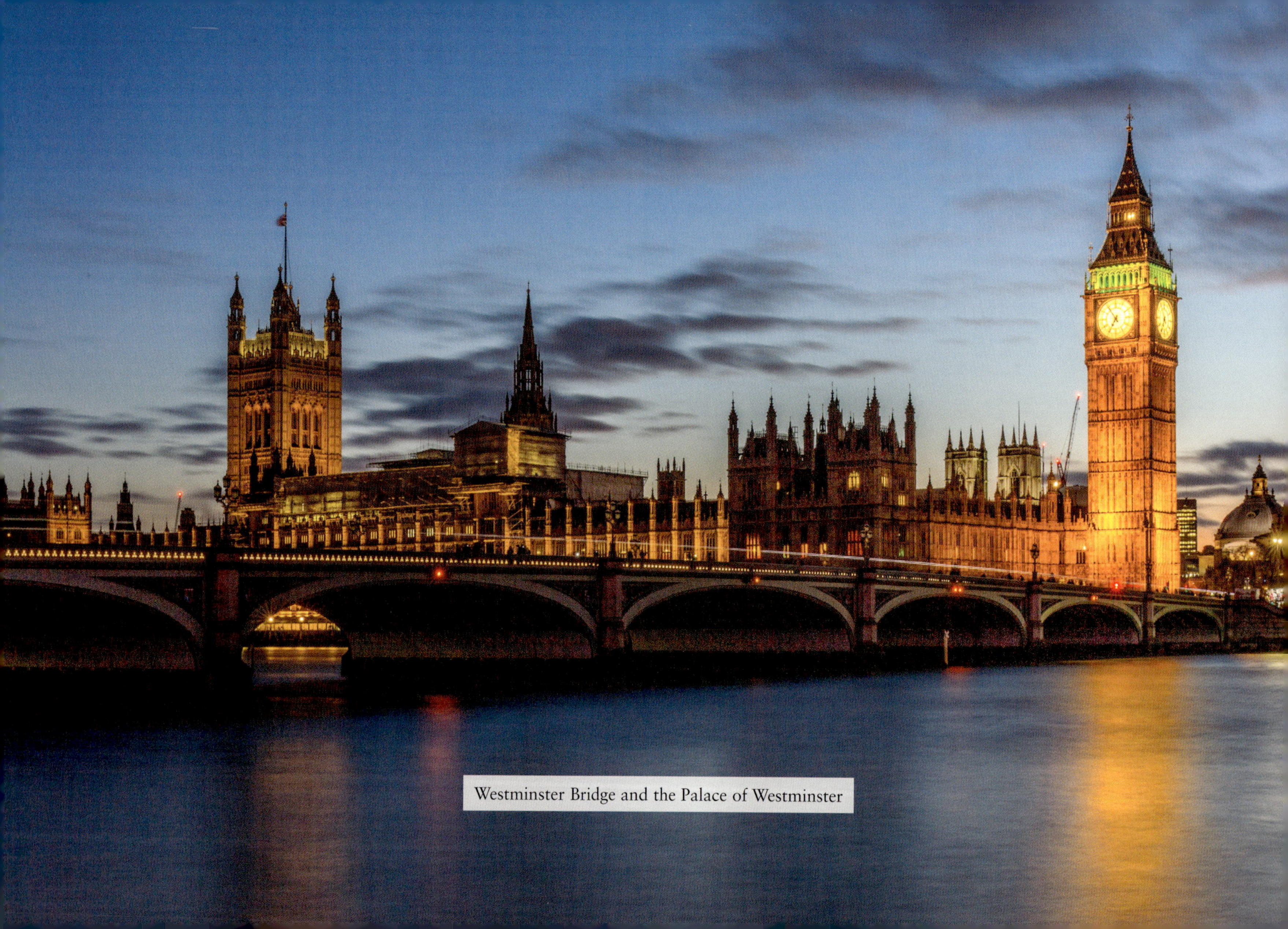

Westminster Bridge and the Palace of Westminster

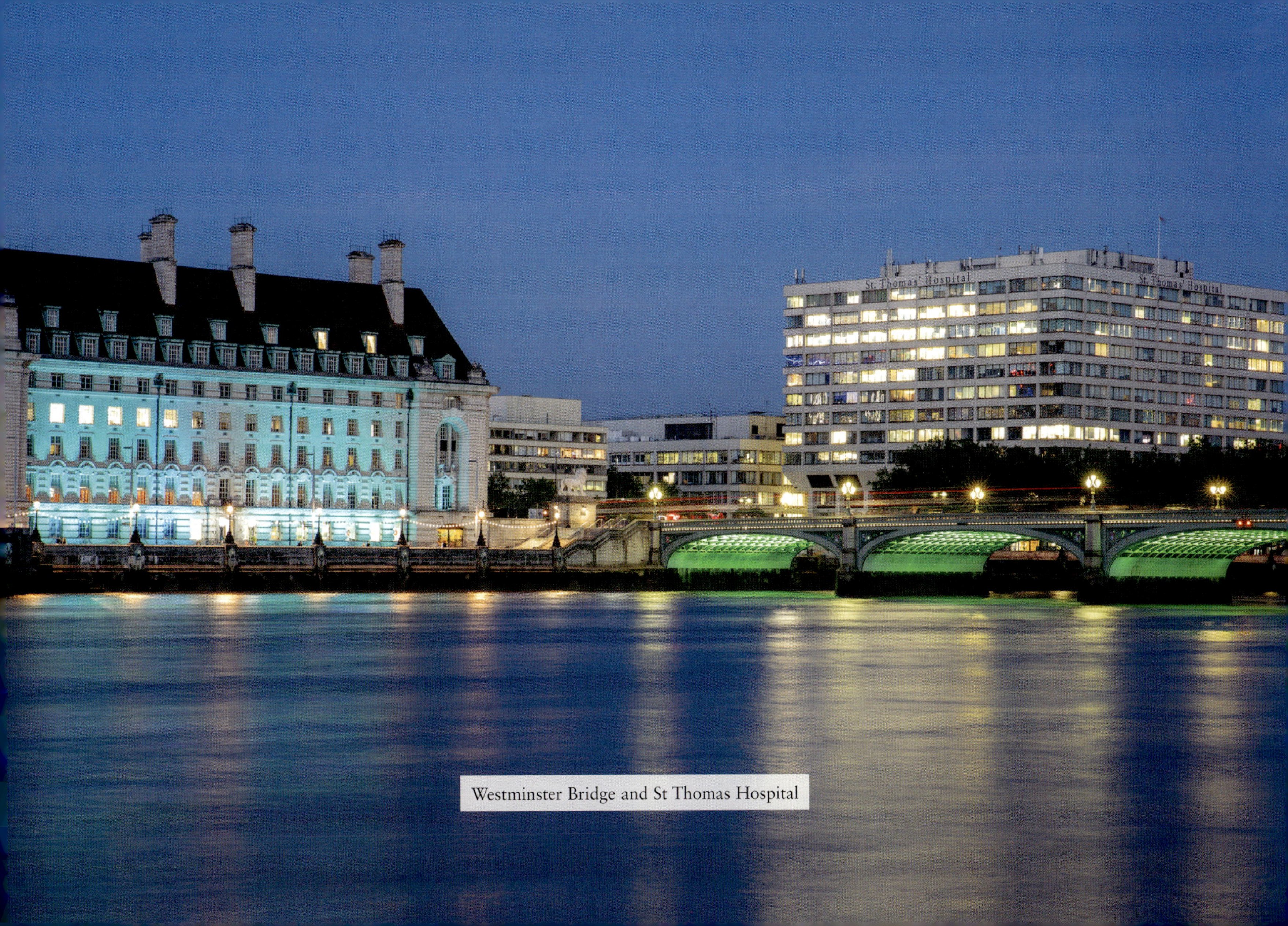

Westminster Bridge and St Thomas Hospital

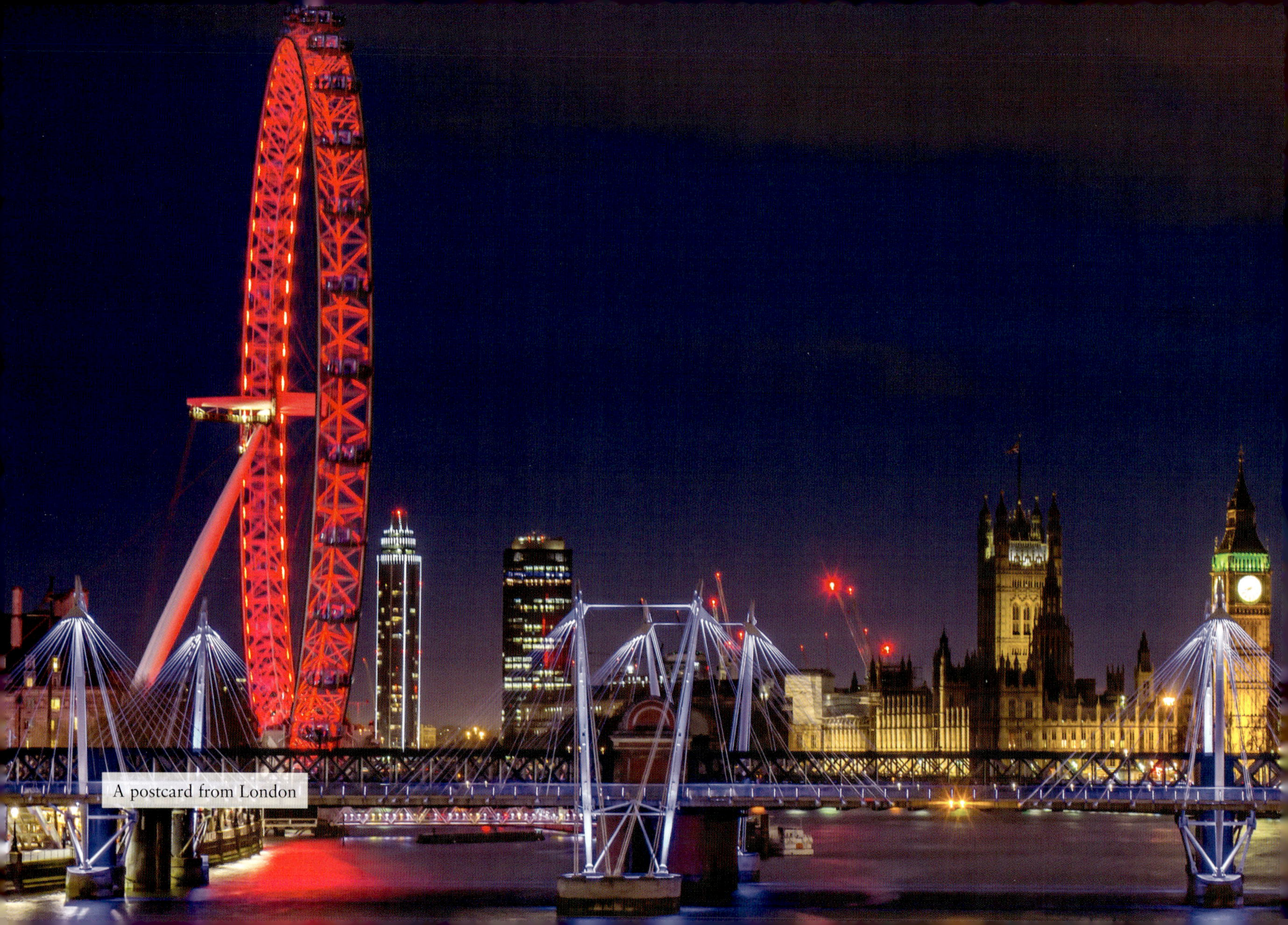
A postcard from London

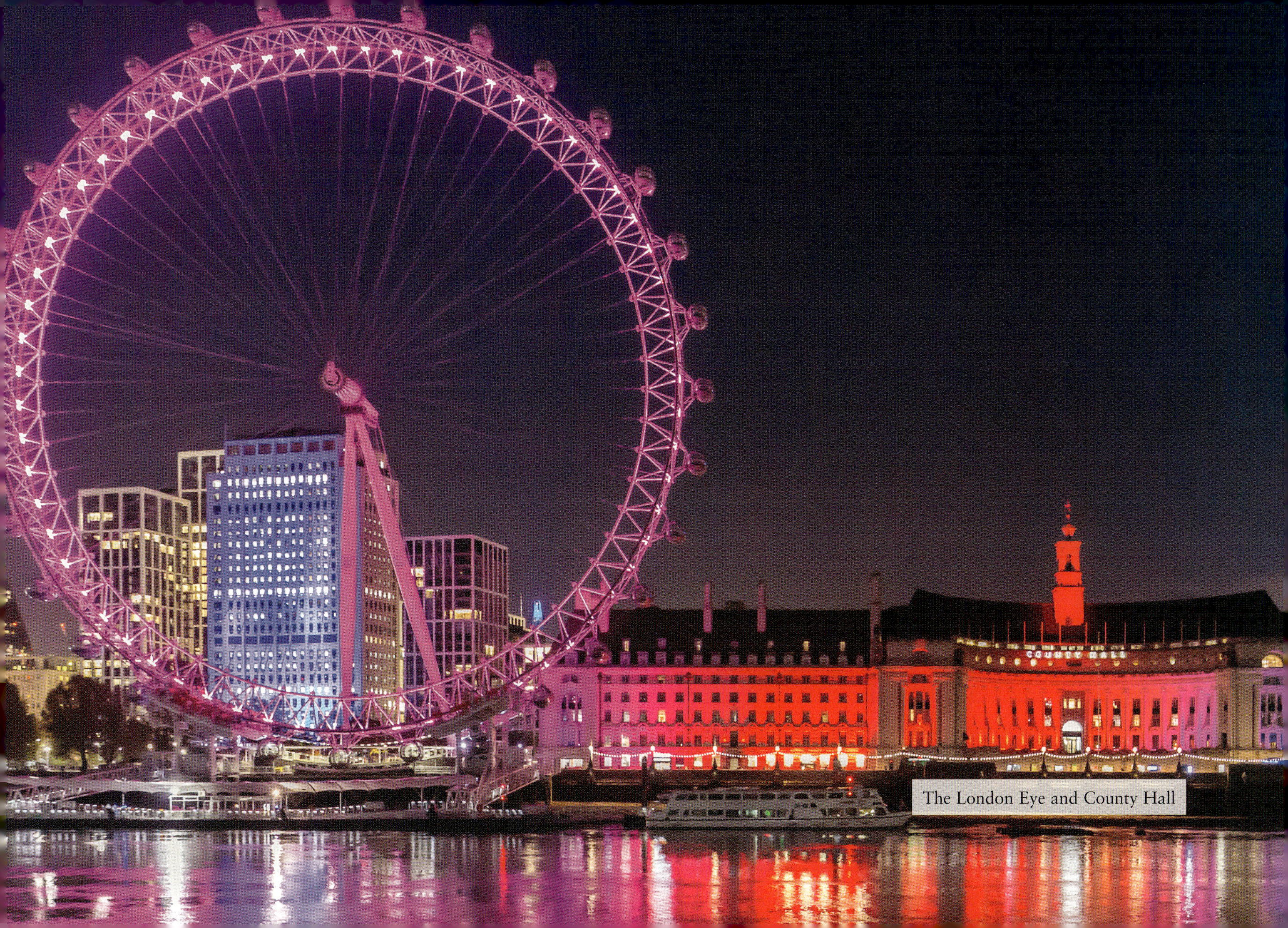

The London Eye and County Hall

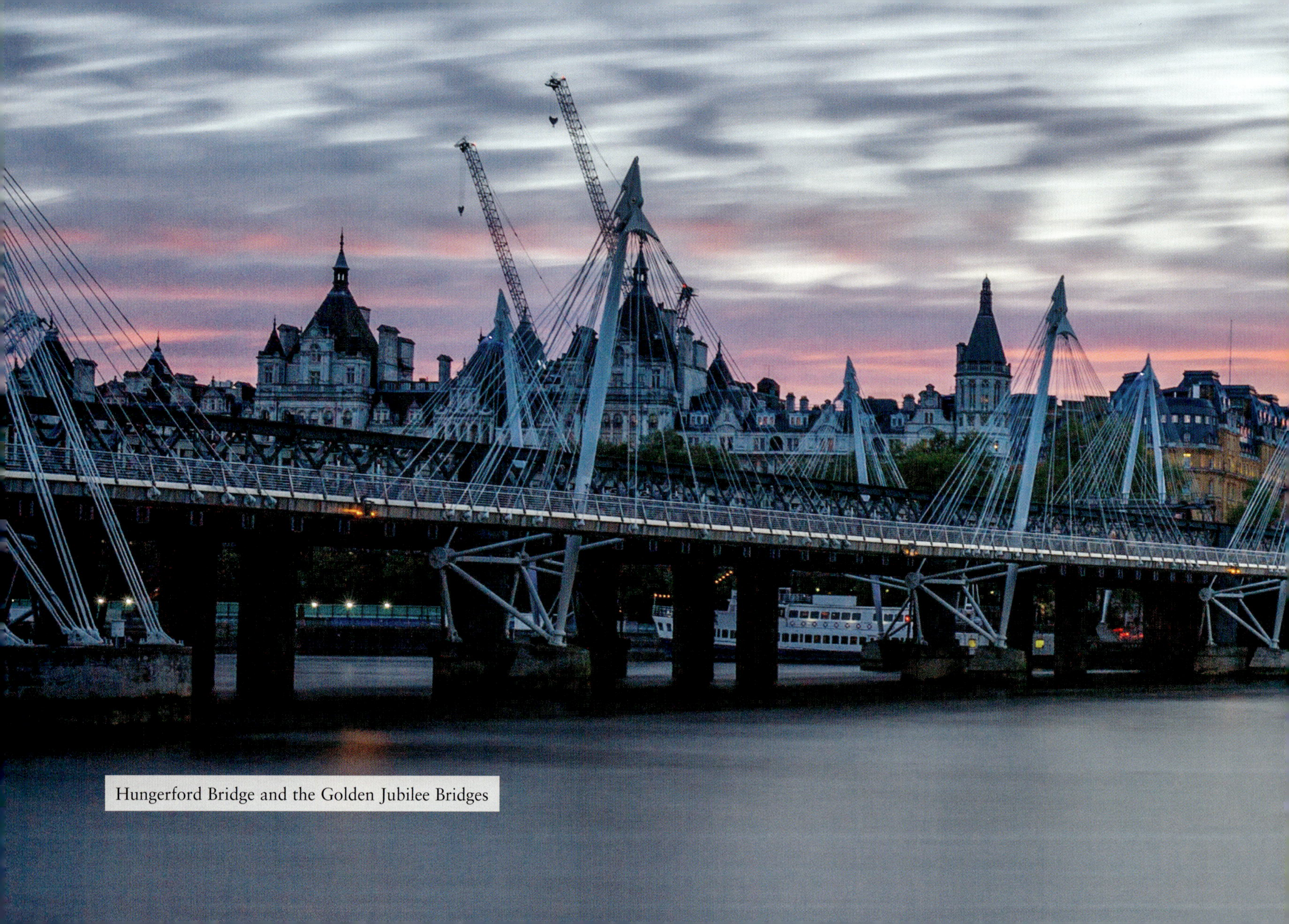

Hungerford Bridge and the Golden Jubilee Bridges

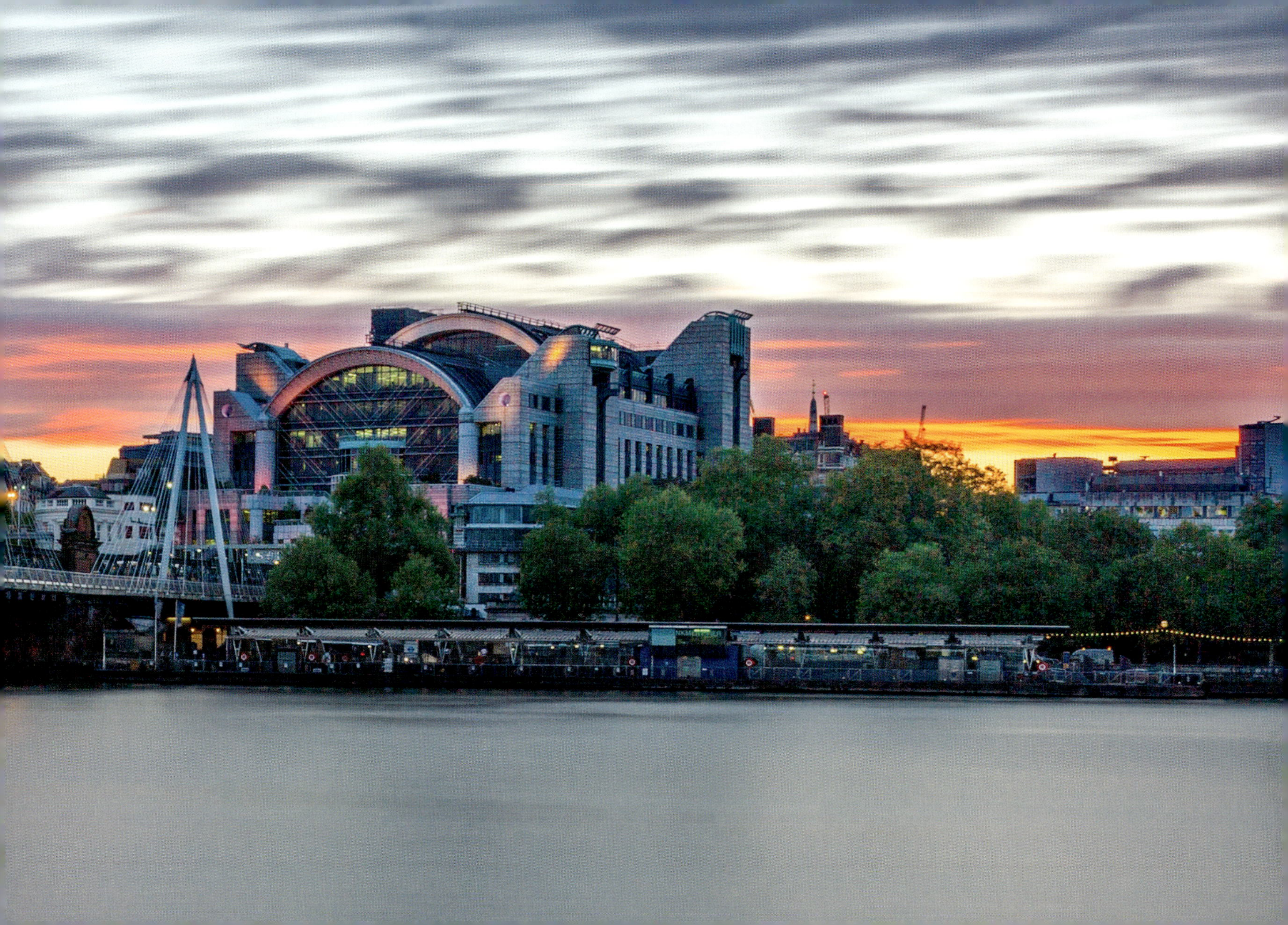

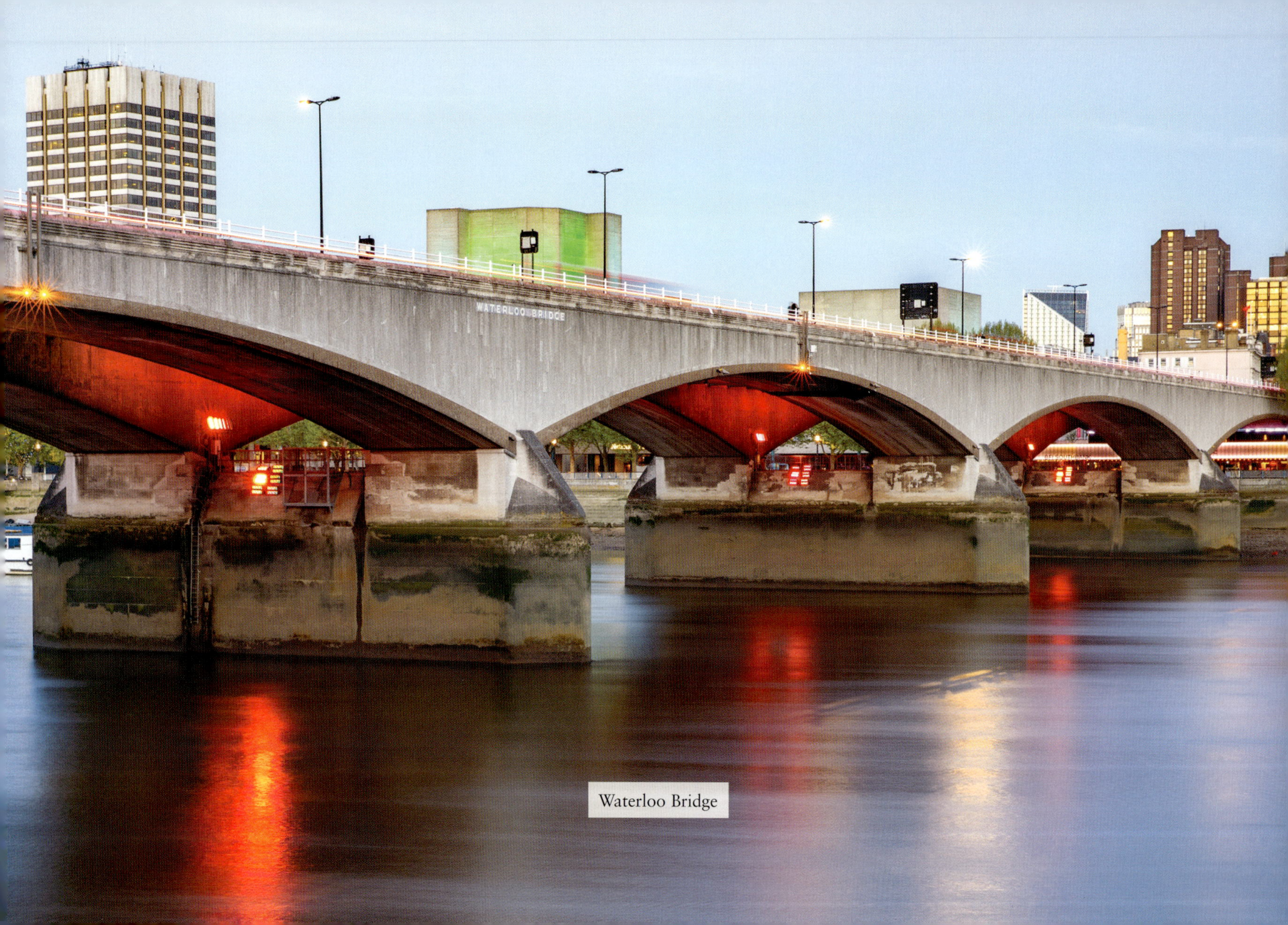

Waterloo Bridge

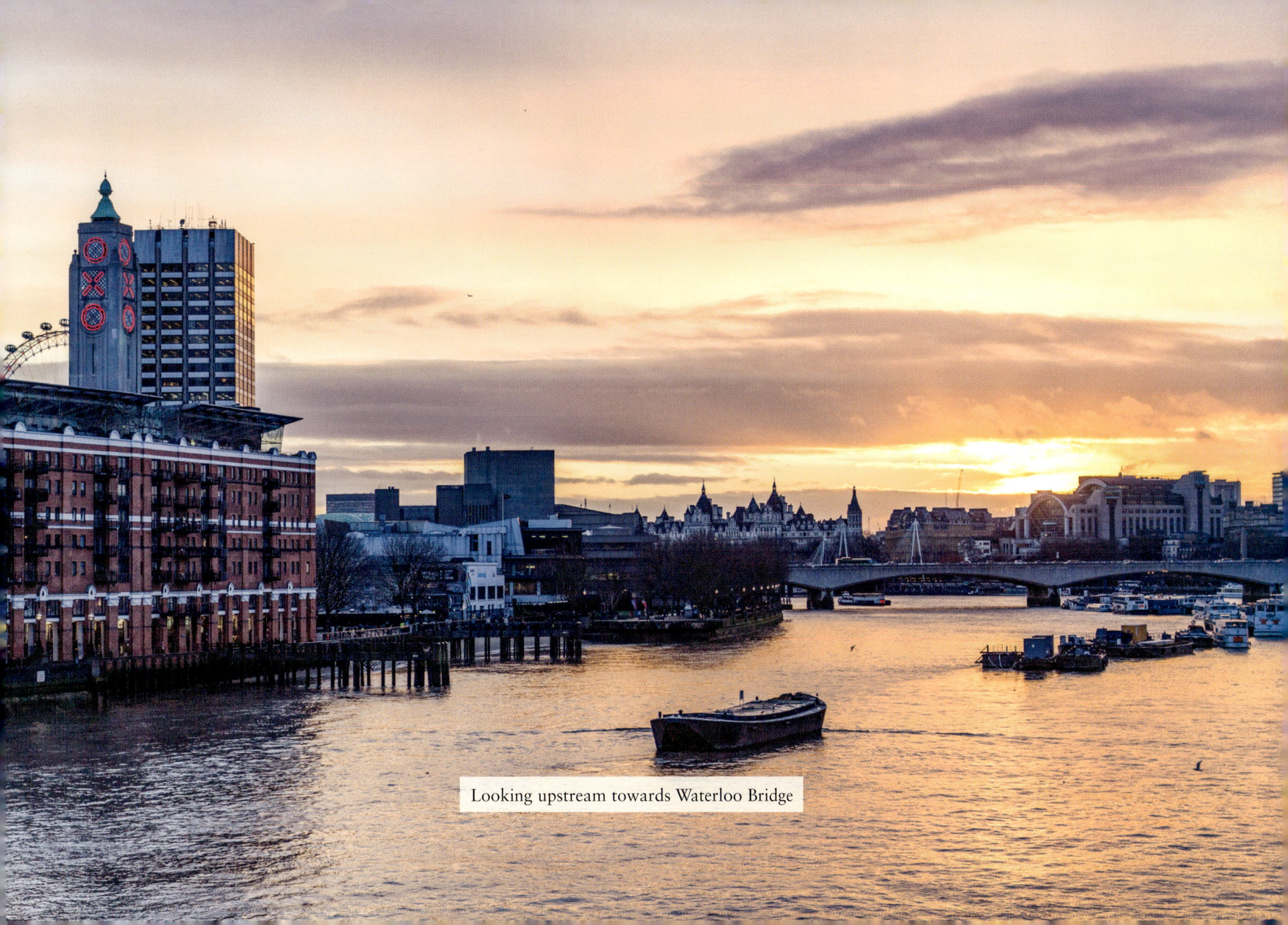

Looking upstream towards Waterloo Bridge

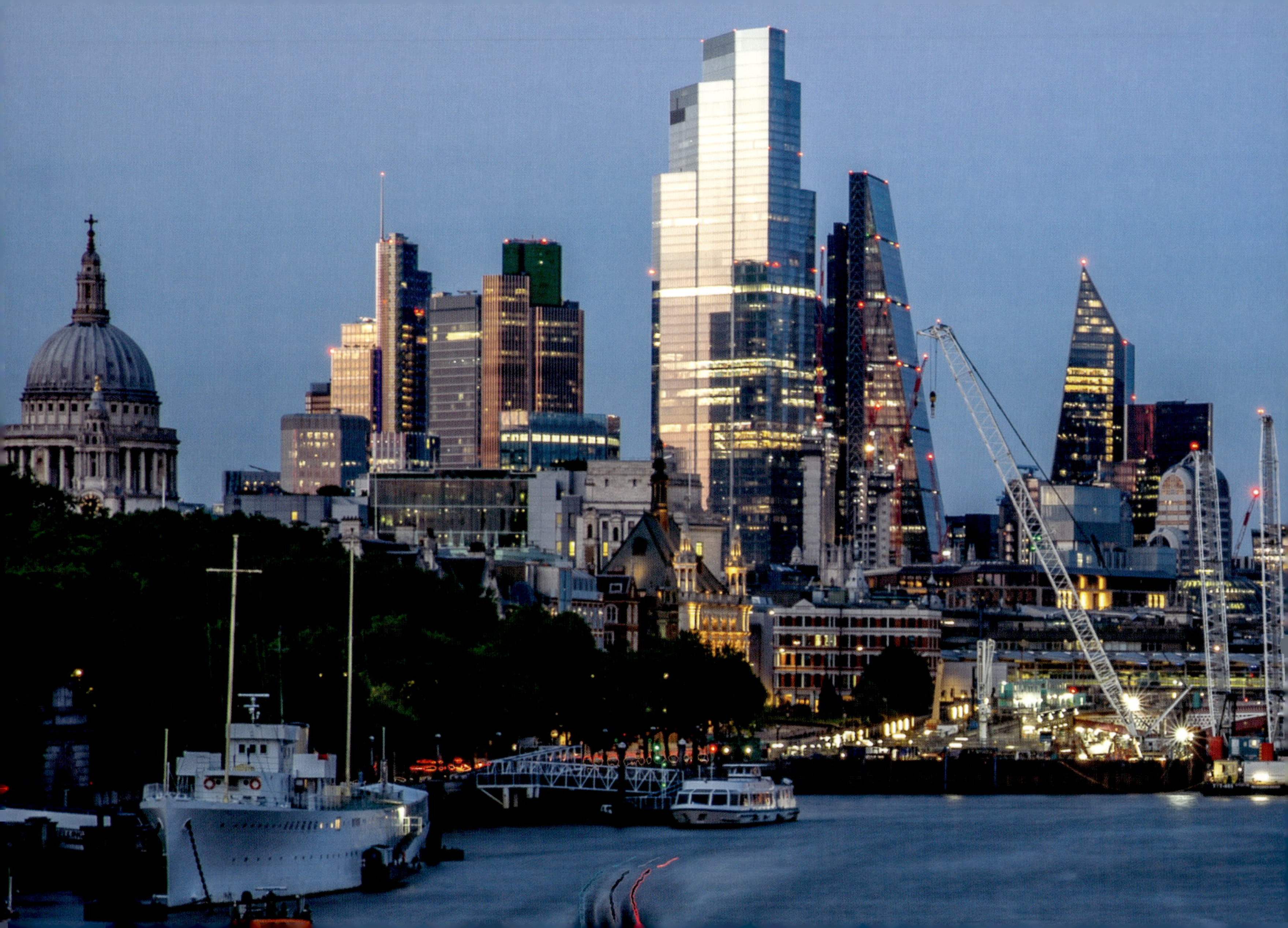

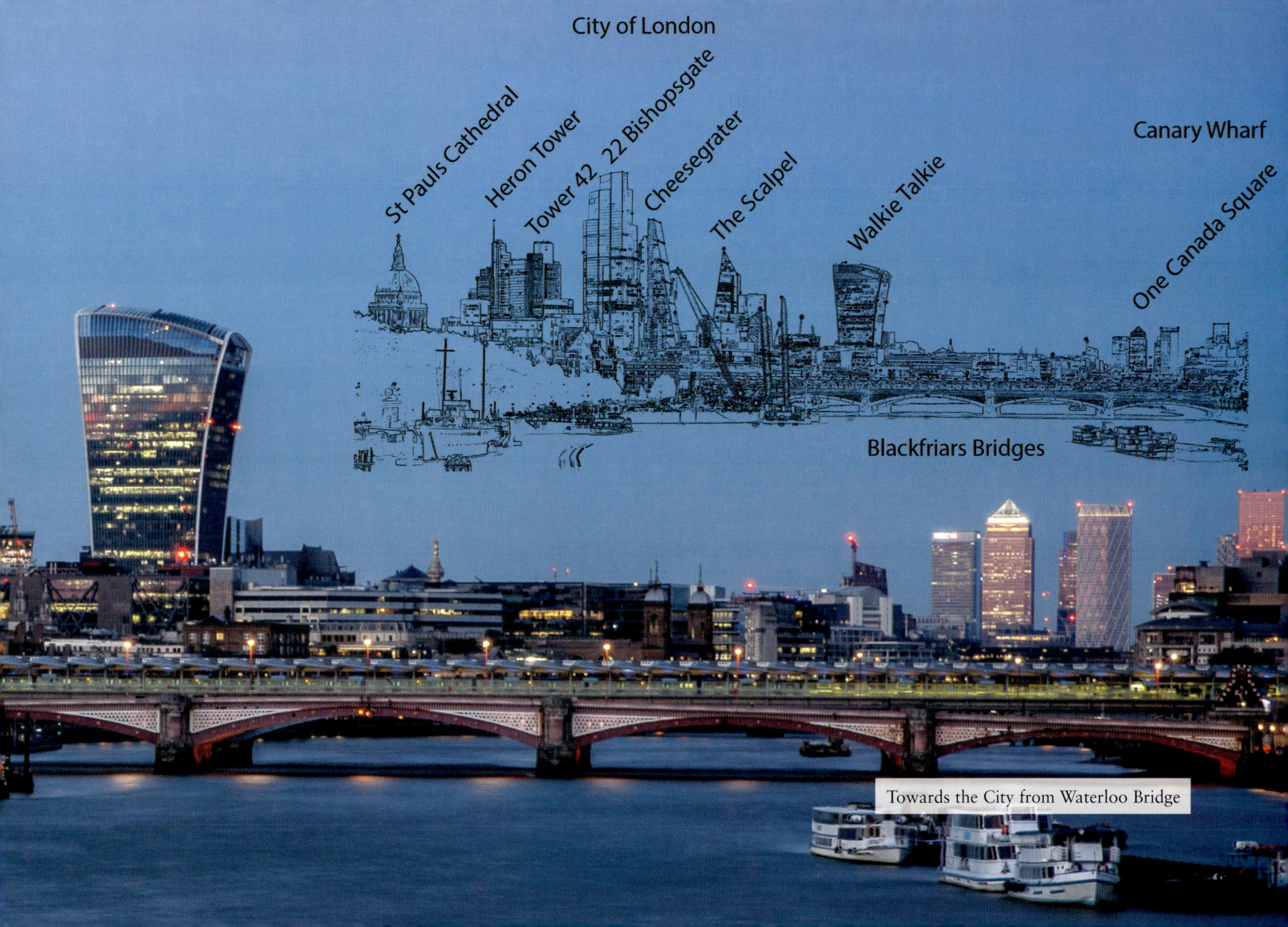
City of London
St Pauls Cathedral
Heron Tower
Tower 42
22 Bishopsgate
Cheesegrater
The Scalpel
Walkie Talkie
Canary Wharf
One Canada Square
Blackfriars Bridges
Towards the City from Waterloo Bridge

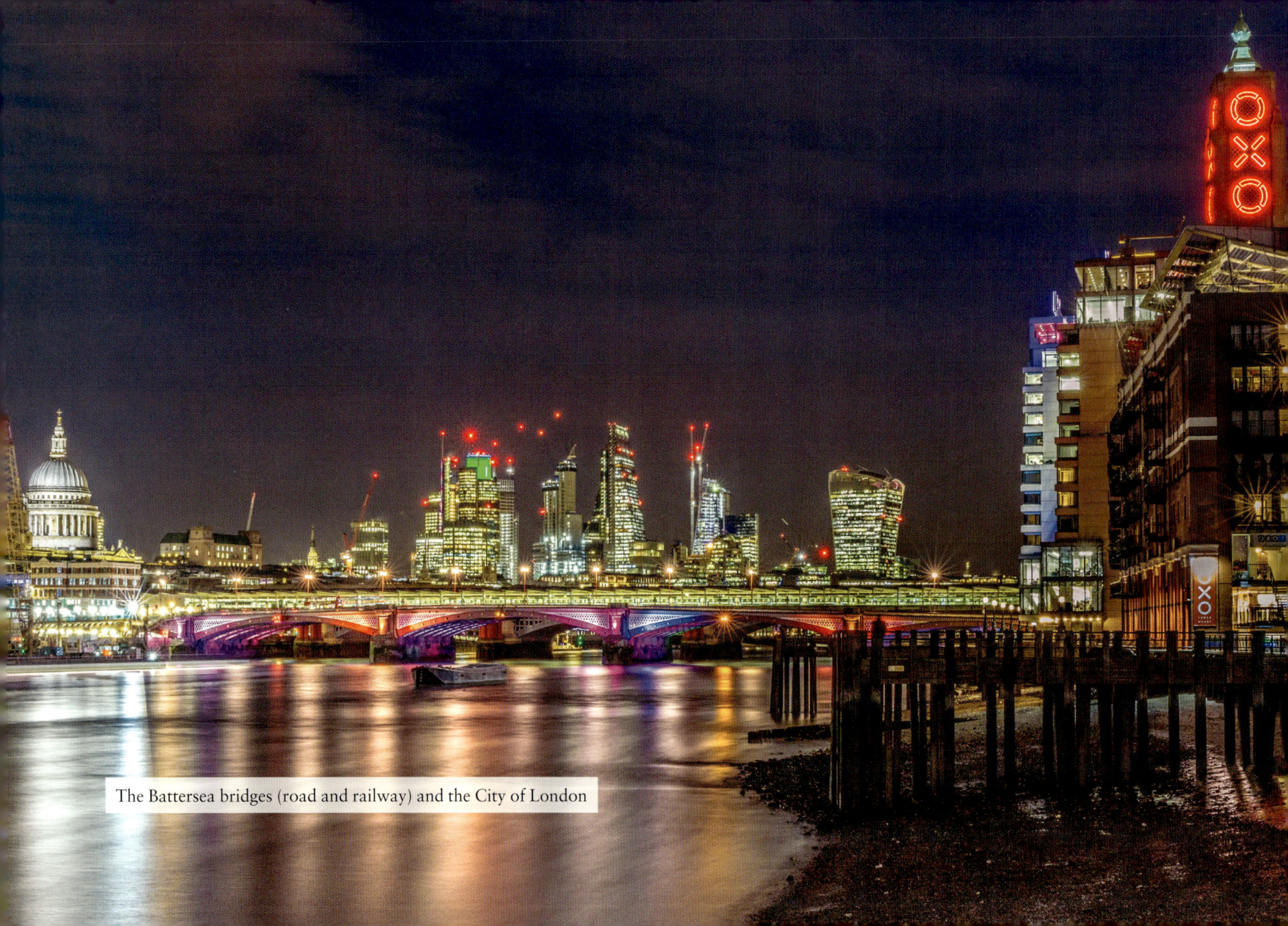
The Battersea bridges (road and railway) and the City of London

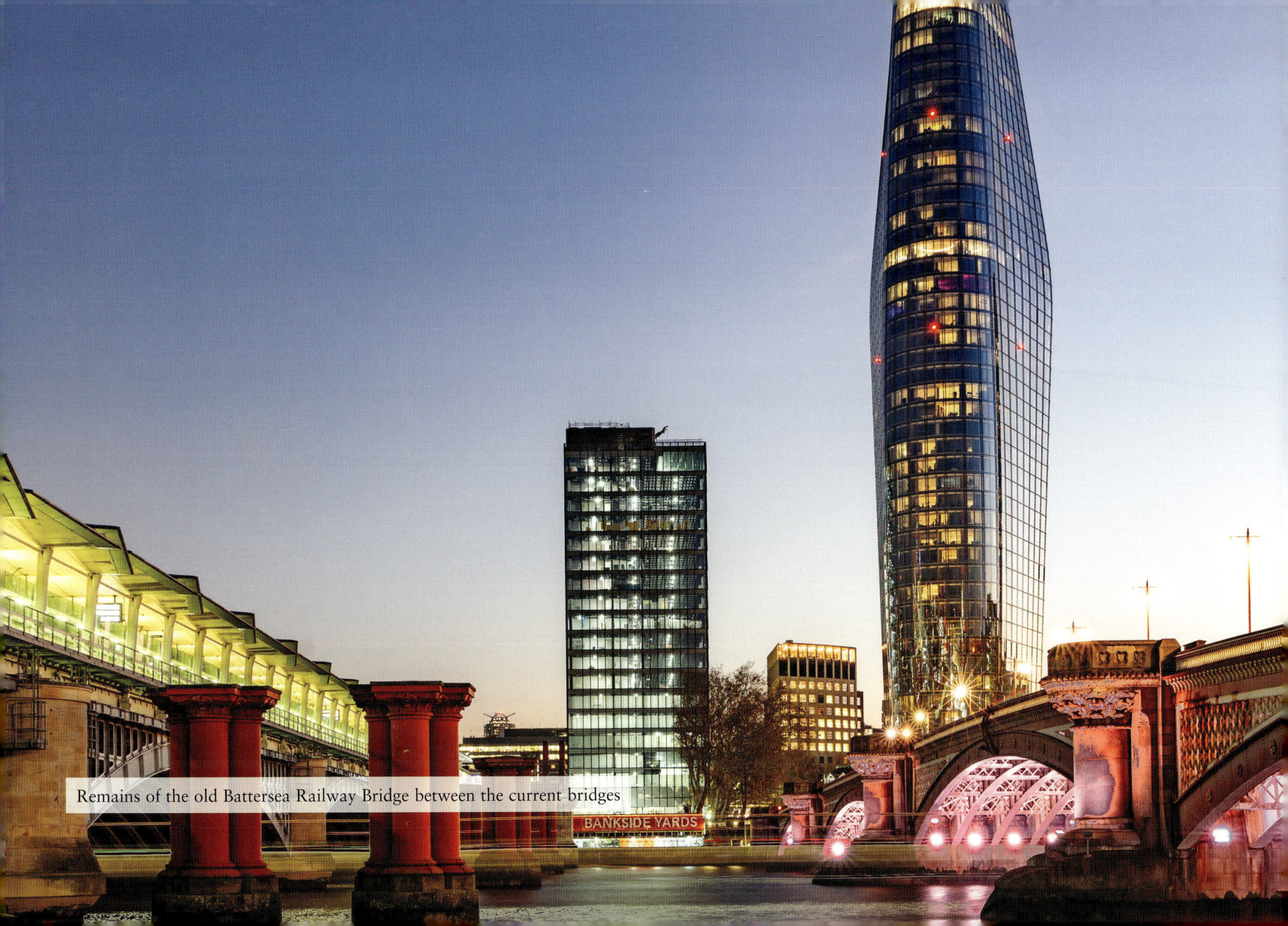

Remains of the old Battersea Railway Bridge between the current bridges

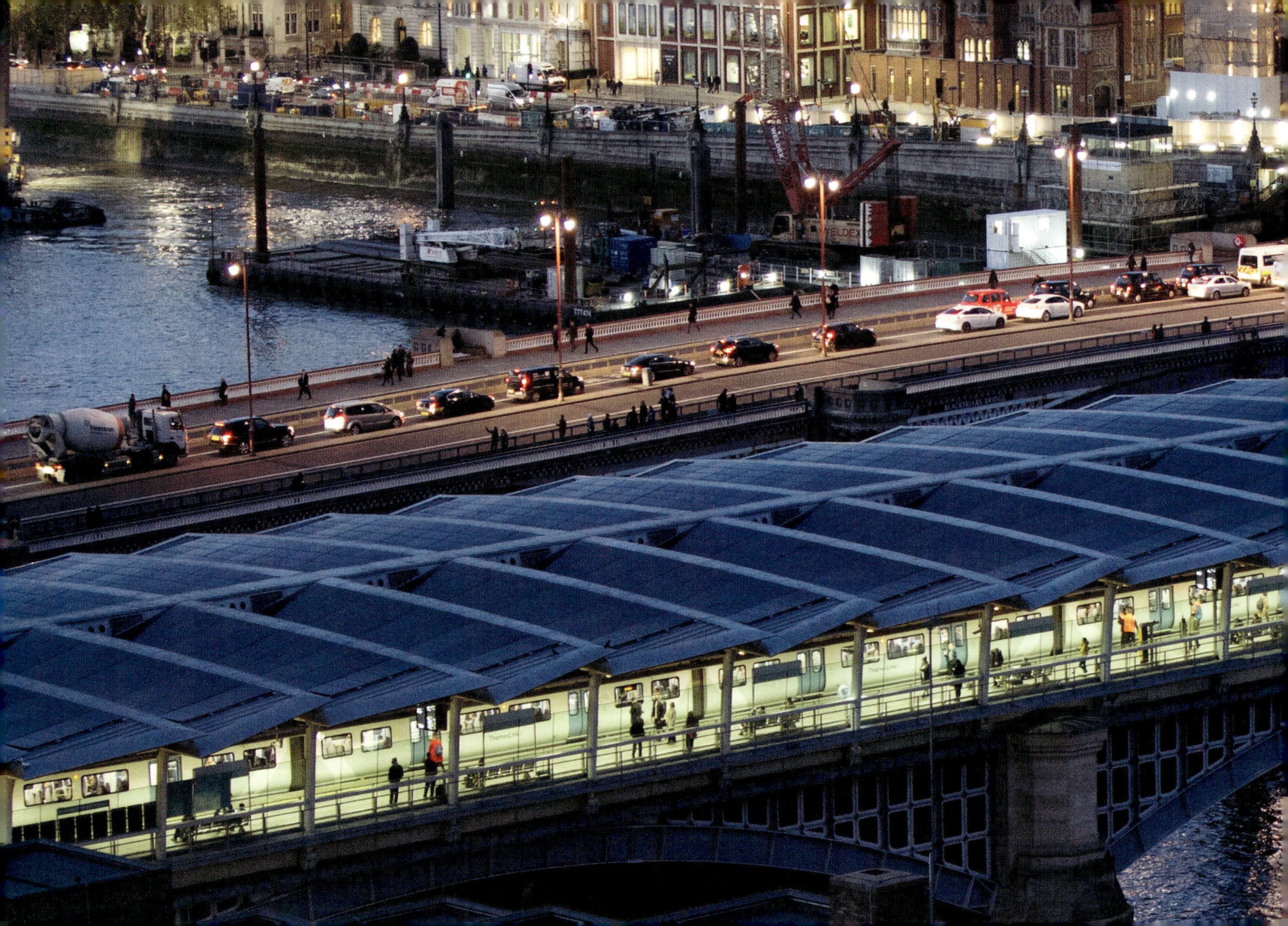

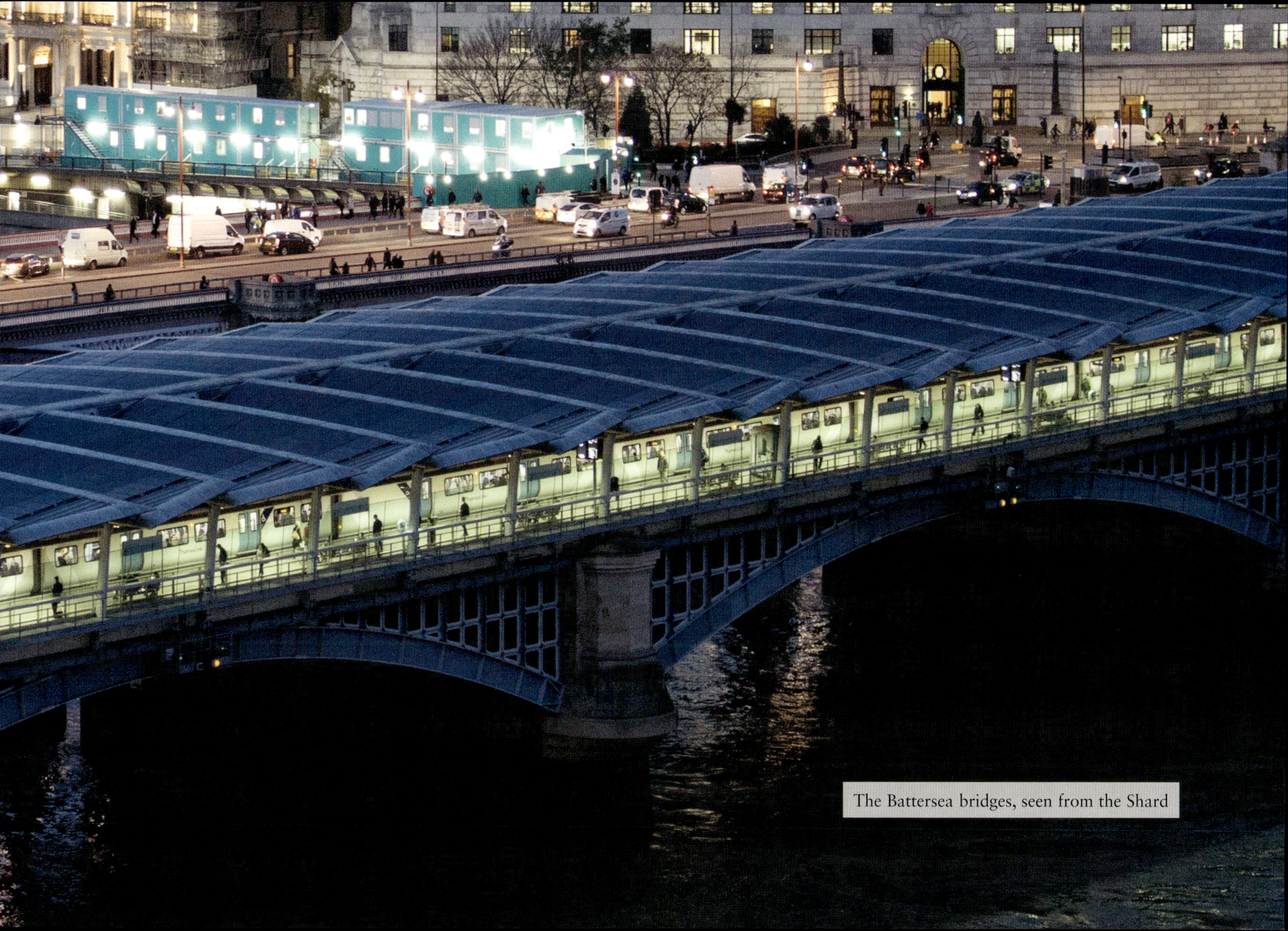

The Battersea bridges, seen from the Shard

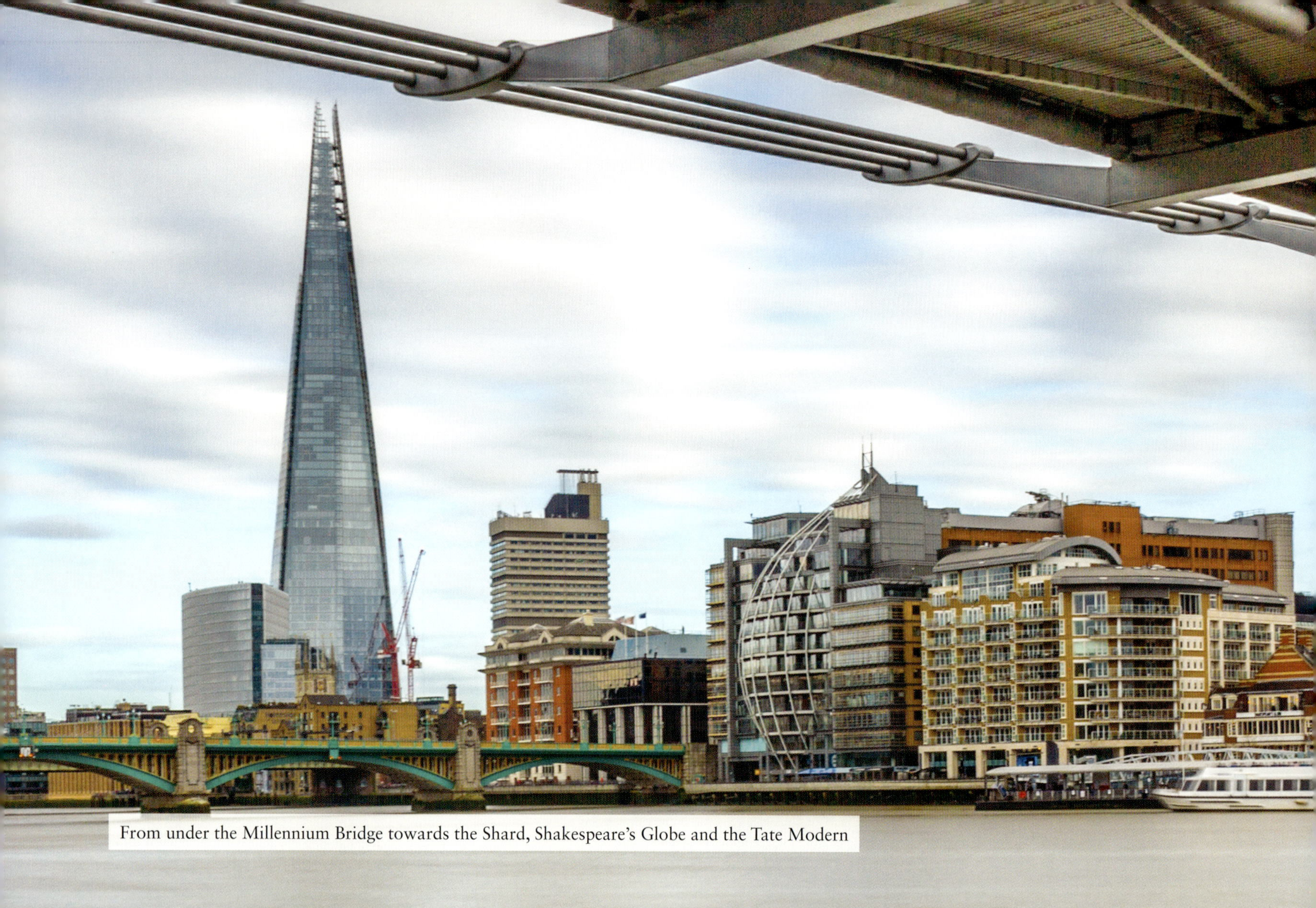

From under the Millennium Bridge towards the Shard, Shakespeare's Globe and the Tate Modern

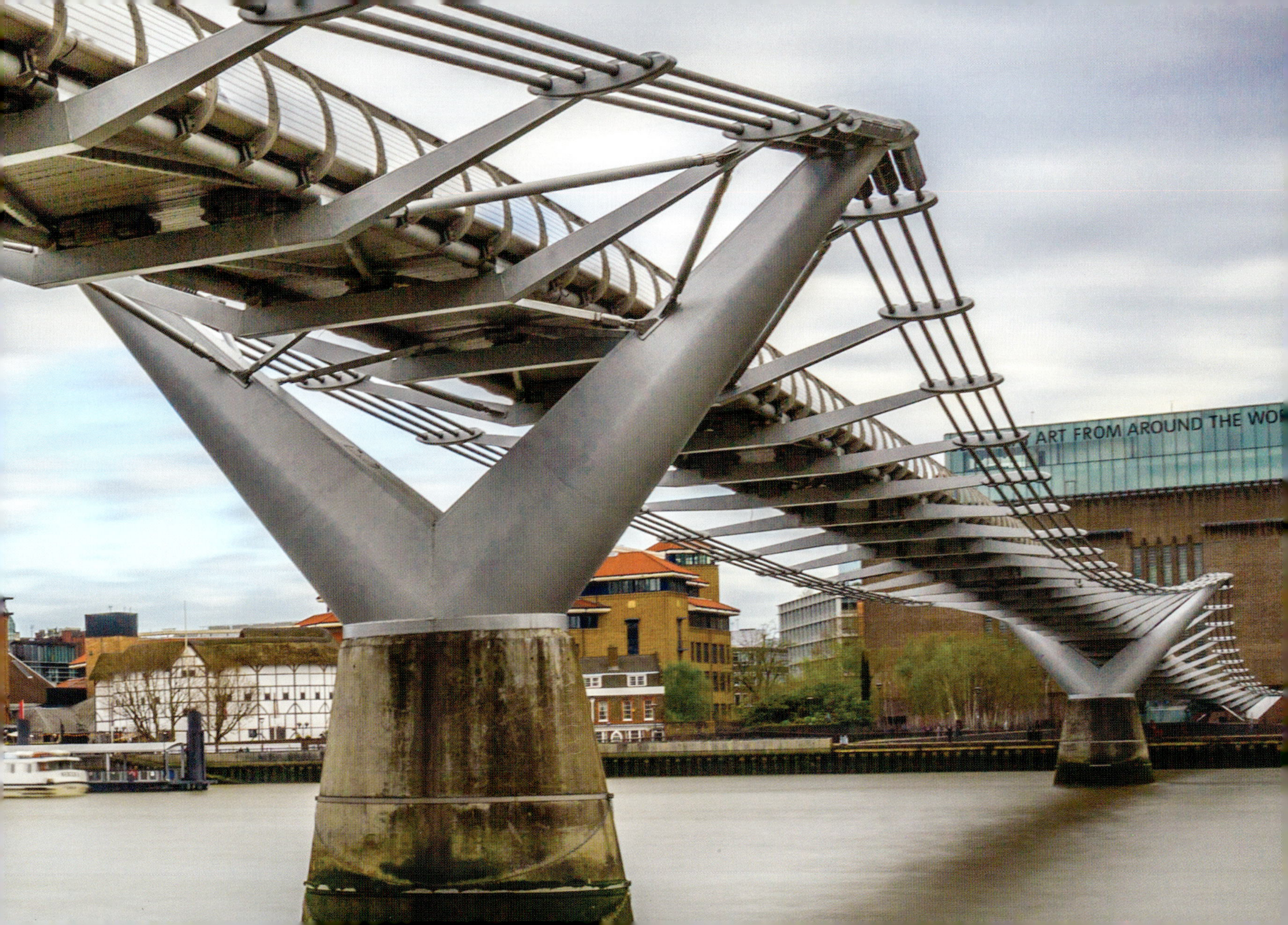
ART FROM AROUND THE WOR

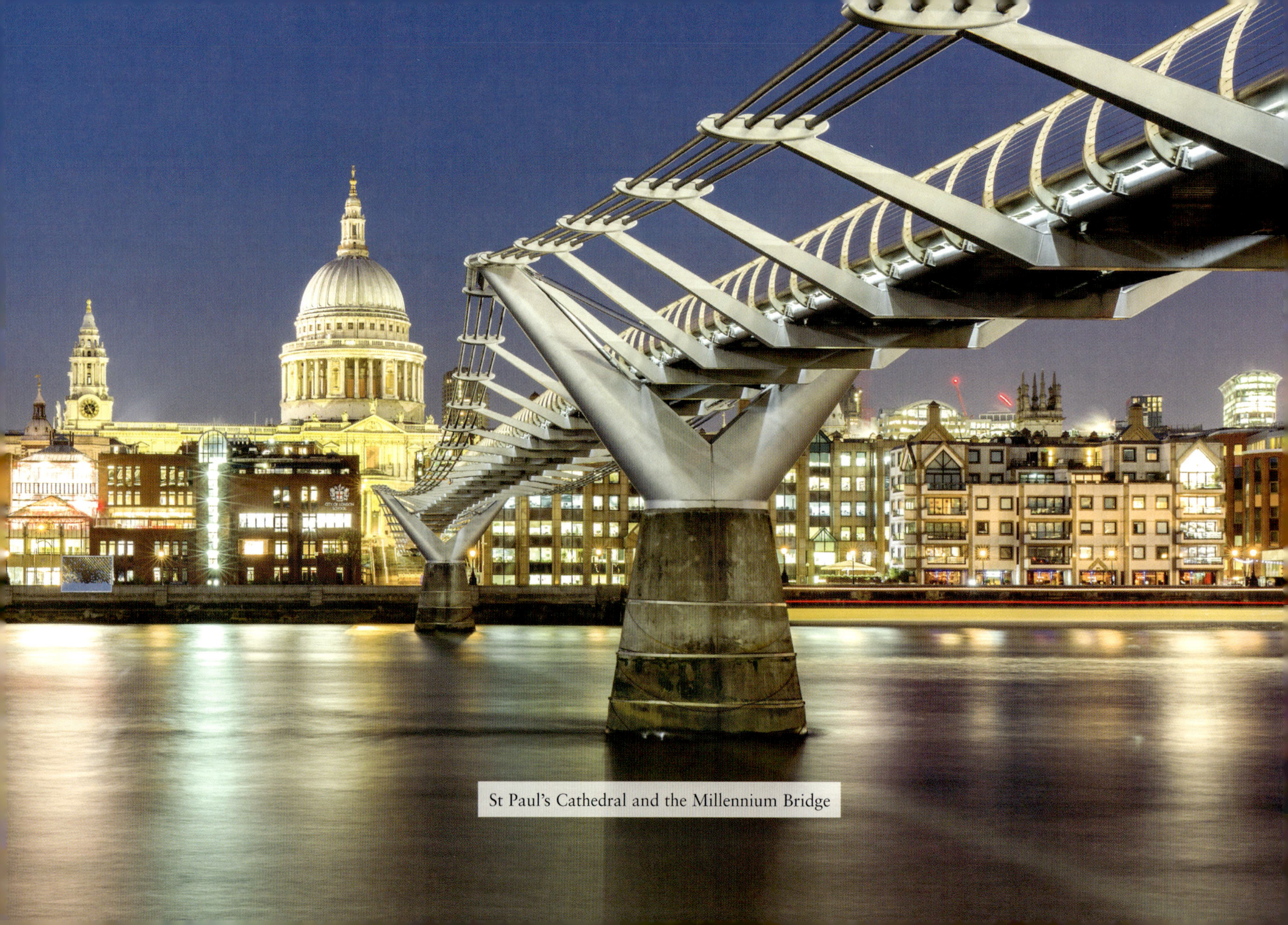

St Paul's Cathedral and the Millennium Bridge

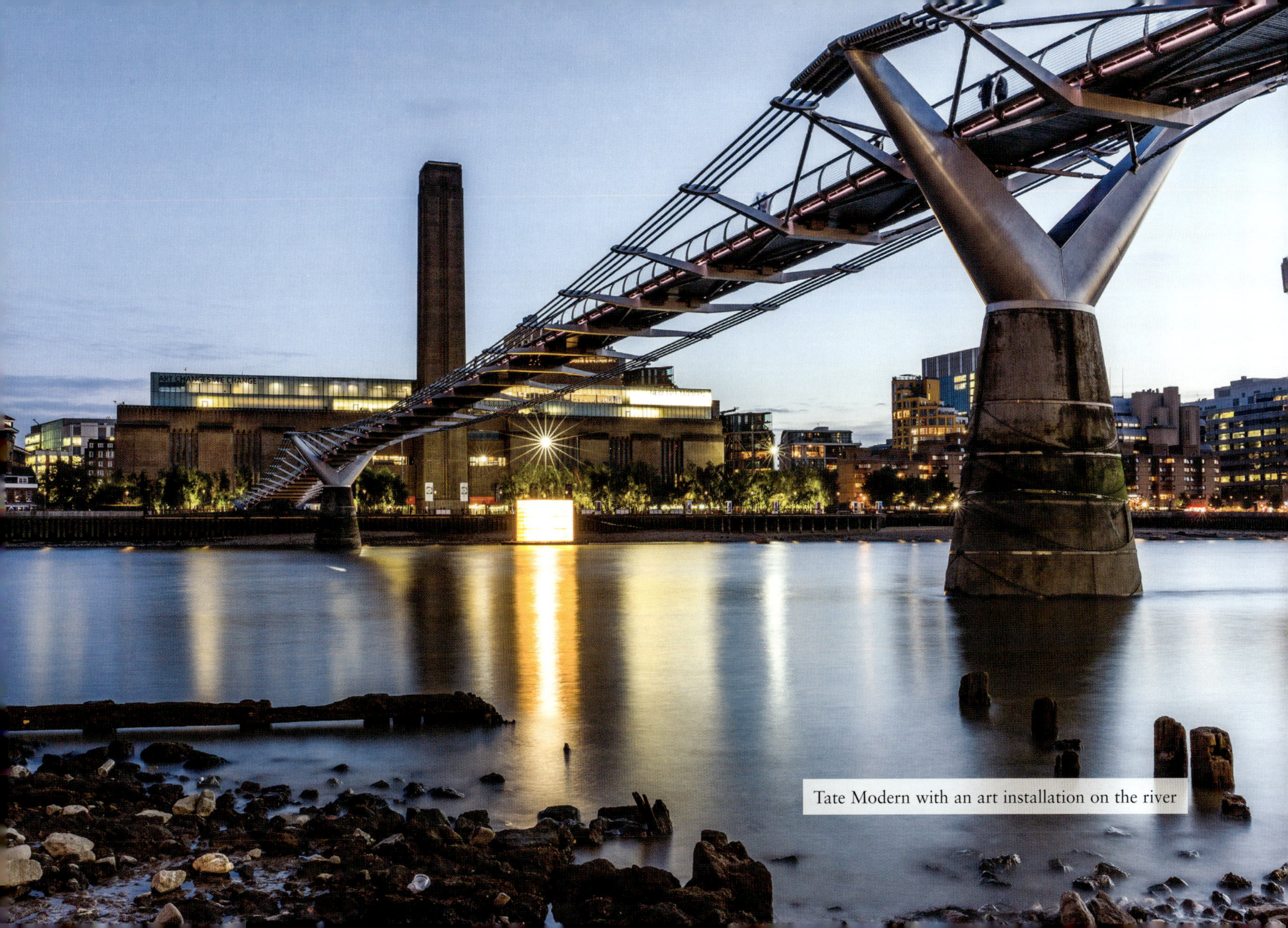

Tate Modern with an art installation on the river

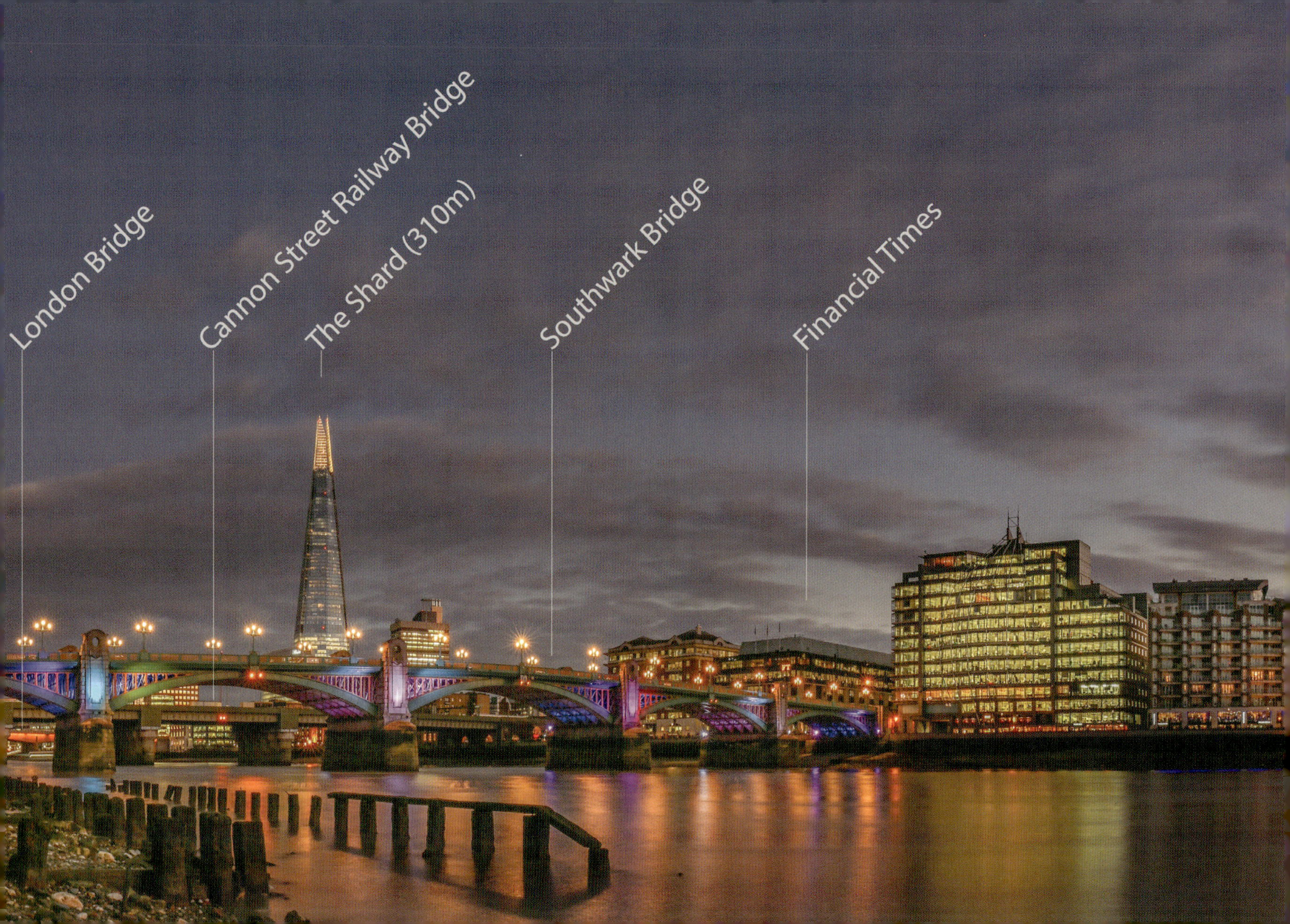

London Bridge
Cannon Street Railway Bridge
The Shard (310m)
Southwark Bridge
Financial Times

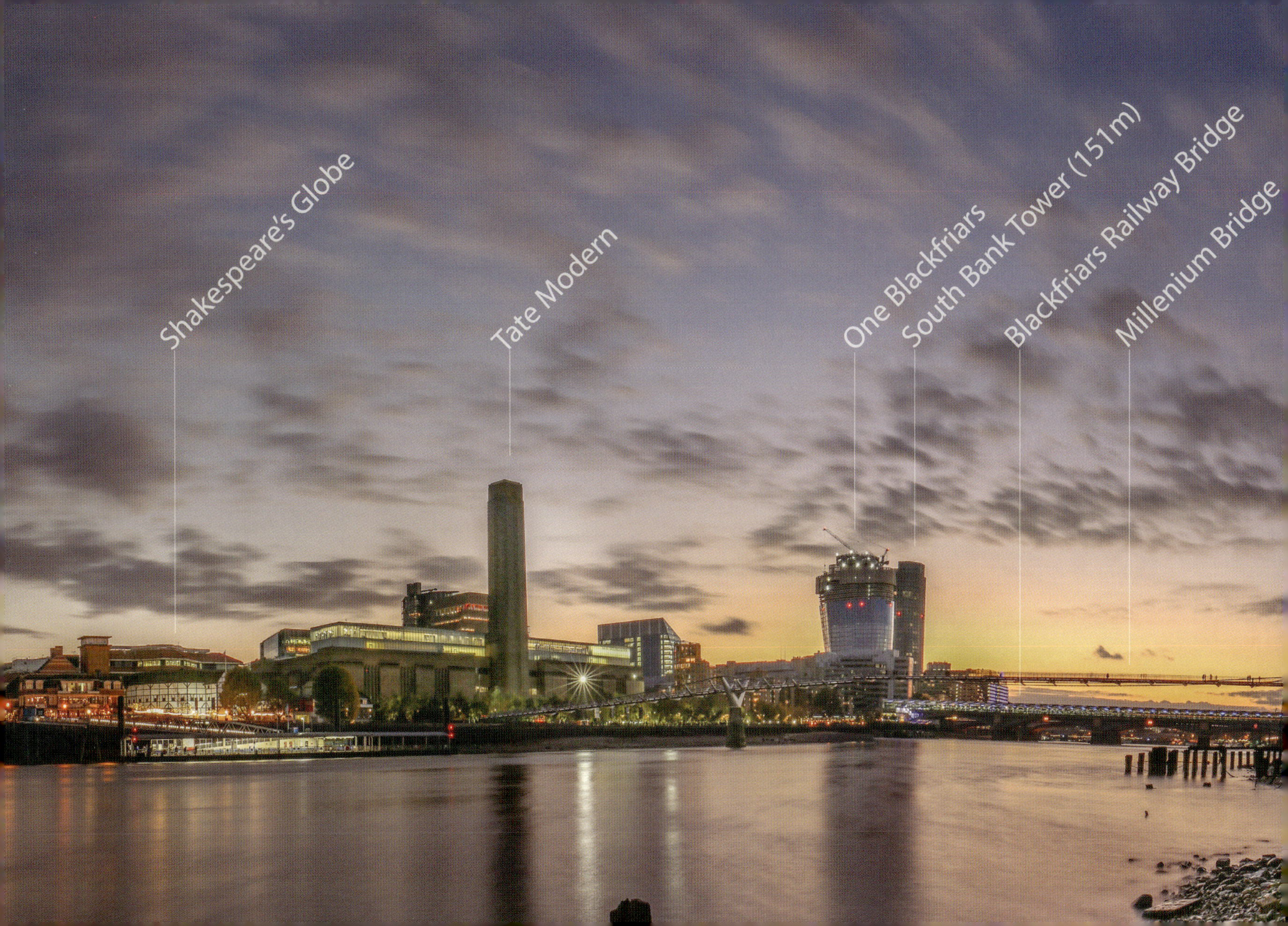

Shakespeare's Globe
Tate Modern
One Blackfriars
South Bank Tower (151m)
Blackfriars Railway Bridge
Millenium Bridge

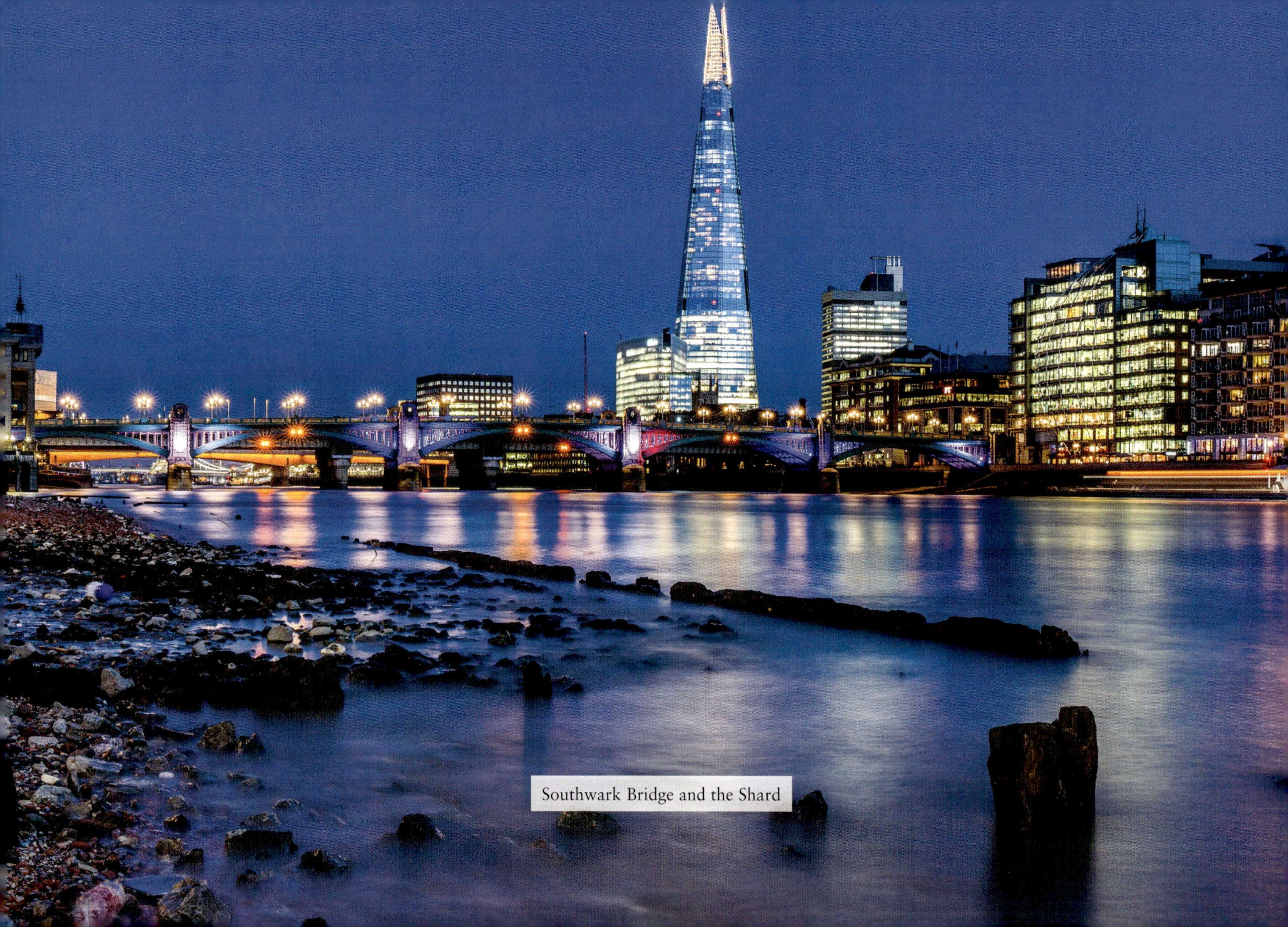

Southwark Bridge and the Shard

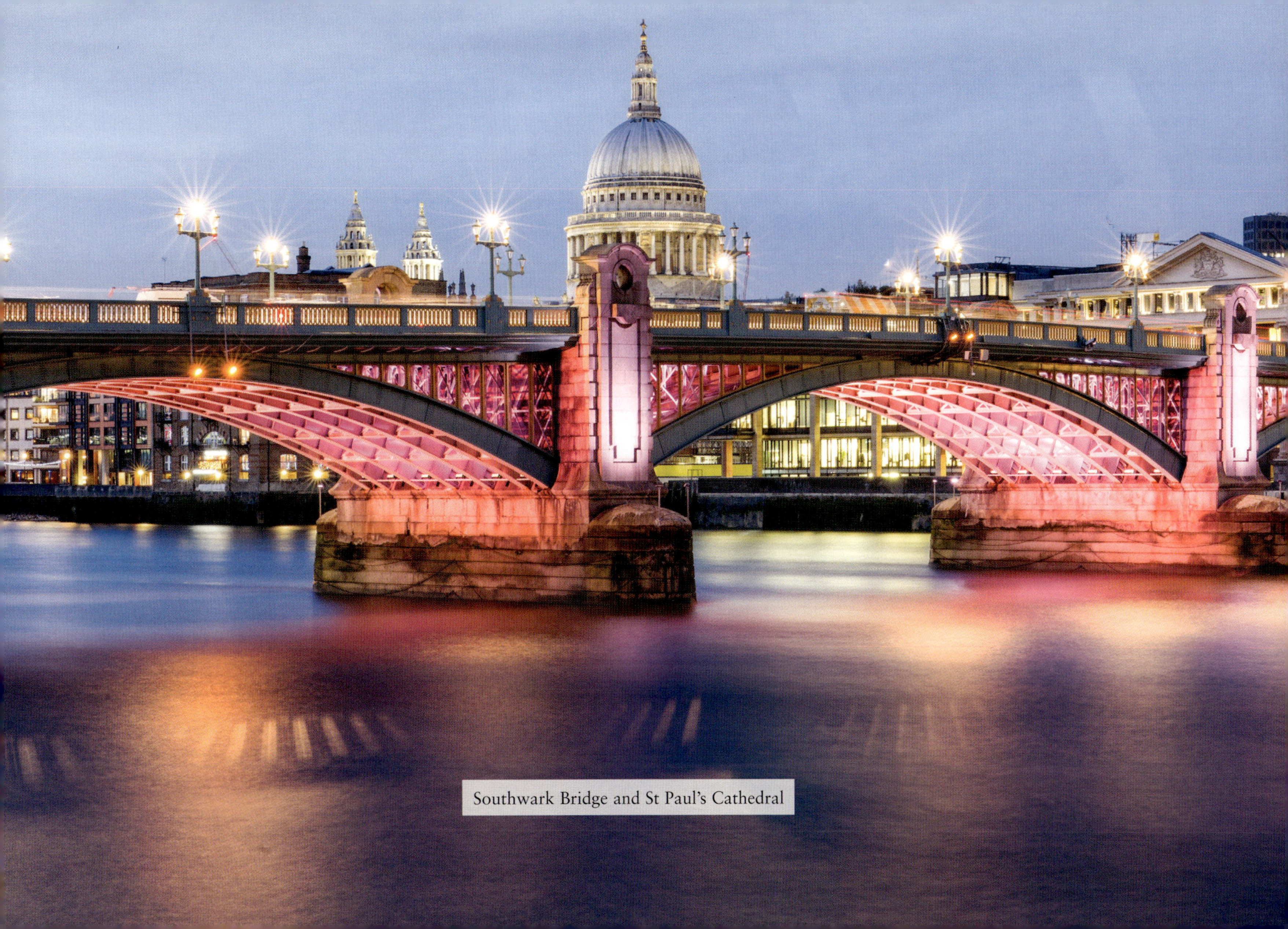

Southwark Bridge and St Paul's Cathedral

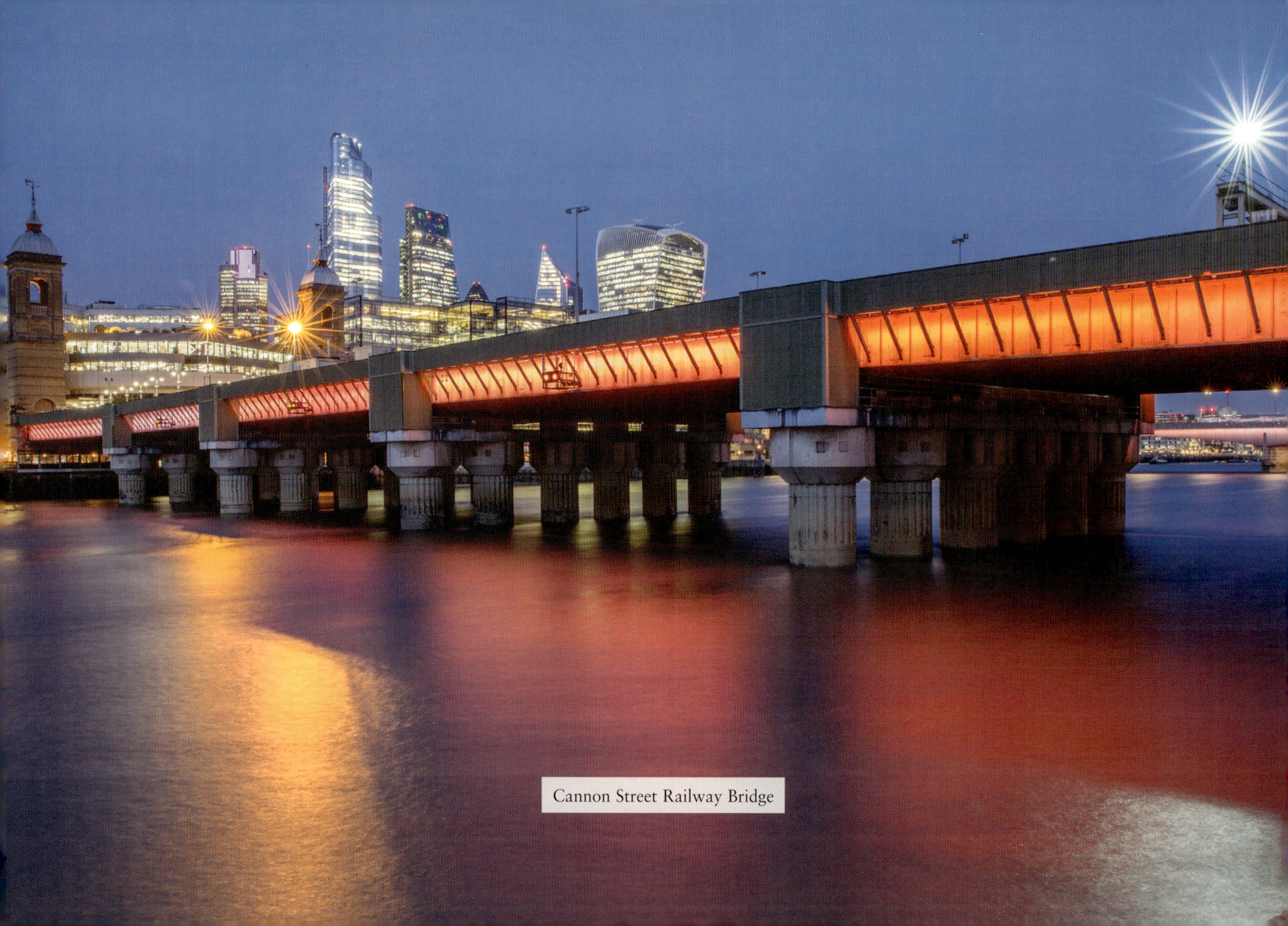

Cannon Street Railway Bridge

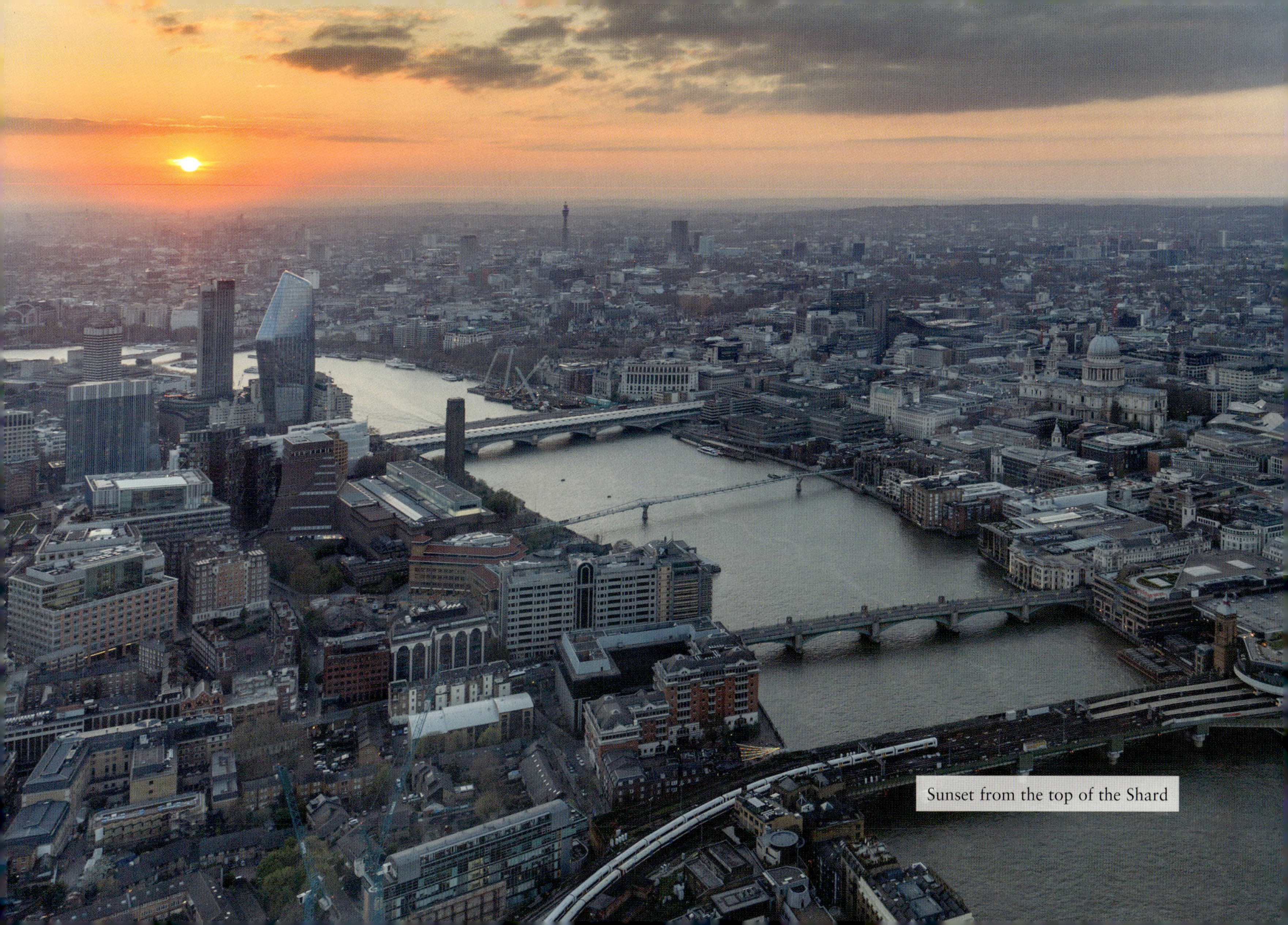

Sunset from the top of the Shard

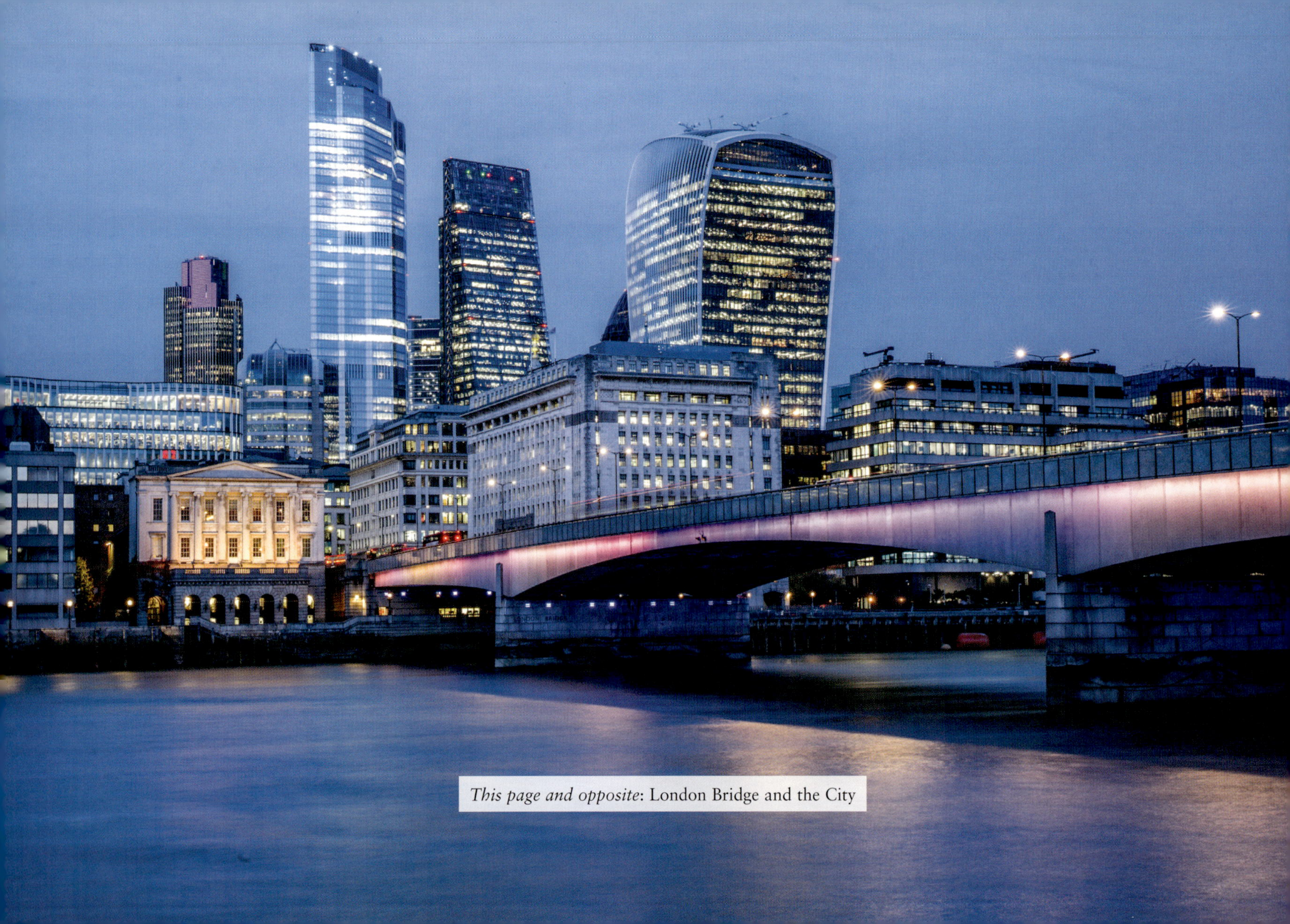

This page and opposite: London Bridge and the City

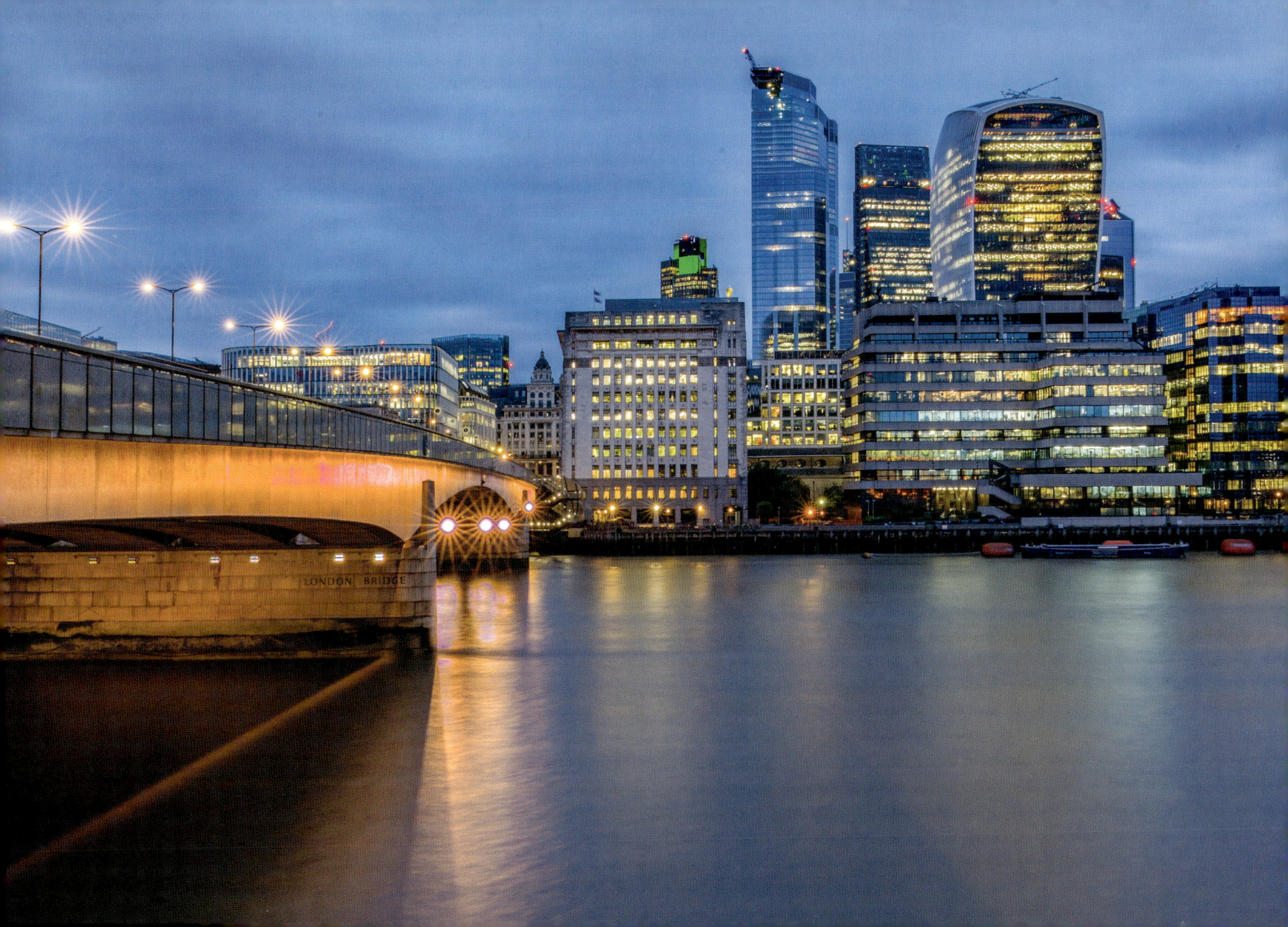
LONDON BRIDGE

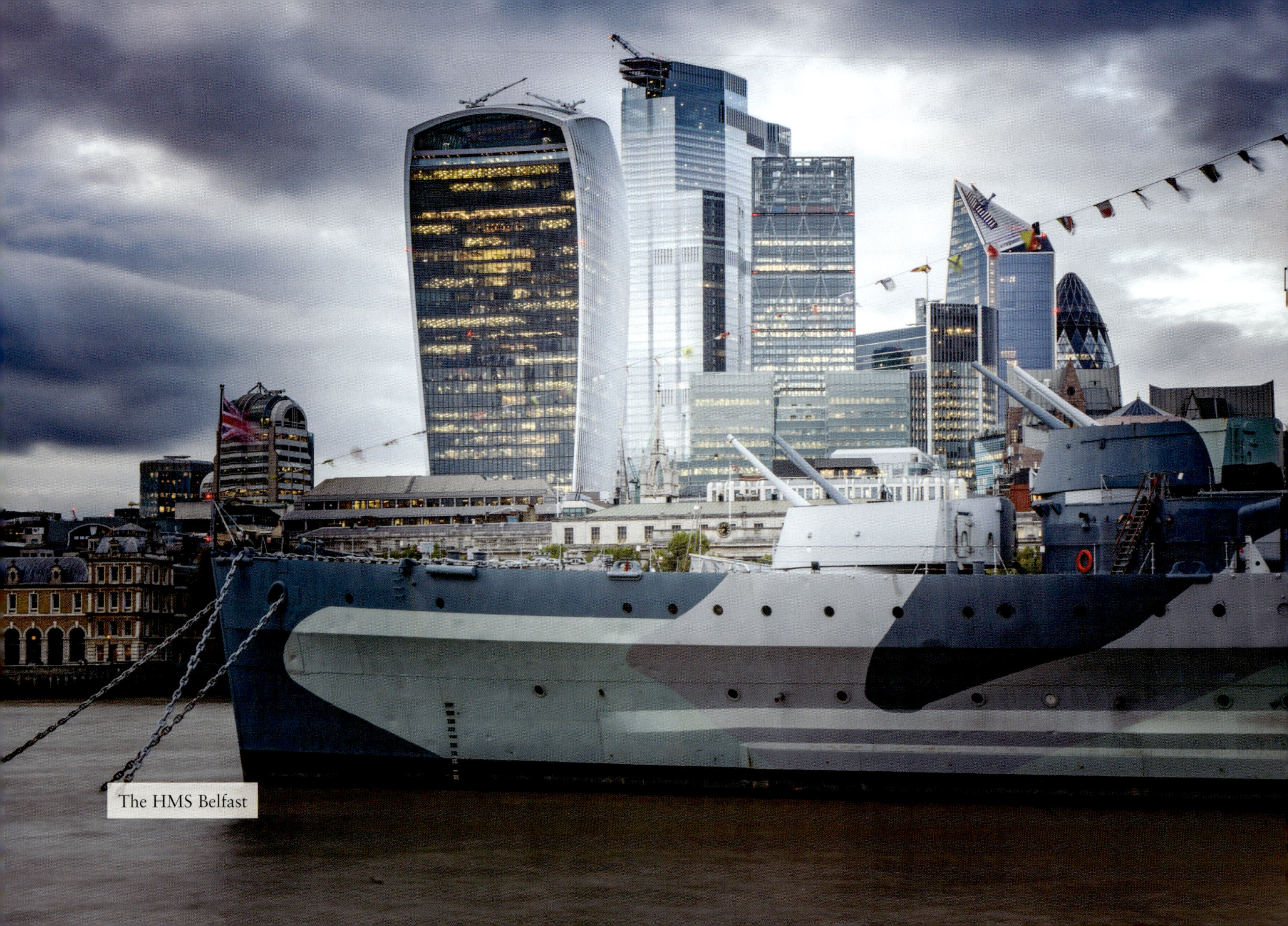

The HMS Belfast

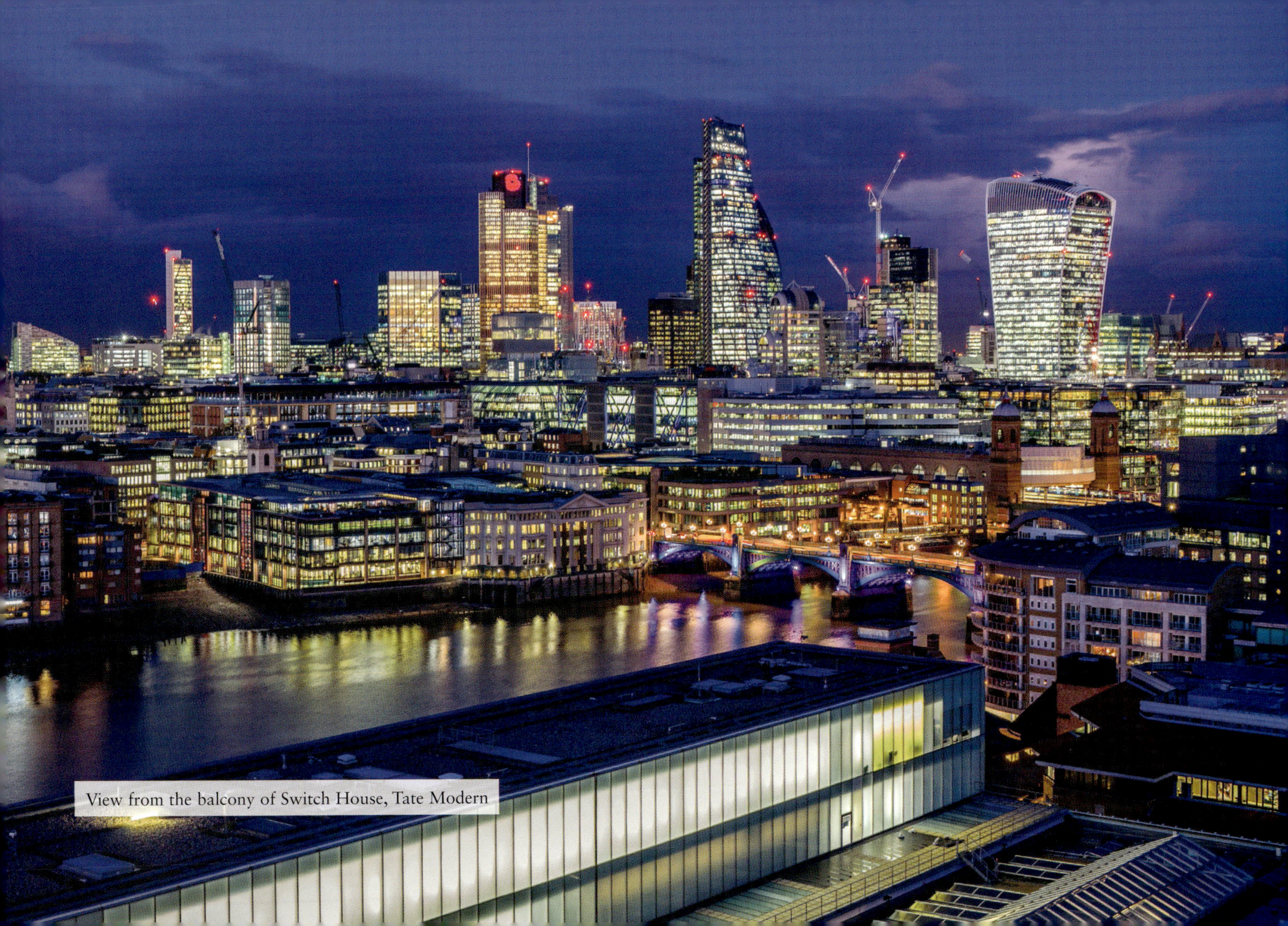

View from the balcony of Switch House, Tate Modern

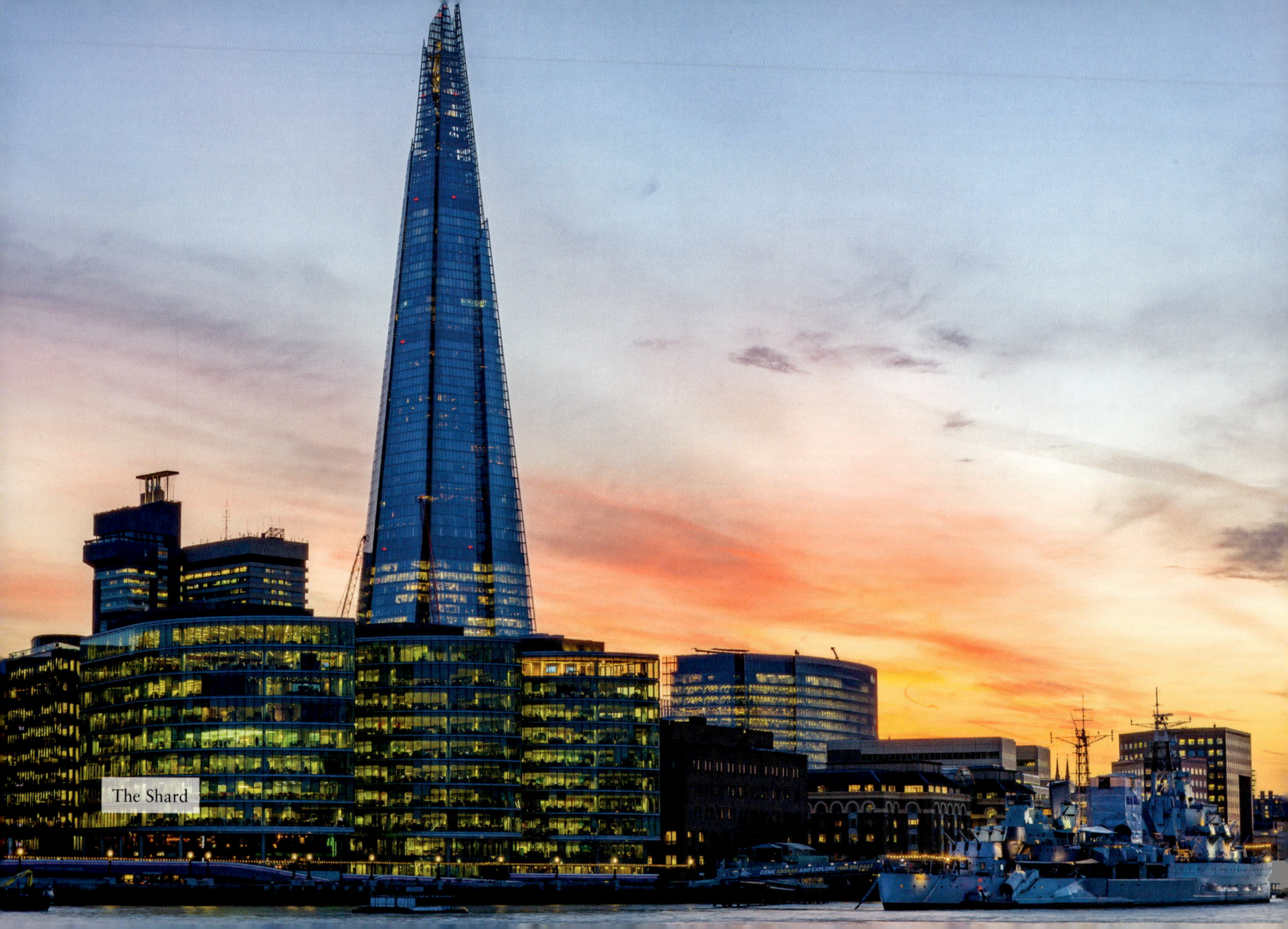
The Shard

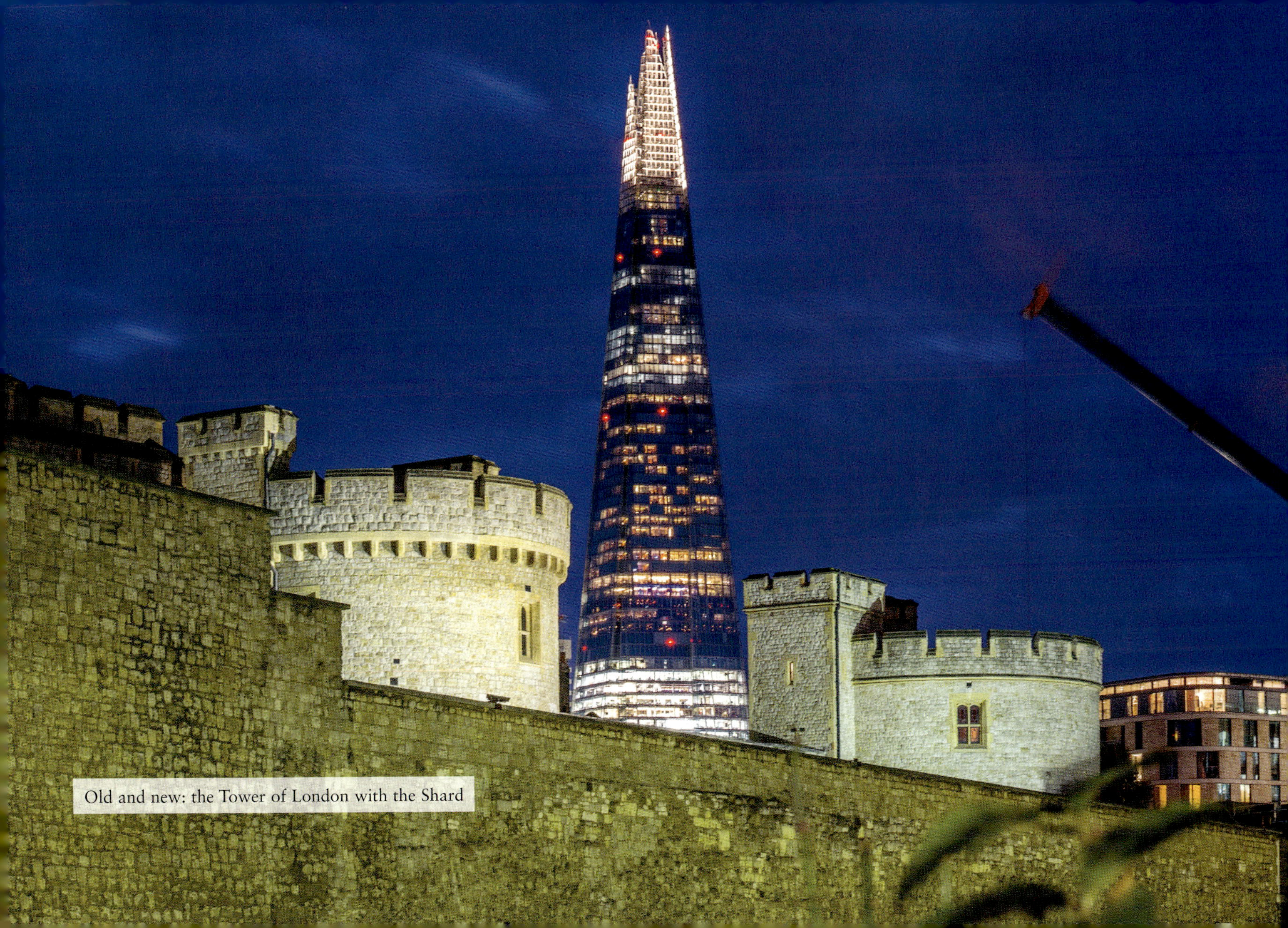

Old and new: the Tower of London with the Shard

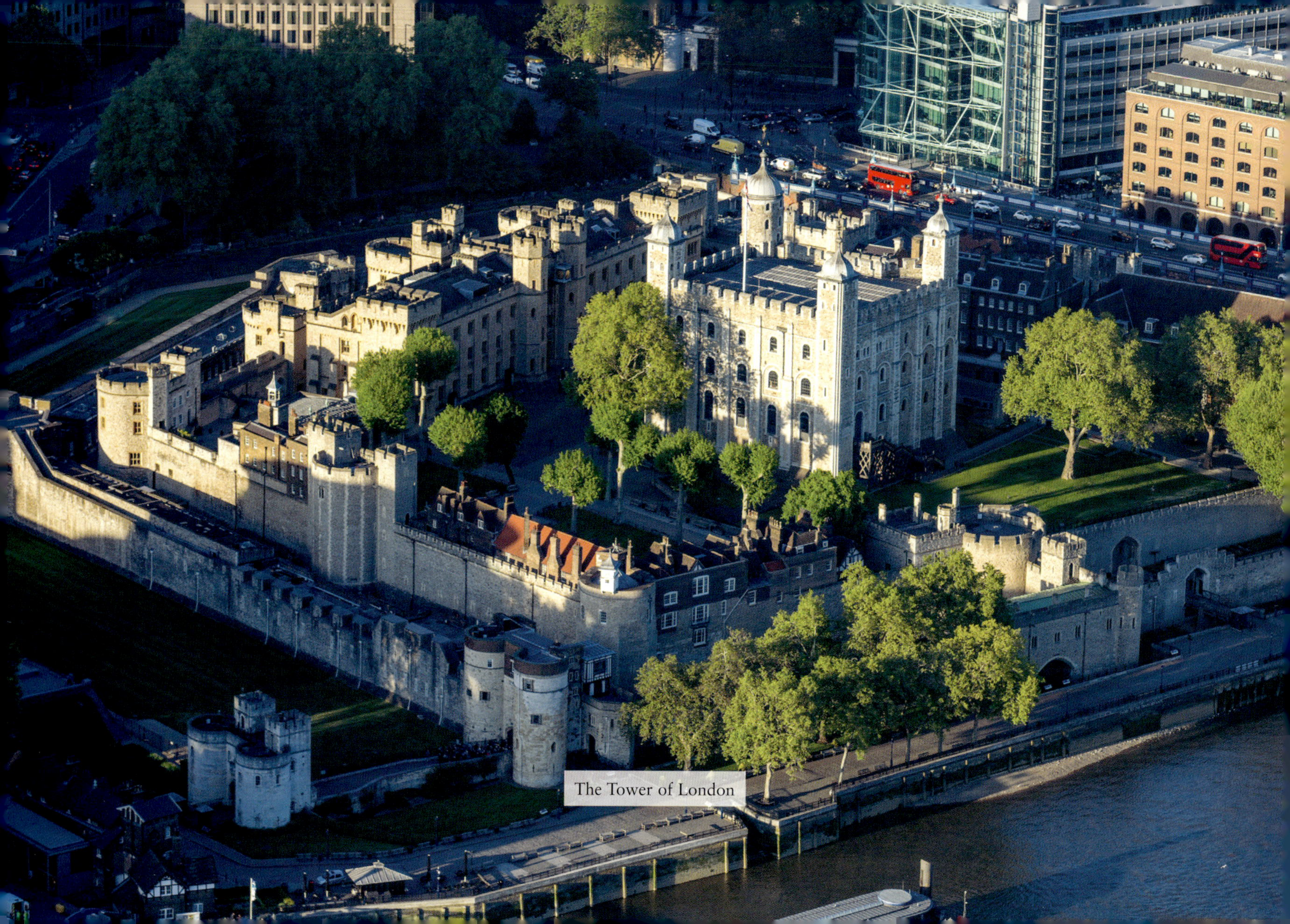
The Tower of London

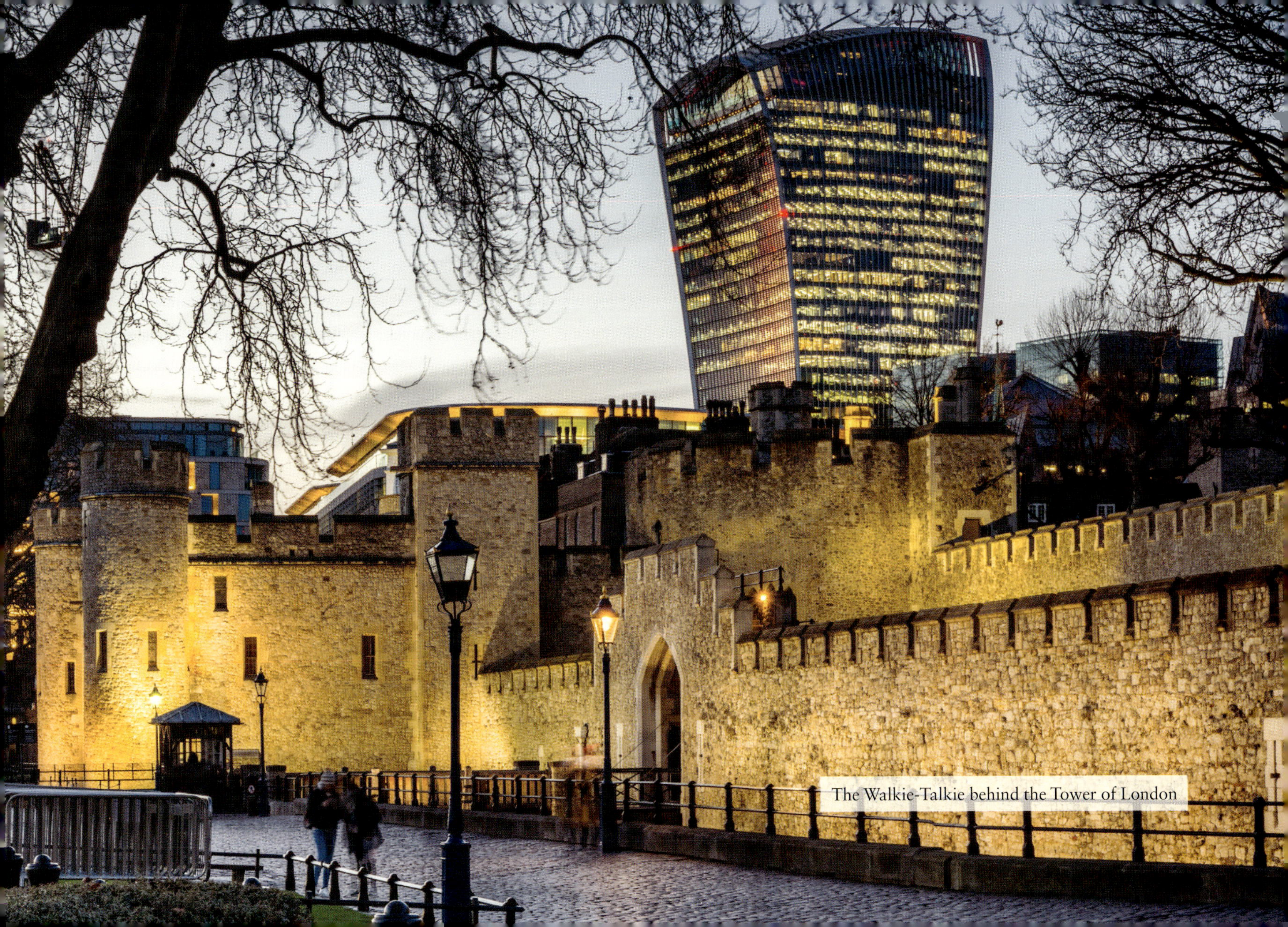
The Walkie-Talkie behind the Tower of London

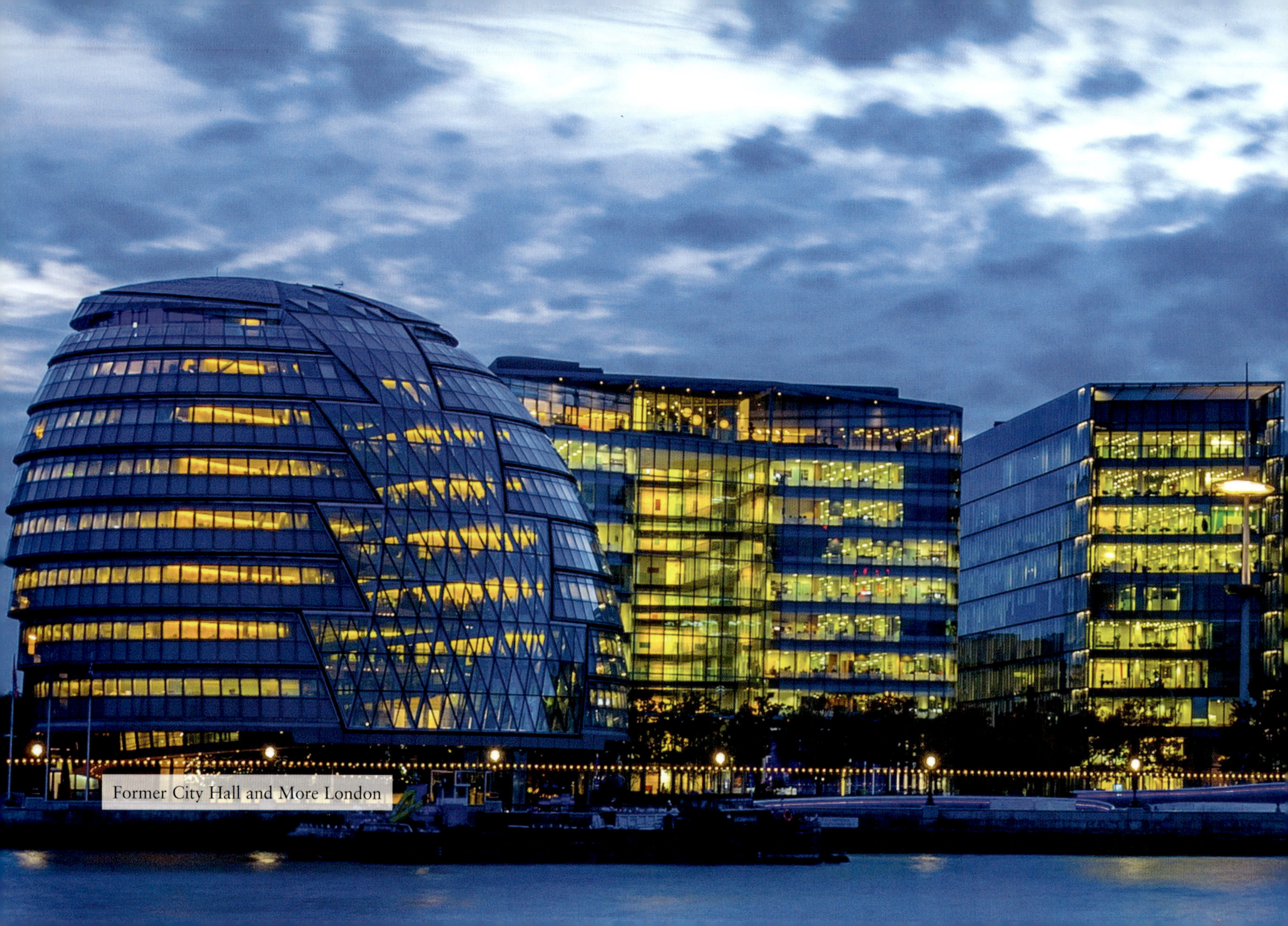

Former City Hall and More London

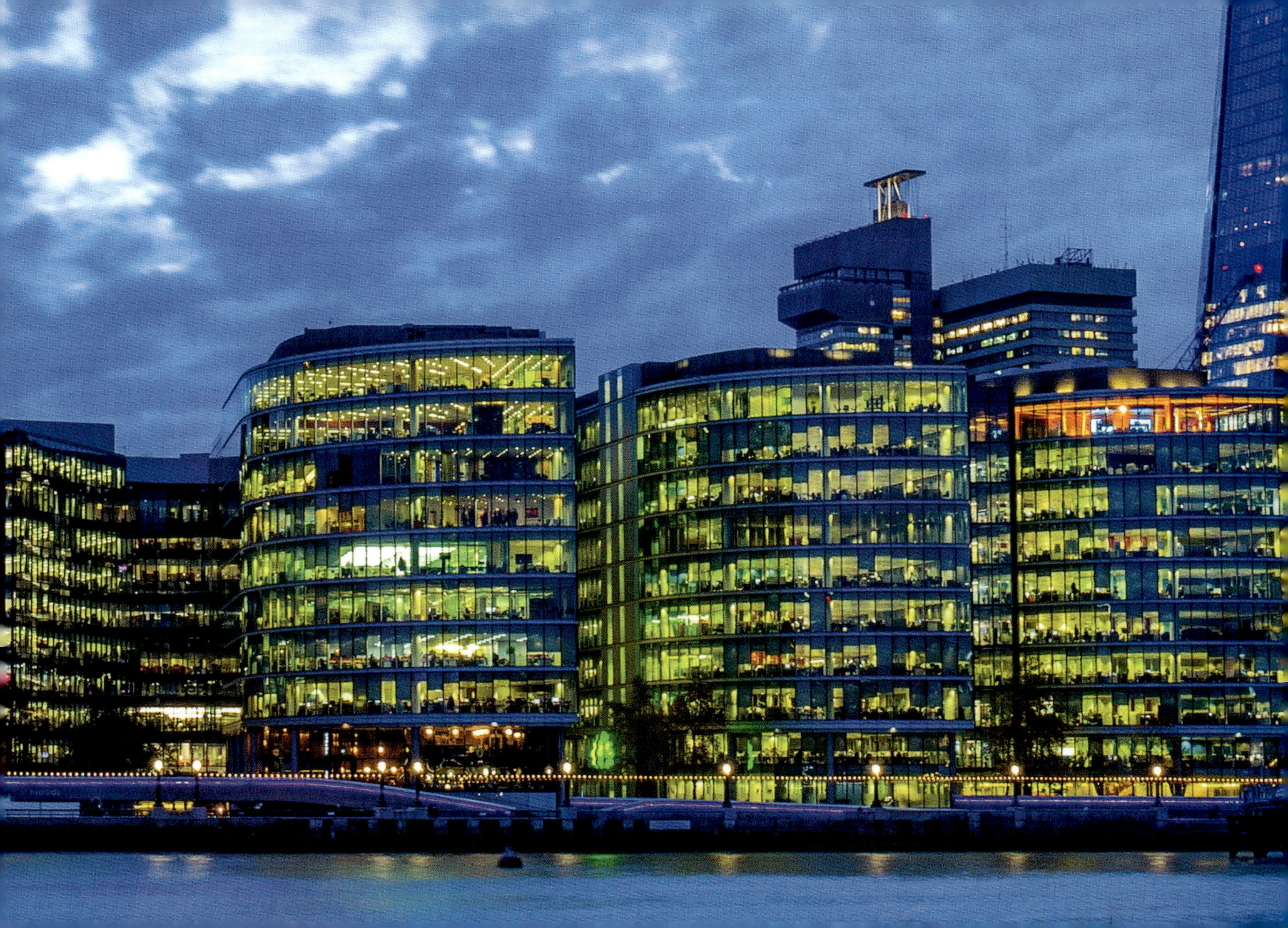

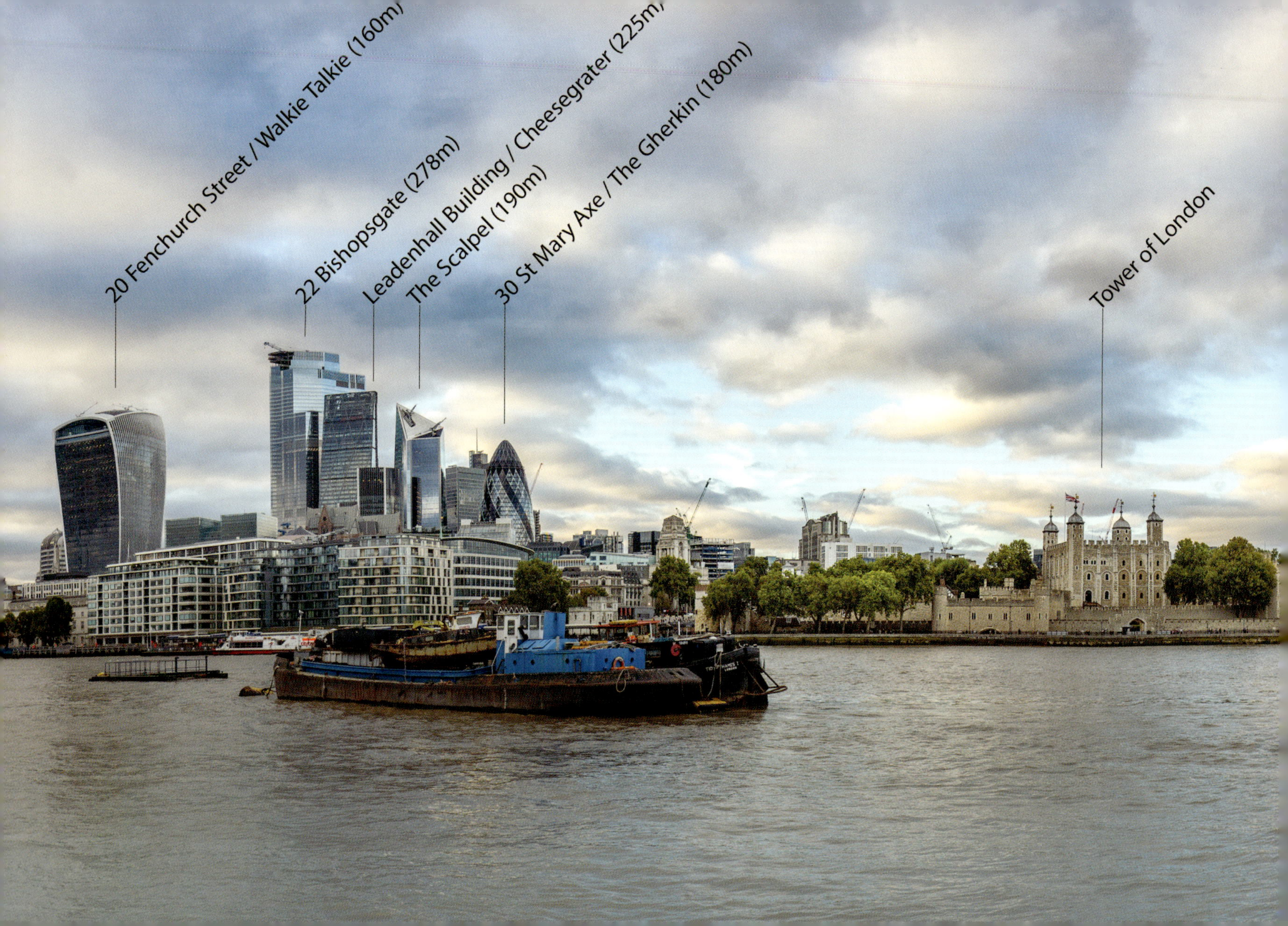

20 Fenchurch Street / Walkie Talkie (160m)
22 Bishopsgate (278m)
Leadenhall Building / Cheesegrater (225m)
The Scalpel (190m)
30 St Mary Axe / The Gherkin (180m)
Tower of London

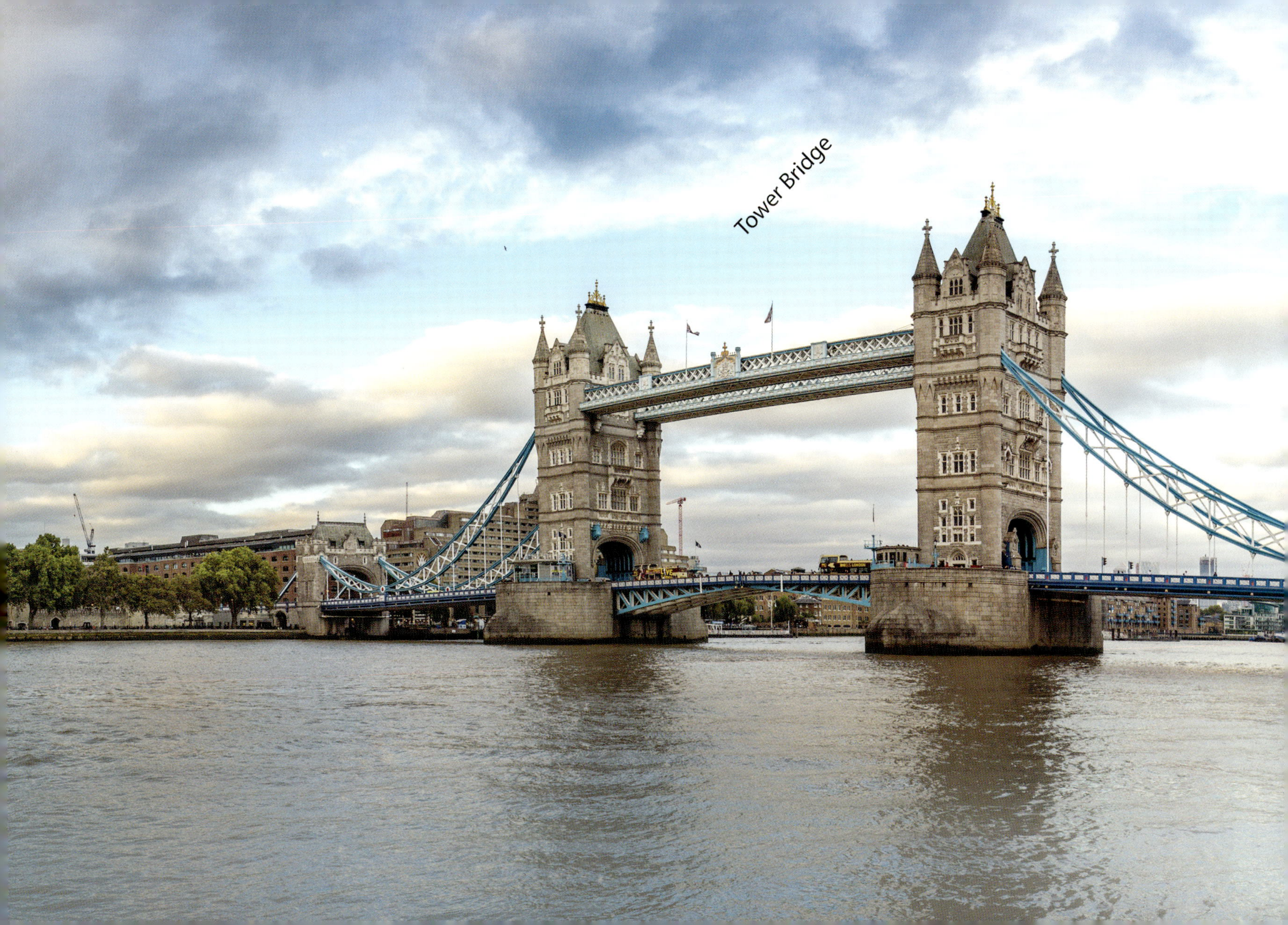
Tower Bridge

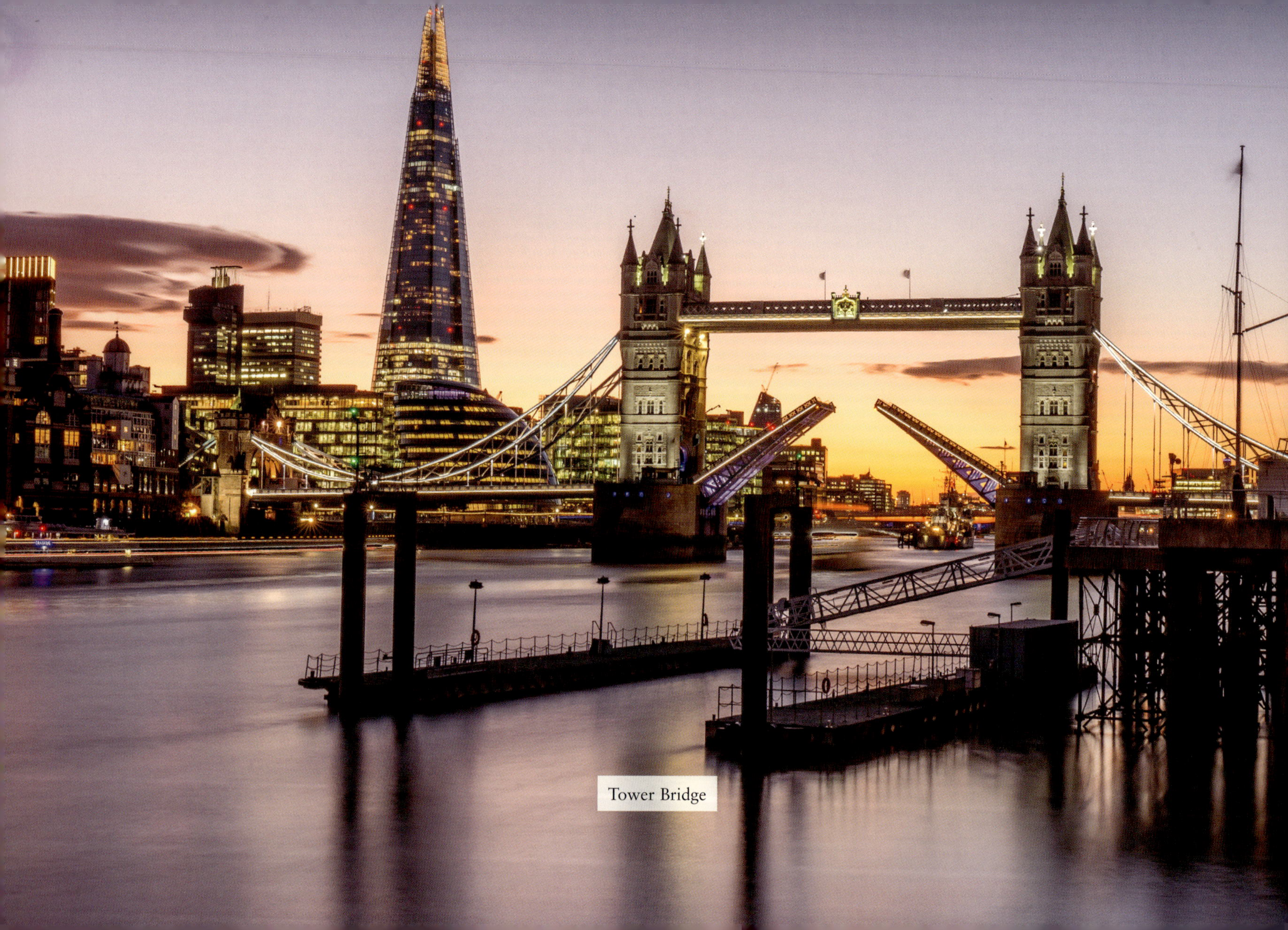

Tower Bridge

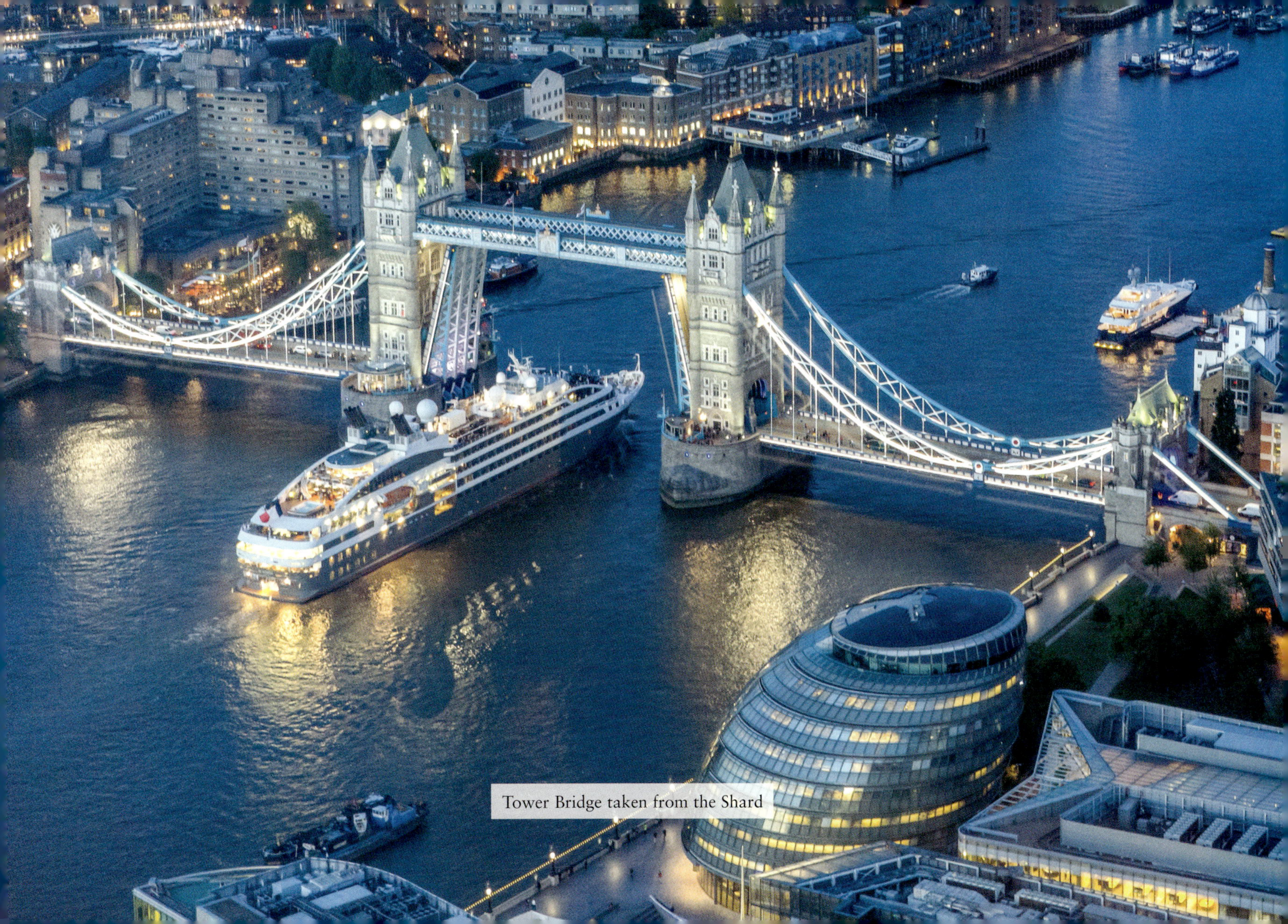

Tower Bridge taken from the Shard

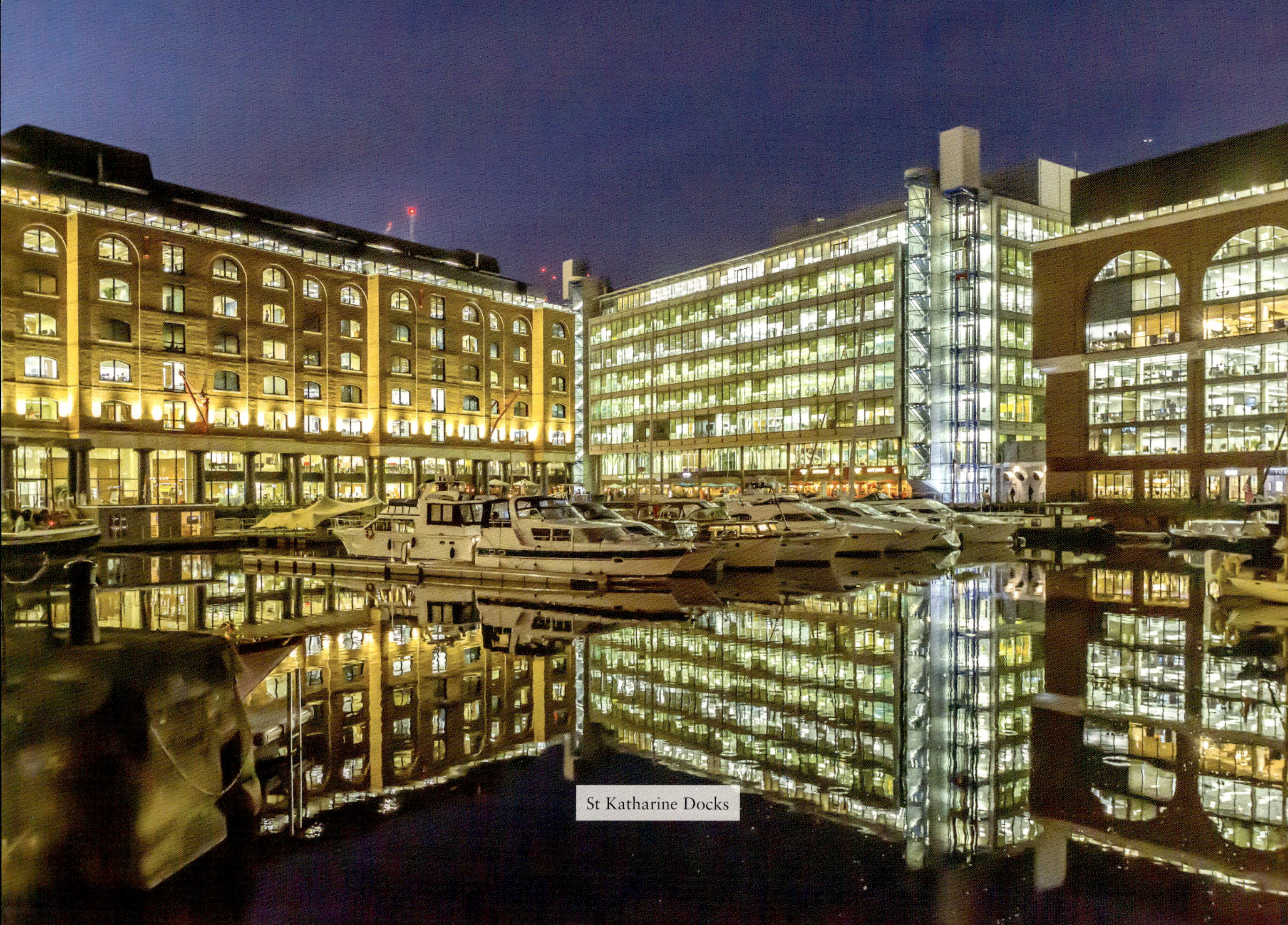
St Katharine Docks

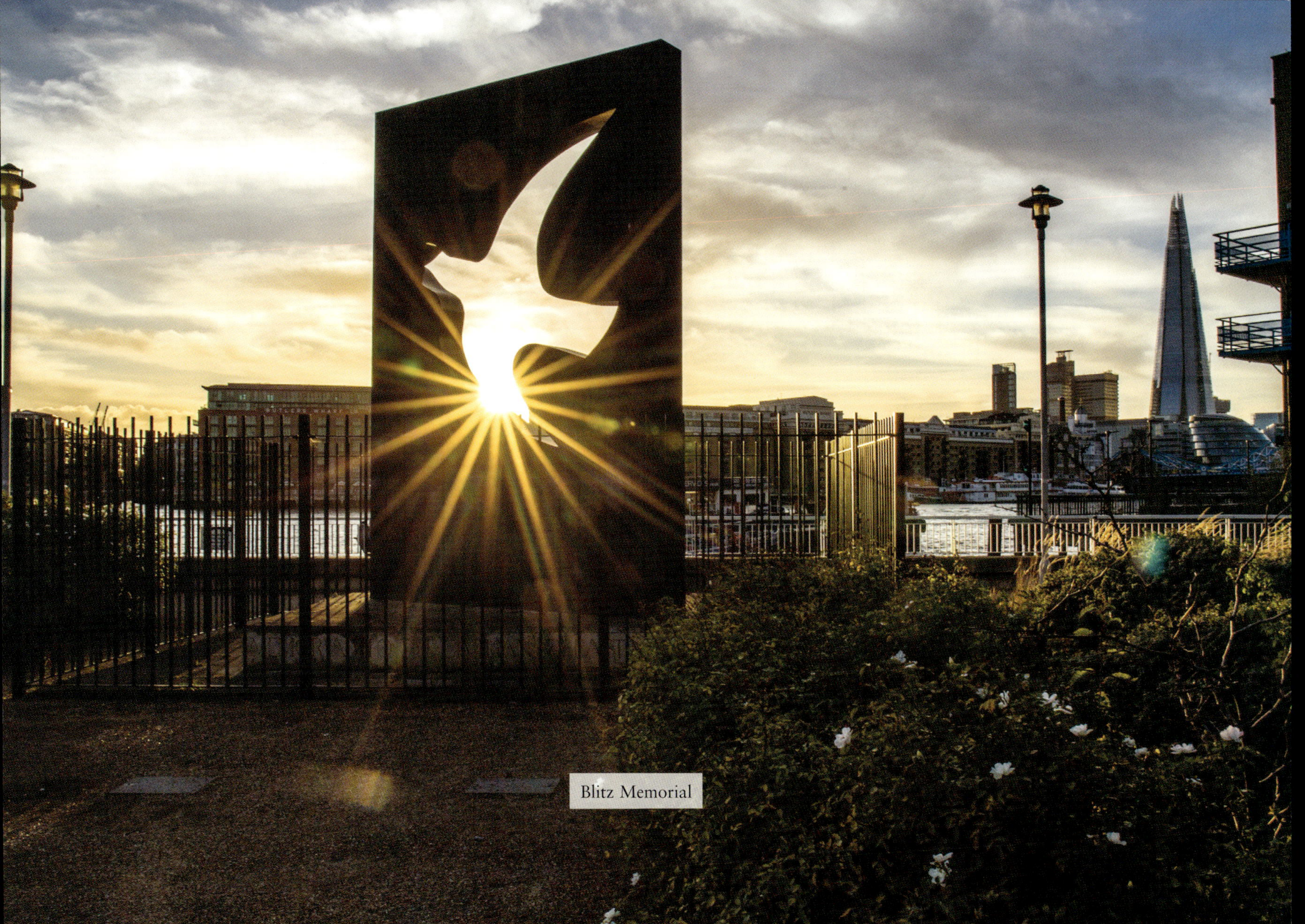

Blitz Memorial

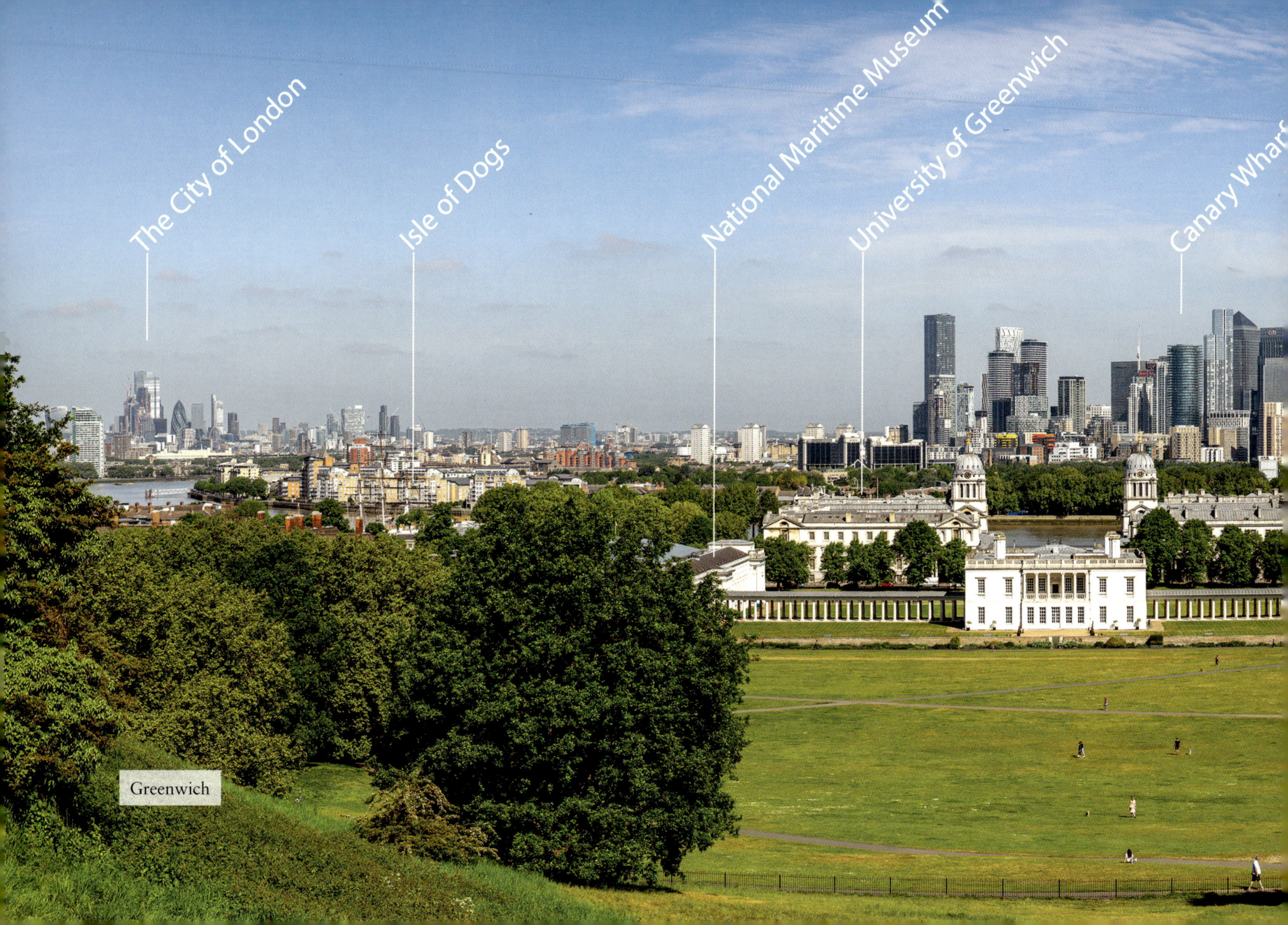
The City of London
Isle of Dogs
National Maritime Museum
University of Greenwich
Canary Wharf
Greenwich

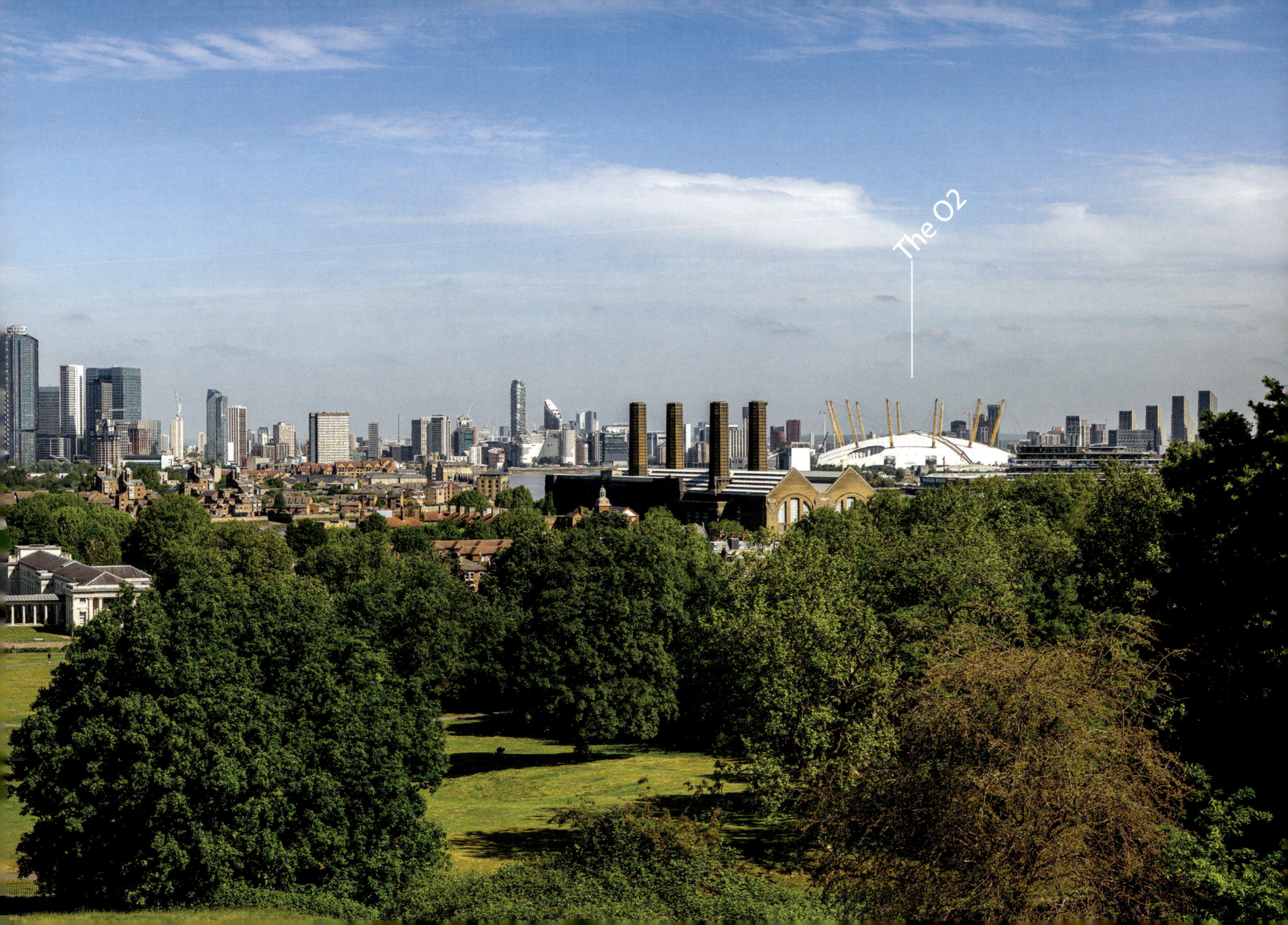
The O2

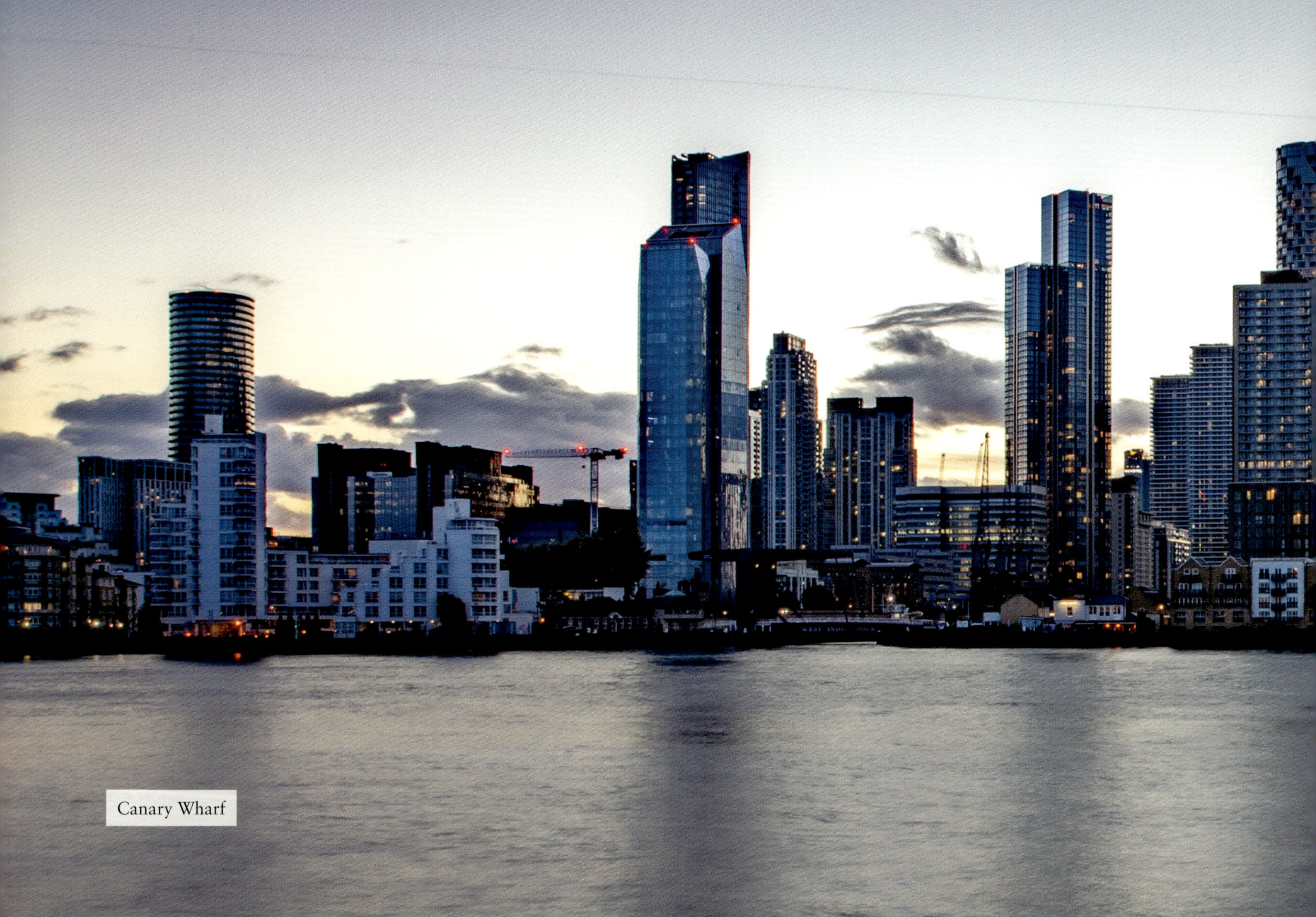
Canary Wharf

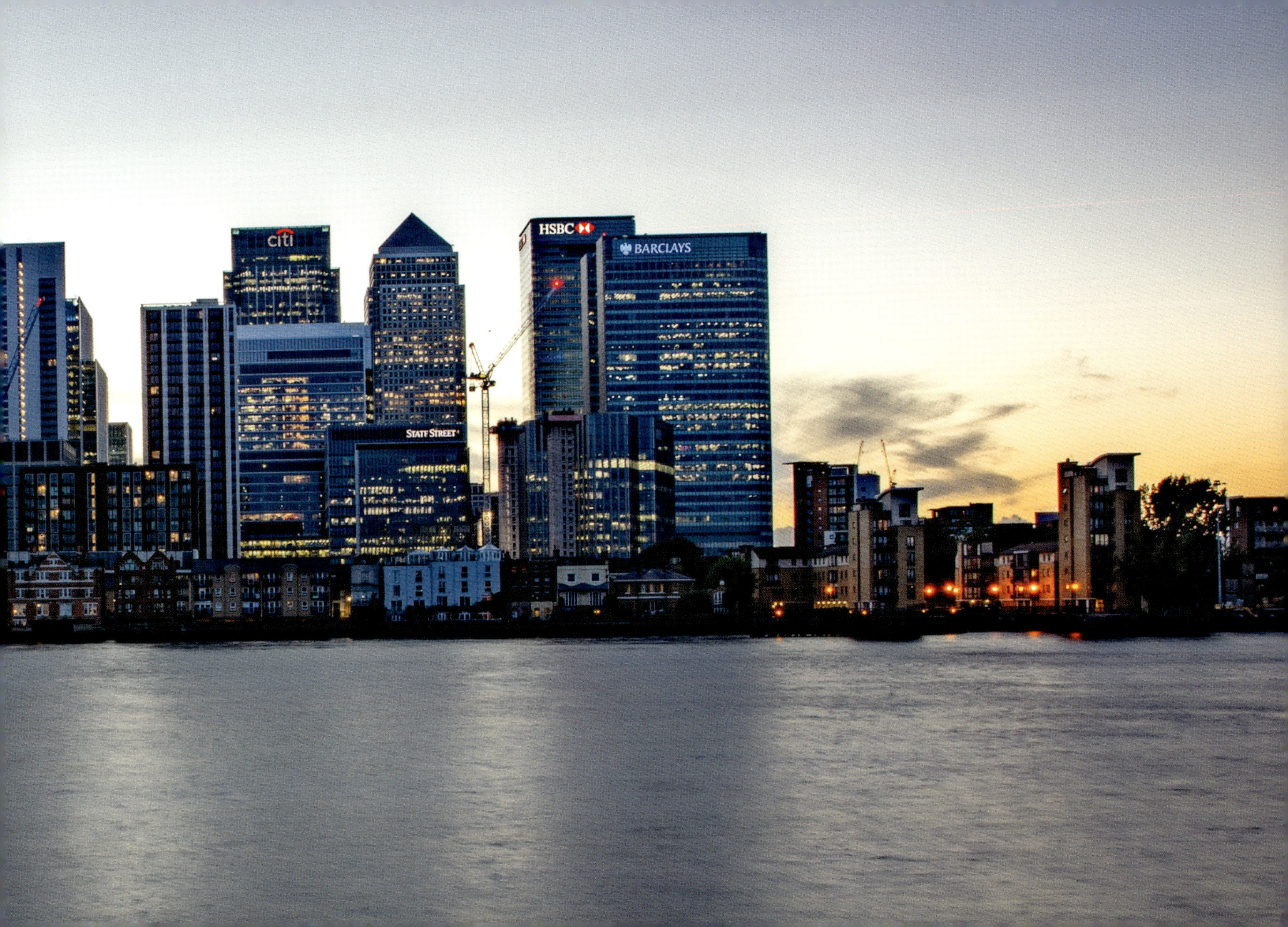
citi
HSBC
BARCLAYS
STATE STREET

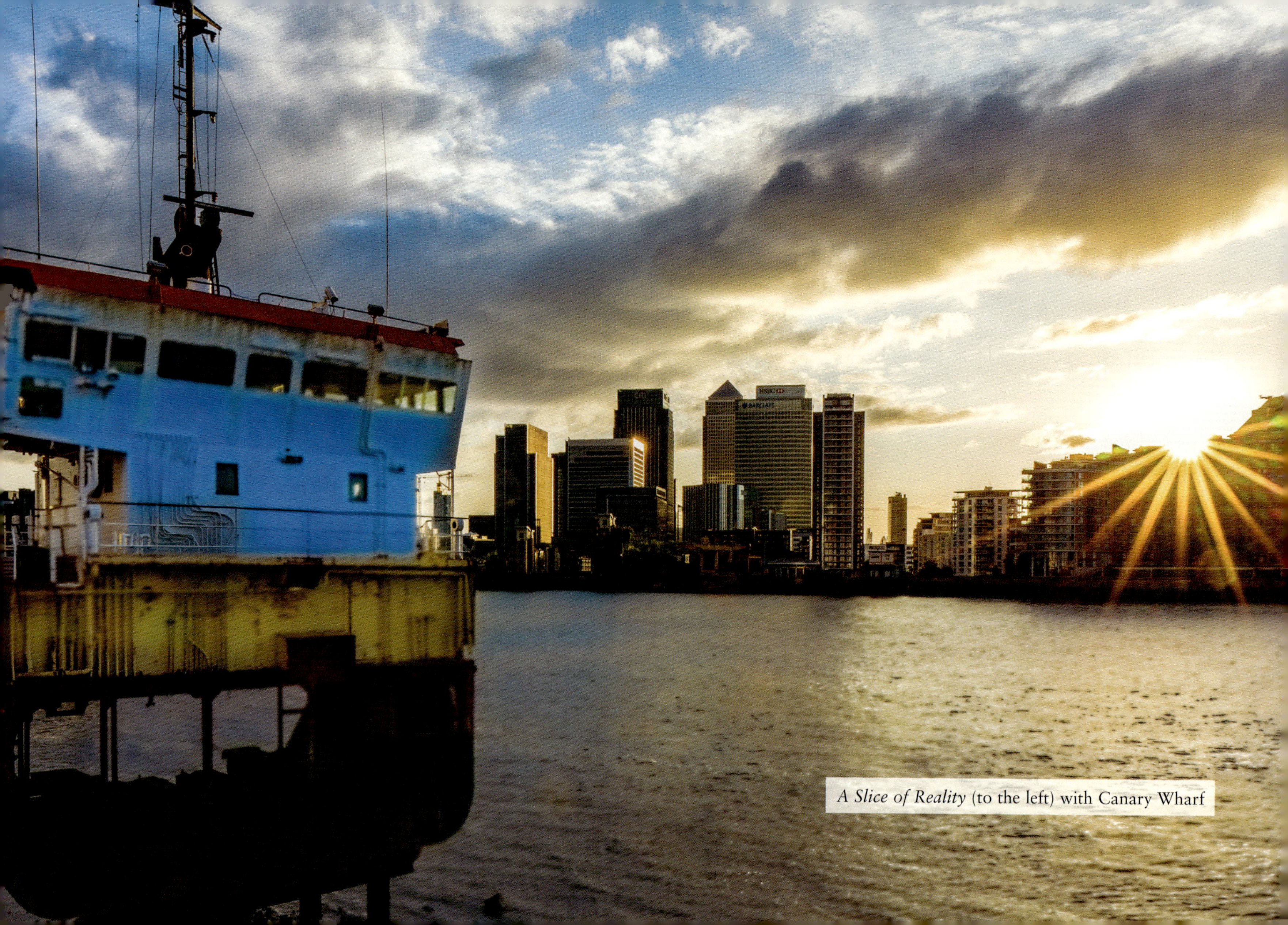

A Slice of Reality (to the left) with Canary Wharf

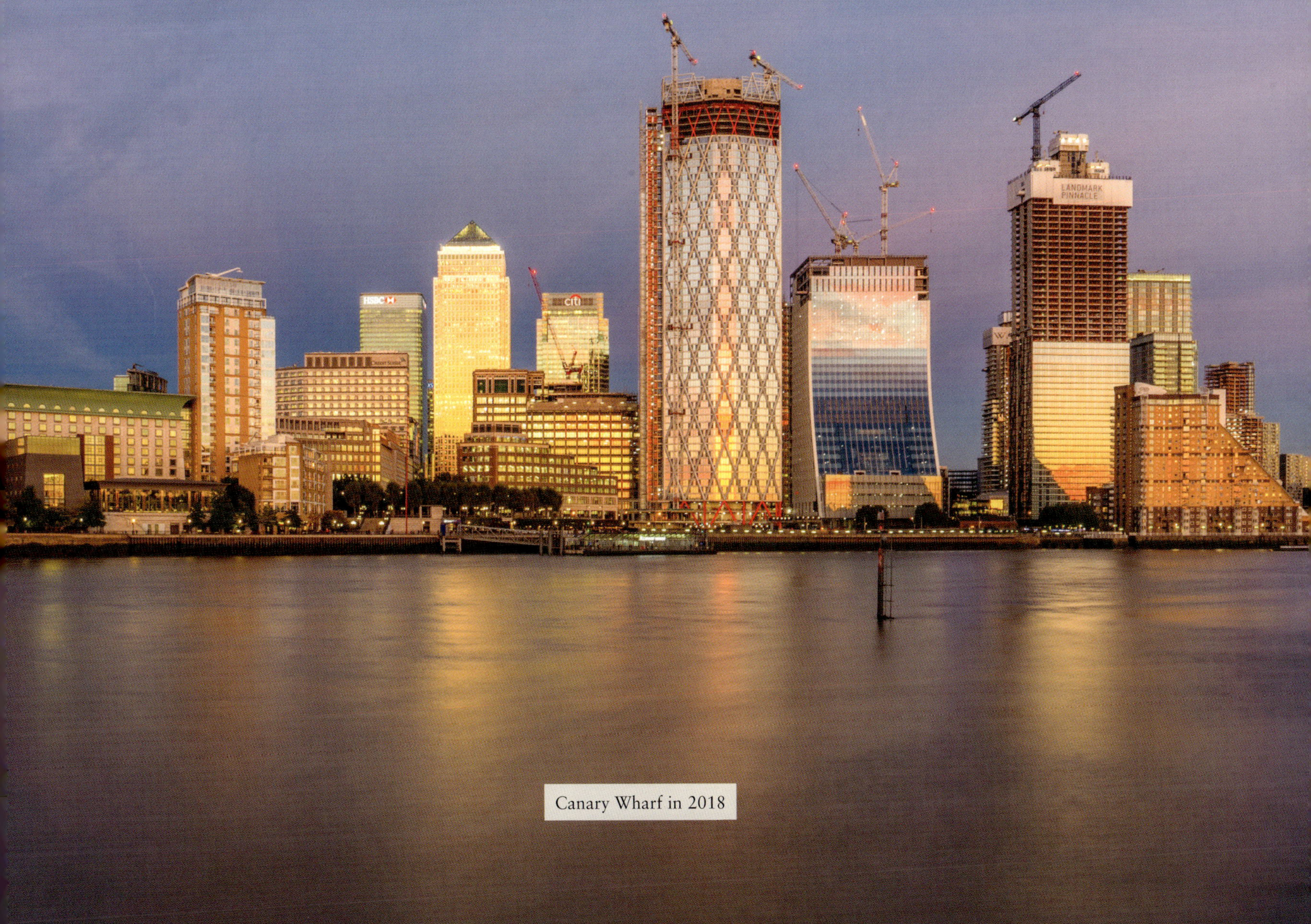

Canary Wharf in 2018

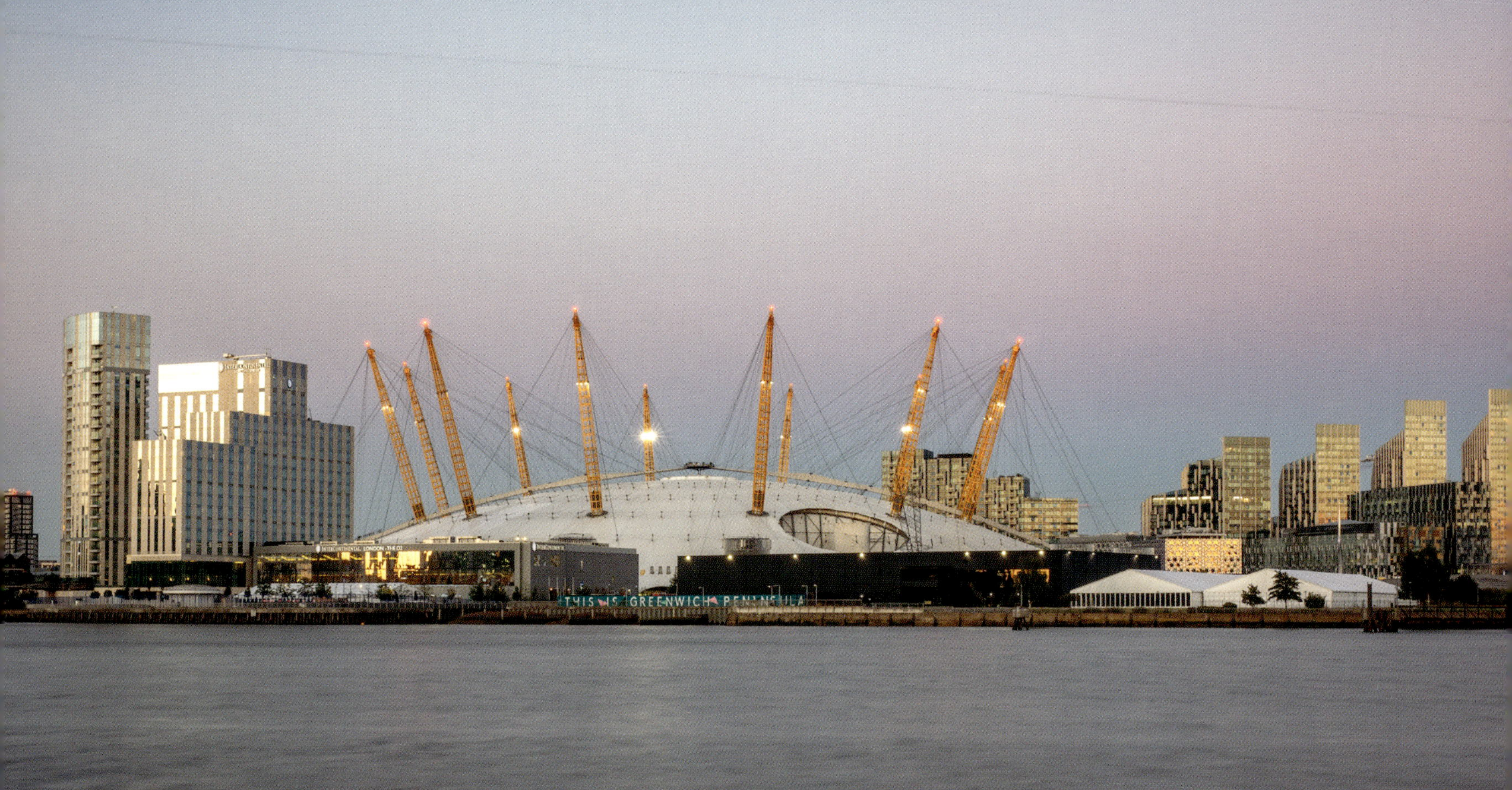

The O2 (formerly the Millennium Dome) on the Greenwich Peninsula

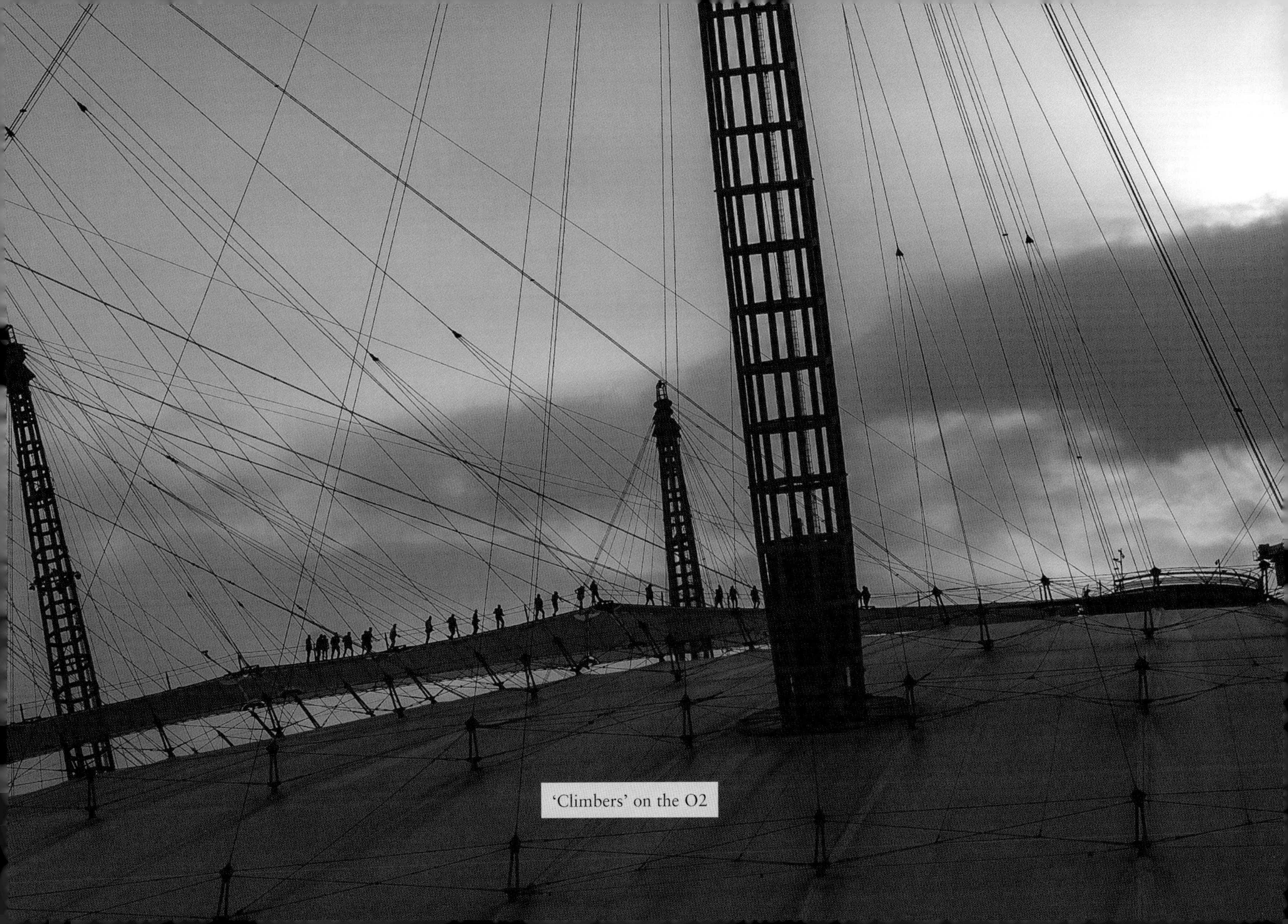

'Climbers' on the O2

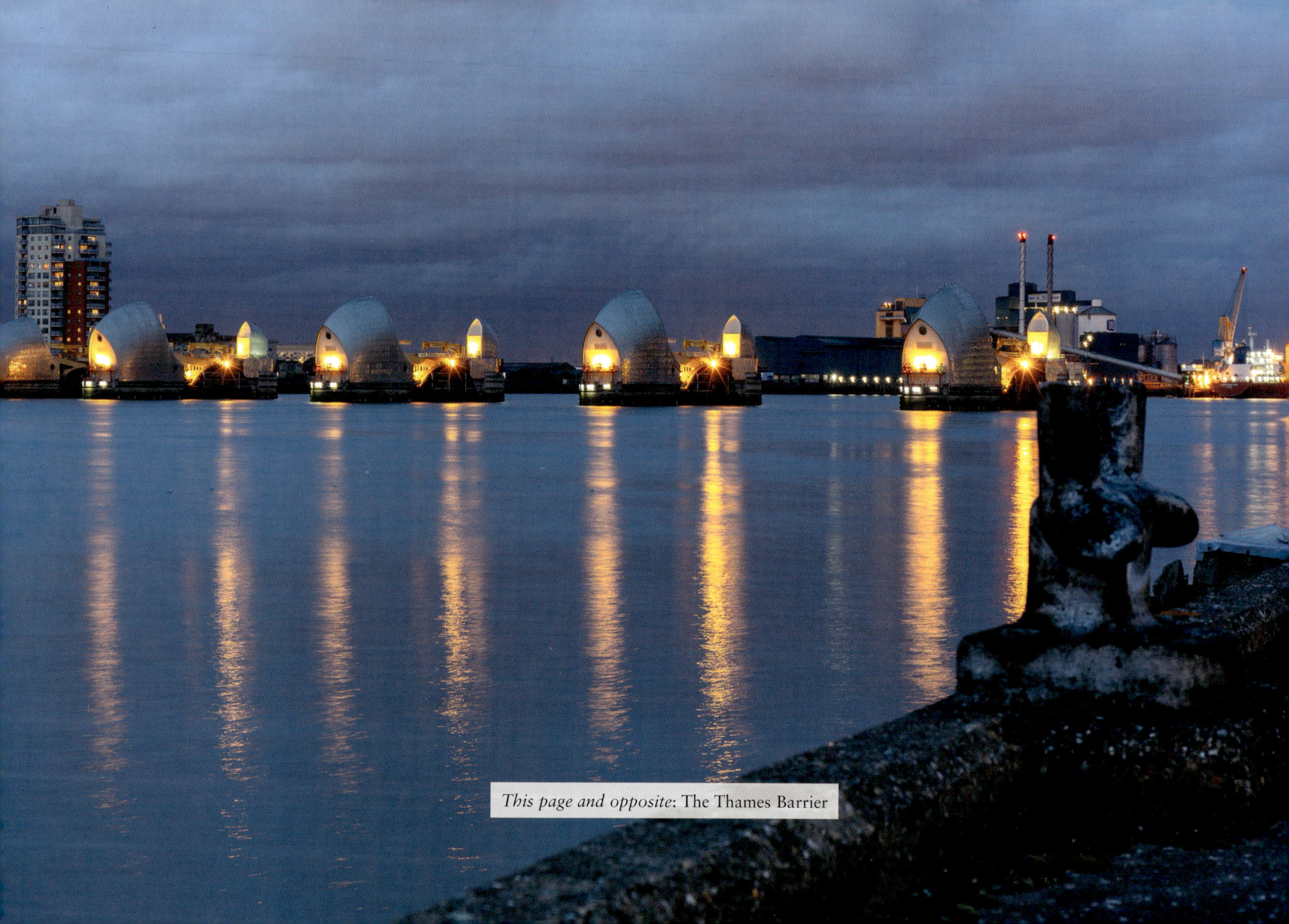

This page and opposite: The Thames Barrier

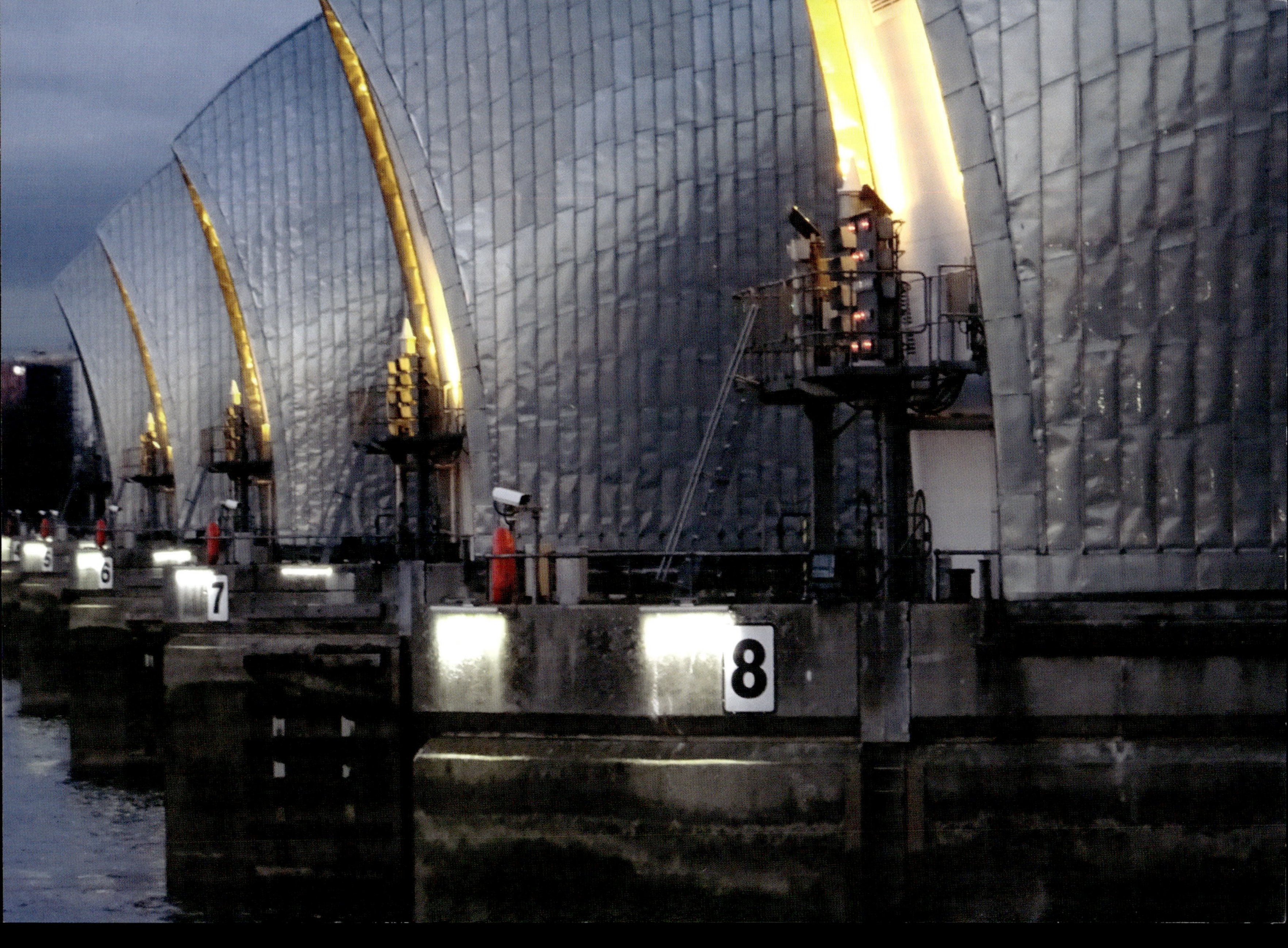
5
6
7
8

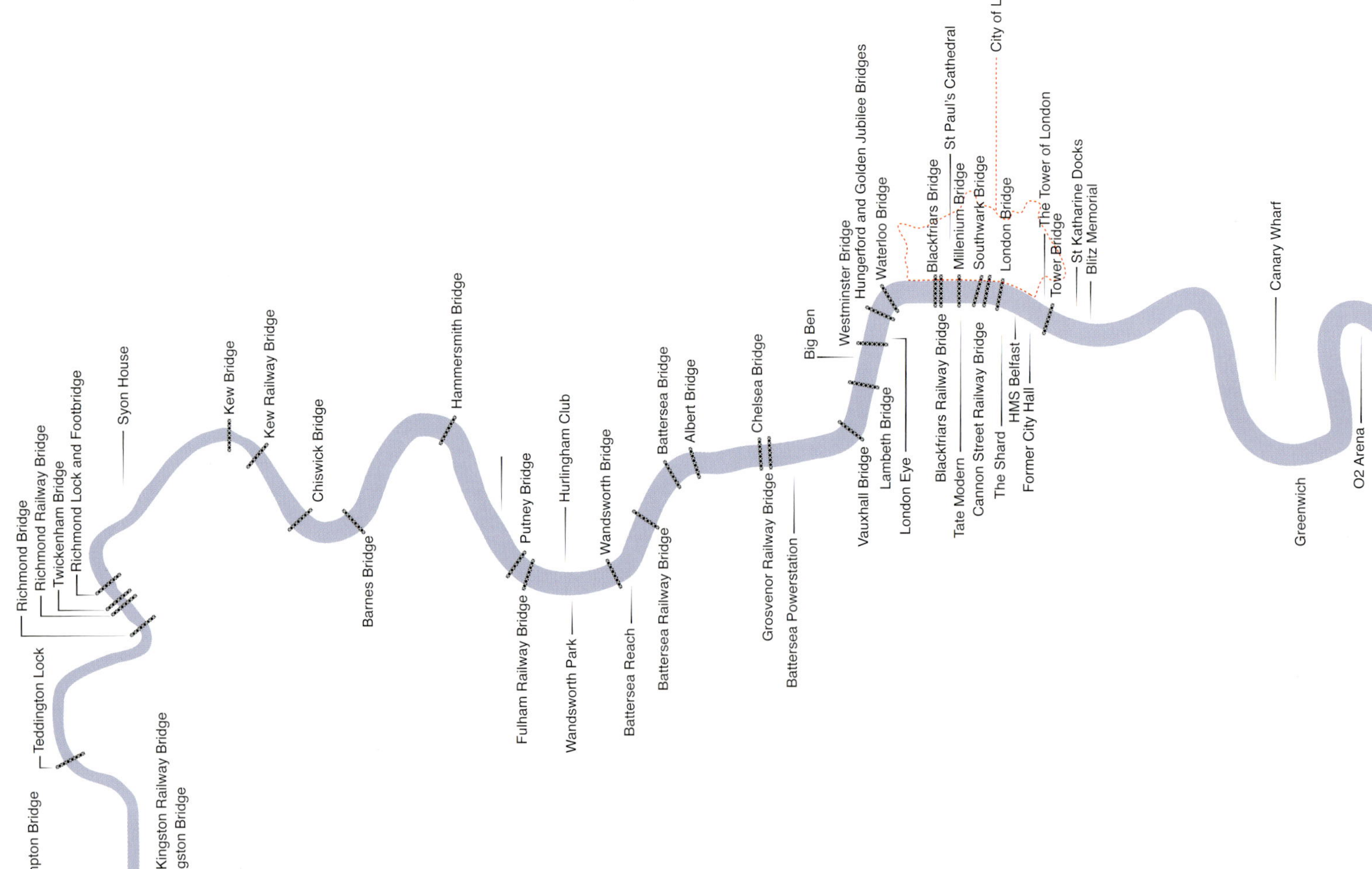

Hampton Bridge
Teddington Lock
Kingston Railway Bridge
Kingston Bridge
Richmond Bridge
Richmond Railway Bridge
Twickenham Bridge
Richmond Lock and Footbridge
Syon House
Kew Bridge
Kew Railway Bridge
Chiswick Bridge
Barnes Bridge
Hammersmith Bridge
Fulham Railway Bridge
Putney Bridge
Hurlingham Club
Wandsworth Park
Wandsworth Bridge
Battersea Reach
Battersea Railway Bridge
Battersea Bridge
Albert Bridge
Chelsea Bridge
Grosvenor Railway Bridge
Battersea Powerstation
Vauxhall Bridge
Lambeth Bridge
London Eye
Big Ben
Westminster Bridge
Hungerford and Golden Jubilee Bridges
Waterloo Bridge
Blackfriars Railway Bridge
Blackfriars Bridge
Tate Modern
St Paul's Cathedral
Millenium Bridge
Cannon Street Railway Bridge
Southwark Bridge
The Shard
London Bridge
City of London
HMS Belfast
Former City Hall
The Tower of London
Tower Bridge
St Katharine Docks
Blitz Memorial
Canary Wharf
Greenwich
O2 Arena
Thames Barrier